T.S   12^{00}

FAITH
OF OUR
FATHERS

VOLUME THREE

The Pilgrims

Dewey D. Wallace, Jr.

A Consortium Book

Library of Congress Card Catalog Number: 77-9507
ISBN: 0-8434-0622-4
ISBN: 0-8434-0635-6 paper

ACKNOWLEDGEMENTS

Raymond W. Albright, HISTORY OF THE PROTESTANT EPISCOPAL CHURCH. Copyright © 1964 by Raymond W. Albright. Macmillan Publishing Co., Inc., New York. Reprinted with permission.

Patrick Collinson, THE ELIZABETHAN PURITAN MOVEMENT. Copyright © 1967 by Patrick Collinson; reprinted by permission of the University of California Press.

John S. Coolidge, THE PAULINE RENAISSANCE IN ENGLAND. Copyright © Oxford University Press, 1970. Used by permission of the Oxford University Press, Oxford.

Reprinted by permission of Schocken Books, Inc. from THE ENGLISH REFORMATION by A.G. Dickens. Copyright © 1964 by A. G. Dickens.

John Tracy Ellis, CATHOLICS IN COLONIAL AMERICA. Baltimore, Maryland, Helicon. Reprinted with permission.

Melvin B. Endy, Jr., WILLIAM PENN AND EARLY QUAKERISM. Copyright © 1973 by Princeton University Press. Reprinted by permission of Princeton University Press.

George Braziller, Inc. - from WITCHCRAFT AT SALEM by Chadwick Hansen; reprinted with the permission of the publisher. Copyright © 1969 by Chadwick Hansen.

Reprinted by permission of Schocken Books from SOCIETY AND PURITANISM IN PRE-REVOLUTIONARY ENGLAND by Christopher Hill, Copyright © 1964 by Christopher Hill.

Reprinted by permission of New York University Press from VISIBLE SAINTS: THE HISTORY OF A PURITAN IDEA by Edmund Morgan, © 1963 by New York University.

NARRATIVES OF EARLY CAROLINA 1650-1708, Alexander S. Salley, Jr. ed. New York, Charles Scribner's Sons, 1911. Reprinted with permission.

To My Father and Mother
Dewey and Junietta Wallace

Preface

I wish to thank many teachers and colleagues who by their instruction and discussion over the years have improved my understanding of Religion in America. I owe a special debt of gratitude to the staffs of the George Washington University and Folger Shakespeare Libraries for their assistance in locating books and materials, to Thomas Pearl of the Consortium Press for his editorial suggestions, and to Laura Brown, Barbara Lettes and my wife Marion for help in preparing the manuscript for publication.

Dewey D. Wallace, Jr.
George Washington University
April, 1976

Table of Contents

Introduction

This book tells the story of the religious settlement of those North American colonies which eventually came to make up the United States. That settlement is basically a seventeenth-century story, although to complete the picture of the coming and establishment of all the main religious groups of the colonial period, it is in some cases necessary to take the story into the eighteenth century: for example, to complete the story of the settlement of the Presbyterians it is necessary to carry the tale to 1729, and with the German religious groups to go into the middle of that century.

The first major theme of this story of the religious settlement of the American colonies is that it represented not primarily (whatever it was to become) so much of a new departure as it did an attempt to carry over intact into a new world patterns of religious thought and practice which had been developed in the old. That those old patterns did not survive their transplantation but rather decayed, opening the way for new patterns, is the major conclusion to be drawn.

Basically the religious settlement of the American colonies involved the bringing to the new world of the struggles and conflicts of British Christianity, which were in turn the conflicts of the whole Reformation era, and which took a long time to reach final resolution in England. These conflicts were not only Protestant-Catholic in nature, but also in-

i

cluded much internecine Protestant strife (and some Roman Catholic) and divided British Christianity into a welter of parties, out of which many of the modern denominations came. These conflicts revolved around the nature, form and government of the Church, and its relation to the state, and also dealt with matters of theology and piety. To make all of this clear as essential background to an understanding of the religious settlement of the American colonies, the first chapter will go into the British religious struggles in some detail, relating that story to certain constellations of religious ideals and practices which can be called Anglican, Puritan, Separatist (which is also a kind of Puritan, but with significant distinctions), Roman Catholic, and Presbyterian (insofar as that term denominates the religious conclusion of the Scottish Reformation). Succeeding chapters will deal with each of those groups in turn, beginning with the Puritans of New England and not the Anglicans of Virginia, who preceded them by a few years, because of the centrality in American experience of that bold experiment and its usefulness as a point of comparison in discussing other groups. At appropriate points in the story other elements which went to make up the religious complexion of the American colonies will be introduced, such as the French and Spanish Catholic missions, the Protestants of the European continent, the small bands of Jewish exiles, and the large numbers of American Indians and Black slaves who were, usually quite unwillingly, incorporated into an emerging religious pattern.

This increasing religious pluralism in the American colonies points to the second major theme of this story, which is that however much the attempt was made to carry intact into the new world certain patterns and programs begotten in the old, many conditions in the new world combined with certain crucial tensions within the exported heritage itself to defeat the attempt at its re-creation in a new environment. Prominent among these factors leading to defeat were certain unresolved tensions and contradictions within Puritanism, probably the most important of all the religious currents having impact upon the religious settlement of the American colonies, as well as certain dimensions of the new world experience itself, such as the seemingly limitless space, the heightened motives for economic and commercial preoccupation (with its attendant secularization), and the religious pluralism and continual conflicts between different groups.

By the end of the initial period of the religious settlement of the American colonies, then, the old patterns were in serious disarray and everywhere breaking down. With what would they be replaced? That must await another volume, for it was in the ferment of Great Awakening, Enlightenment and American Revolution that new and characteristically American patterns of religious life and thought were to emerge. But the breakdown of the older patterns by the early eighteenth century must not blind us to the fact that the religious settlement of the American colonies was not primarily a radical new departure and breaking away from the long established forms of European Christendom, but rather the attempt to transport those long established forms to a new world and maintain there the state churches and religious uniformity known before. If there was any majority opinion among the earliest colonists in most of the colonies it was that religion was something which concerned the state and that the state ought to maintain religious uniformity.

PART ONE

British Background

1

Religious Conflicts in England

The religious life of the colonies in British North America began and continued through the first century of settlement as an extension to a new world of the religious conflicts of the mother country. Thus the story of religion in what was to be the first part of the United States is first the story of the transference to America of the complex religious struggles of British Christianity, and accordingly some understanding of those struggles is essential in order to understand colonial American religion. To be sure, there were exceptions to this in the various non-English speaking groups, but even where their settlement preceded that of the British, in the long run they had to adapt to British patterns and fight to retain their own identities.

Out of the conflicts within British Christianity there emerged several distinct groups or at the least distinct religious impulses, Anglican Protestants, Puritan Protestants, Separatist Radicals (also Protestant), Presbyterians and Roman Catholics.

The English Reformation and Anglicanism

Anglican Protestantism refers to that combination of groups and interests which came to control the established Church of England. It was the product of the Protestant Reformation in England, at which we must therefore look,

3

calling attention first to those religious dissatisfactions upon which the English Reformation, like the Reformation on the continent, was built. These dissatisfactions, which were also in varying degrees new styles of Christian thought and feeling, can be briefly identified as lay anticlericalism, the urge for ecclesiastical independence, scholarly Humanism, and Augustinian pietism.

Anticlerical attitudes were held by laymen almost everywhere in European Christendom by the end of the Middle Ages, so that it is not surprising that such views were current in England. Many ordinary folk simply disliked the Church as an institution because of its coercive power, monetary demands and the bad moral example of so many of its clergy, high and low. But in England lay anticlericalism also took the more specific form of Lollard or Wycliffite protest. This movement, inspired by John Wycliffe who in the late fourteenth century had denied the legitimacy of the Church's worldly power, had in the next century taken root among many lay people, especially of the artisan and merchant classes of the eastern counties and the area around London. These Lollards, many of whom were brought before local church courts and compelled to recant, and some of whom were martyred for their beliefs, criticized the wealth, pomp, and worldliness of the Church. Christ and his apostles, they declared, had been poor men preaching a simple faith—how did a corrupt institution dare to call itself their successors? Their protest was not primarily theological, although they denounced the mass and transubstantiation as idolatrous and far removed from the simplicity of primitive Christianity, but was an exaltation of the plain words of Christ which they sought to follow, as they read, treasured and distributed portions of the Bible in English. Wycliffe himself had begun work on the translation of the Bible into English. There was, then, in England on the eve of the Protestant Revolt a substantial body of common folk dissatisfied with the Church.

Alongside of this lay anticlericalism there was also present in England on the eve of the Reformation an urge for the independence of the church from foreign control and the independence of the laity from ecclesiastical control. Both burgeoning nationalism and monarchical desire to consolidate power resented the drain of finances out of England to Rome and the subservience of England to foreign ecclesiastics. Such attitudes were nursed by rulers and nobility jealous of interference by the Church in their own governmental activities, by lawyers concerned over the conflicting jurisdictions of civil and ecclesiastical courts, and by reformers who hoped that greater local control over church affairs would remedy administrative abuses in the church. The conciliarist ideals of a century before, according to which supreme authority in the church was exercised by the whole body of the bishops rather than by the Pope alone, had contributed to the urge for independence.

The Humanist movement in Renaissance scholarship was one of the main currents which flowed into the Protestant Reformation. The new learning of Renaissance Humanism involved scholarly inquiry into Christian sources which soon branched out into a call for moderate reform within the Church. At the beginning of the sixteenth century it spread rapidly through Northern Europe from its Italian origins. On the eve of the Reformation it was best represented by the Dutchman Erasmus, who labored to produce an accurate Greek text of the New Testament and who declared his hope that someday even ploughboys and milkmaids at work would sing the words of scripture in their own tongues. Erasmus spent considerable time in England, planting seeds of humanism there, but the most characteristic English humanist was John Colet who after 1496 lectured on the Bible at Oxford, treating it in the new humanist way, with plain, contextual exposition rather than in the disputatious manner of medieval scholasticism. The humanists were interested in the practical meaning of the biblical text, which they thought should be studied in the original languages and then made accessible to layfolk in the vernacular. Colet's lectures on Paul's epistles were considered revolutionary, and attracted Lollard interest. The new Renaissance learning was taken up by many others in England too, including Thomas More, a friend of both Erasmus and Colet. Such humanists often objected to the crasser elements and abuses of late medieval piety, such as its legalism and dependence on the external— relics, pilgrimages and mechanically performed devotions.

Augustinian pietism refers to yet another religious current of the early sixteenth century, an emphasis upon man's sinfulness before God and absolute need of God's grace for salvation. This outlook is termed "Augustinian" because the theology of St. Augustine had placed such great emphasis upon man's dependence upon grace, and as a theological tradition, Augustinianism occasionally appeared throughout the Middle Ages, becoming more common in the scholasticism of the later part of that era when the scholastic theology had become predominantly nominalistic, defining God in terms of sheer power and will. Thomas Bradwardine was an English scholastic theologian whose strongly Augustinian theology had considerable influence. Wycliffe too had emphasized predestination, many of the later medieval mystics spoke of the sole dependence of the individual upon God, and some humanists pointed in the same direction when they showed interest in the study of the writings of St. Augustine. When Luther appeared upon the scene he too represented Augustinian pietism, stressing as he did the agonizing search of the lonely soul for a gracious God. By the early 1520's Luther's books were being smuggled into England, probably at first by persons of Lollard sympathies, and a small circle was being formed at Cambridge University of young men who were interested not only in church reform and the new learning but also in the specific ideas of Luther about justification by grace alone. This group included Friar Robert Barnes, soon to go to Germany and make the acquaintance of Lutheranism first hand, Hugh Latimer, eventually to distinguish himself as a bishop, Thomas Bilney, and William Tyndale, a graduate ,of Oxford who came into contact with this Cambridge circle and was shortly to be known for his work of Bible translation. At the other university, John Frith, who became the author of the ablest early English Protestant tracts, was active. In time every one of these was to suffer martyrdom for his convictions.

It is not surprising, then, that when King Henry VIII chose to throw off the papal allegiance for reasons of his own, the movement away from Rome quickly snowballed, influenced as it inevitably was by these forces conducive to change. Henry's break with the Papacy became the occasion for the Reformation in England, and, as A.G. Dickens writes, "we must avoid the temptation to equate the Henrician Schism with the Protestant Reformation. The divorce-suit did not create either Protestantism or those anti-papal and anti-sacerdotal forces which smoothed its path."[1]

The religious revolution in England began when Henry, desiring the annulment of his marriage with Catherine of Aragon, pushed through a series of acts of state which separated England from the papal allegiance. This he did because he was convinced of the need to be succeeded by a male heir if his dynasty was to survive and because he was unable to get live male issue through Catherine. Perhaps also he genuinely if superstitiously felt that his marriage to Catherine had been cursed by God since she had previously been wife to his deceased brother Arthur; at least he claimed this as a reason for annulment of their marriage and in the hope of getting his relationship with the astute Anne Boleyn legitimated, that he might have a male heir by her. Unable to get an annulment from Pope Clement VII who was under the control of the Hapsburg ruler Charles V, nephew of the spurned Catherine, through a series of royal decrees and parliamentary acts Henry divorced the English Church from the Papacy and himself from Catherine. Now "supreme head" of the English Church, he was free for further matrimonial adventures and free to accede to the wishes of reformers for the purging of the church of some of its worst abuses. One of his most revolutionary ecclesiastical acts was the suppression of the monasteries, done more for financial reasons than any-thing else, although the dire social effects of this have probably been greatly exaggerated. To the end of his life, however, Henry, who had been dubbed "defender of the faith" in 1521 by the pope for writing against Luther, was adamantly opposed to most of Protestant doctrine, having Protestants burnt at the stake as heretics for the denial of the doctrine of transubstantiation. Much of the official teaching of the English church remained traditionally Catholic, and Henry's approach was supported by churchmen like Stephen Gardiner, bishop of Winchester, who both accepted Henry's supremacy in the church and rejected the introduction of Protestant teaching into England. Those like Gardiner how-ever gradually drew back from the radical consequences of the break with Rome, and returned to the Catholic Church, as Gardiner himself did.

Henry VIII died in 1547 and his sickly son by his third wife, Jane Seymour, came to the throne as Edward VI. Only nine years of age, the nation was ruled under the regencies first of the "Protector" Somerset and then of the Duke of Northumberland, and under their leadership a more thor-ough "Protestantization" of the realm was carried out, with Protestants advancing to positions of power in the church and with the adoption of a Protestant creed and liturgy in the *Forty-Two Articles* and the *Book of Common Prayer*. But Edward's reign was to be short, his death coming in 1553, when he was succeeded by his older half-sister Mary, daughter of the Catholic Catherine. Mary took steps to re-store the land to papal religion, executing many of the Pro-testant leaders of the preceding reign, but her rule too was short, ending with her death in 1558. The new monarch, Elizabeth I, daughter of Anne Boleyn, like her father was politically astute and her religious policy was to return to a moderate Protestantism which would support her rule but not unnecessarily alienate those of somewhat different outlook, including even some who had supported Mary. England had thus achieved a Protestant settlement which was to remain in spite of later threats.

Up to this point the story of the English Reformation sounds as though it were almost entirely a matter of political arrangements, but the shifting political arrangements provided the occasion for a Protestant religious movement to mature. Anglicanism, as a type of Protestantism, developed in a church in which the structural and constitutional changes often preceded the theological ones, and was a product of both kinds of change, which perhaps accounts for some of its characteristic peculiarities, especially the close control of religion by the political order. But nonetheless its inner character was most profoundly shaped by the growth of English Protestantism.

Men of Protestant sympathies were encouraged by the steps which Henry took, and some of them rose to prominence in his church, such as Hugh Latimer, named bishop of Worcester in 1535, and Thomas Cranmer, who served as Archbishop of Canterbury for over twenty years of Henry's reign. Cranmer seems to have held to Luther's justification by faith alone throughout all this period, and even to have tried to convince Henry of its truth; somehow he survived even those periods of reaction when the king cracked down on Protestant belief. Other more radical figures among the early English Protestants were to give their lives for the cause: Robert Barnes, for a while useful to Henry in seeking negotiations with German Lutherans, was burnt at the stake for heresy when his efforts proved fruitless. Earlier William Tyndale was burnt for heresy at Antwerp, where he lived as an exile because of his radical Protestant beliefs. Henry, who had approved his burning, was shortly thereafter to have the English translation of the Bible, for much of which Tyndale was responsible, distributed in the parish churches of the realm.

In the later years of the reign of Henry VIII an important change was taking place in the thinking of English Protestants, more rapidly among those in exile than among those in England. They had begun as reforming humanists, "Erasmians," who were receptive to Luther's ideas, but gradually they were turning away from the Lutheranism of Germany towards the theological outlook of Swiss and Rhineland Protestantism, derived originally from Zwingli's Zurich Reformation, but after Zwingli's death led by Heinrich Bullinger, Zwingli's successor at Zurich, Martin Bucer, the reformer of Strassburg, Johannes Oecolampadius, theologian of Basle, and eventually John Calvin, protégé of Bucer and reformer of Geneva. What this meant for the English Protestants was that while still stressing Luther's central teachings of justification by faith and the sole authority of scripture they abandoned his doctrine of the real presence of Christ in the Eucharist for the Swiss doctrine which interpreted that presence in more symbolic terms as the eating and drinking of the signs of Christ's sacrificial death, which conveyed to the believer the benefits of Christ's death but not his very body and blood. The Swiss reformers were also more radical in their application of the principle of scriptural authority, programmatically seeking to strip the outward face of the church of all non-scriptural accretions, and in their development of a lay-centered, synodal approach to the government of the church, not surprising granted the origins of the Swiss Reformation in free city-states with traditions of oligarchic self-government. These "Reformed" theologians (so they were called in distinction from "Lutheran;" later the term "Calvinist" came into currency to designate them) also put more emphasis than Luther had on the doctrine of predestination, which taught that God's grace had preceded even the faith of the "elect", and on the process of sanctification, the actual holy living of the believer who expresses his faith by good works done in obedience to the law of Christ. The Reformed theologians believed that God had chosen some persons for salvation in order that they might be a holy people doing His will on earth.

Already before Henry's death Archbishop Cranmer had apparently traded in Luther's doctrine of the Eucharist for that of the Swiss, and during the reign of Edward the English Reformation as a whole turned abruptly in that direction. In its official Articles of Religion and the teachings of its theologians the English church adopted the Swiss theology on the Lord's Supper and the other matters which separated Lutheran from Reformed. Only in the conservatism of its liturgy and the firm control of the church by the state did it resemble Lutheran Protestantism. Leading continental theologians were invited to England, and Martin Bucer, now exiled from Strassburg, came to teach at Cambridge and Peter Martyr, exiled Italian Protestant and erstwhile associate of Calvin at Geneva, came to Oxford. Thoroughgoing outward religious changes were also carried out, such as the removal of all images from churches, the replacement of altars by holy tables, and the abandonment of the special Eucharistic vestments.

This headlong rush into complete Protestantism was halted in 1553 with Edward's death, and English Protestantism was then to seal its faith in blood. At Mary's accession many Protestant leaders fled to the continent, finding refuge in places like Zurich and Geneva, but others either refused or were unable to escape. The Queen was determined to purge England of the stain of heresy and persecuted even against the counsel of her advisers, some of whom saw that it alienated the populace, turning them against a half-Spanish monarch and associated Catholicism with foreign cruelty. And so out of the burnings came that fierce and proud identification of loyal Englishman and Protestant, and for that Mary was largely responsible. Up to this point Protestantism had probably been the work of an energetic minority, but as the executions proceeded the crowds who witnessed them became more and more ominously sympathetic to the victims. The persecution also showed the heroism of the followers of the new doctrines and gave those doctrines greater prestige than they had had when merely promoted by authority not entirely free from self-seeking. Among the victims of the stake were the formerly powerful—bishops Latimer, Ridley, Hooper and Cranmer; and the lowly—including artisans and apprentices of London and at least fifty women, reminiscent of the tenacity of the Lollard type of protest against the old church among the ordinary folk. Most dramatic was the story of Cranmer, who under unrelenting pressure had recanted his Protestant faith only to retract his recantation at the last minute, and who at the stake sought to expiate his frailty by holding the hand which had signed the recantation in the rising flames until it burnt away. And the details of the whole grisly episode of persecution were etched into the minds of Englishmen through the voluminous pages of the martyrologist John Foxe, who told and retold these stories in edition after edition of his "Book of Martyrs," heightening each tale with such memorable details as the last words of Latimer to his fellow sufferer, "Be of good comfort Master Ridley, and play the man. We shall this day light such a candle, by God's grace, in England, as I trust shall never be put out." Thus the persecution "became an integral part of the memory of a people; it took its place alongside King Alfred, the Black Prince and Agincourt as a factor in the evolution of our national self-consciousness."[2]

Anglican Protestantism was shaped by these theological changes and events. But it was especially and directly shaped by the religious settlement carried out by Queen Elizabeth after 1558. Politically cautious, moderate in her own religious opinions, her reign saw England once again become fully Protestant. The *Thirty-Nine Articles*, a modification of the creed of Edward's time, were thoroughly Protestant, definitely leaning in a Swiss direction on such matters as predestination, sanctification and the presence of Christ in the sacrament. Beginning with bishop John Jewel's classic

Apology of the Church of England this "Reformed" character
of Anglican theology continued throughout most of Elizabeth's reign, with continental theologians such as Calvin and
Bullinger being the guilding lights for English theology. Far
then from being some kind of compromise between Catholic
and Protestant, the Elizabethan Church of England was a distinctly Protestant church with a decided lean in the direction
of Switzerland.

But there were elements retained in the Elizabethan church
which pointed in another direction, and which at a later time
were to be more fully developed. Elizabeth herself desired as
moderate a Protestantism as possible, allowing matters to go
as far in a Swiss direction as they did because she was
dependent upon men of such opinions to fill positions within
her ecclesiastical establishment. Where possible the Queen
preserved medieval elements, and chose as her first Archbishop of Canterbury Matthew Parker, who had not left the
country during the Marian persecution and was accordingly
less influenced by continental theology. With the aid of those
like Parker she tried to maintain a Church which while necessarily and clearly Protestant would at least on its outward
face resemble the old order as much as possible, partly
perhaps because she hoped such a policy would be less alien-
ating to a population confused by the many religious changes
it had witnessed. Thus the liturgy of the *Book of Common
Prayer* was a more traditional service book than those used
by continental Protestants, except, perhaps, for some Lutherans. With regard to what has been termed ""the scenic appa-
ratus" of worship", [3] vestments and ceremonies, for example,
she hoped to keep as much of the traditional as possible, even
long retaining candles and a cross in her private chapel in
spite of the objections of her bishops (she found it useful to
keep Catholic ambassadors guessing as to where her real
sympathies lay). The traditional governmental structure of
the church remained intact, although the monarchy stood at
its head (as "supreme governor" now) in place of the Pope:

the episcopate remained, the church courts and administrative system, with the use of canon law, continued to function, and such offices as deans, prebendaries, and archdeacons, abolished in the Reformed churches of the continent, were kept. If the English church was a compromise church, it was in this sense: a church in which while the inner core was distinctly Protestant the outer fabric retained much of the character of the medieval church, and if that is what is meant by the "via media", then Elizabeth was its architect.

By the end of the reign of Elizabeth there began to appear a school of Anglican writers who did more than grant the legitimacy of these concessions to old ways—they came to value this conservative fabric, especially liturgy, ceremonial and episcopacy, for its own sake, and to look about for a theology more appropriate as its buttress than the prevailing Calvinism. This was at first a change of tone more than a change of doctrine, visible in the thought of Richard Hooker in the 1590's, who without abandoning Reformed theology granted more value to the time-honored practices of a national church and more validity to the usages of the ancient church than was typical. Richard Bancroft, Archbishop of Canterbury early in the seventeenth century, probably first began the exaltation of episcopacy to divine right as the one legitimate mode of governing the church—earlier Anglicanism had merely argued that bishops were convenient and allowable. And in the decades after 1600 a radically new theology appeared with such theologians as Lancelot Andrewes and William Laud, who placed the focus of religion not on the Reformed scheme of predestination, justification by faith and sanctification but upon the sacraments of the church, introducing along with that theology a ritualism and ceremonialism unknown in the earlier Reformation. This new Anglicanism or "High Church" Anglicanism did not deny itself to be Protestant, but sought to develop a more "catholic" Protestantism attuned to the traditions of the ancient church as enshrined in the Councils and Church Fathers of antiquity.

This new Anglicanism was abhorrent to the Puritans in the English Church, and thus it is to them that we turn.

The Puritans

Only gradually did Puritanism emerge as a distinct movement within English Protestantism and the Church of England which can be set over against something called "Anglicanism," and in fact there continued to be much overlapping of these two religious impulses to the end of the seventeenth century. Puritanism may be defined initially as the Protestant dissatisfaction with the extent to which reform of the English church had gone. It was therefore a movement within the Church of England for its further reform which was rooted in the more radical Protestantism of the earlier English Reformation and inspired by the model of continental Protestantism and by its own thoroughgoing adherence to the Bible. Beginning in the early years of Elizabeth's reign, Puritanism was an attempt to purge the Church of England of the last vestiges of the old order. As such, Puritanism continued as a party and program in English religious life until the end of the seventeenth century, developing characteristic ideas about the polity of the church, the work of pastoral ministry, the nature of true piety, the central beliefs of Christian theology, the shape of the Christian state, and the unfolding of God's future work in the world.

As we have already seen in the cases of leaders like William Tyndale and Robert Barnes, there had been Protestant dissatisfaction with the pace of religious change in the English Reformation from the very beginning. Many of those who first took up Protestant opinions in England found themselves at odds with the authorities even after papal control had been abandoned. Advanced English Protestants were continually impatient with reluctant steps taken in the direction of change by a leadership more interested in political than religious matters and surprisingly conservative in religion in spite of the breach with the papacy. Tyndale, an exile on the continent because of his impatience, wanted his countrymen to have access to the Bible in their own language before the King could be persuaded to move in that direction, and so he proceeded to carry out his own illicit work of translation, even though it cost him his life.

Discontent with the pace of change appeared even in the reign of Edward VI, as the cases of John Hooper and John Knox show. Hooper, chosen a bishop by the king, refused to be consecrated to his office wearing the special vestments of a bishop, for which he thought there was no scriptural warrant, although after a few months imprisonment he consented to be a bishop on the king's terms! John Knox started a controversy at the end of the reign by insisting that the new edition of the *Book of Common Prayer* make quite clear that by kneeling to receive the bread and wine of the Lord's Supper nothing more was implied about Christ's presence than what was consonant with Swiss doctrine.

Puritanism emerged at the beginning of Elizabeth's reign with the memory and spirit of these earlier radicals. But meanwhile, during Mary's reign, many of the English exiles on the continent had become more radical than they had been when they left. Some of these radicals broke away from other more moderate English Protestants resident at Frankfort over the legitimacy of certain things in the *Book of Common Prayer*. One of these, John Knox, eventually went to Geneva, calling it "the most perfect school of Christ that ever was in earth since the days of the Apostles." The exiles in Geneva produced a new translation of the Bible complete with extensive annotations providing Calvinist interpretations; known as the "Geneva Bible," it was long popular in England. The whole experience of exile strengthened the Swiss and Calvinist influence in English Protestantism, and when many of these exiles returned to England and took up positions of influence in the Elizabethan church they were eager to press on in the task of reform.

These exiles on the continent and their predecessors in the

Henrician years had an international outlook on reform, and this was to be characteristic of Puritanism. With the model of such places as Geneva before them, they were deaf to those defenders of the slow pace of change in England who argued for the independence of national churches in making their own arrangements about ceremonies and church government. The Puritans shared with Calvin a vision of a united and militant international Protestantism, with churches free from state dictation and interference.

As an internationalist movement, Puritanism was also a movement of intellectuals with ideal rather than practical and political visions about the shape of the church. Not surprisingly Puritanism took firm root in the universities, especially at Cambridge, and there, with the founding in 1584 of Emmanuel College, "that happy Seminary both of Piety and Learning," it had a kind of headquarters. Theological writers naturally looked to the Protestant scholarship of the continent for models, and so became conscious of their ideas on reform and theology, and such university theologians were important as Puritan leaders.

Early radical Protestants, later exiles, and university Puritans alike searched the scriptures for directions concerning the proper beliefs and practices of the church, and thereby Puritanism came to have a very intense biblicism. On one level, this was merely the continuing study and translation of the Bible which had always been central to Protestantism, but on another level such continual searching of the scriptures could be a dangerous vocation, as new ideas were frequently thrown off by this intense biblicism, a process which is one of the most remarkable aspects of Puritanism. Sabbatarianism is an example, for after the publication in 1595 of Nicholas Bownde's *True Doctrine of the Sabbath* Puritans were generally convinced that the Sabbath legislation of the Old Testament still applied to the Christian Sunday and did their best to live up to the details of the scriptural commandments. The Puritan interest in a theology of the "covenants" (the covenants being primarily those of law and grace, of the Old and New Testaments) was also a result of their biblicism, for this gave them categories of theological interpretation which were biblical. John S. Coolidge has argued that Puritan seriousness about the Bible was so great that we may fruitfully see the whole movement as primarily a "reapprehension and development of biblical thought." [4]

Based on earlier English Protestant radicalism, continental influences strengthened by the years of Marian exile, and a strenuous biblicism, Puritanism developed in the early years of Elizabeth's reign as a program for further reform, erupting frequently into protest. Such an eruption of protest was the vestiarian controversy. The Queen, seeking to keep as much of the old fabric of church tradition as possible, wanted ministers in the celebration of the Eucharist to wear at least the surplice, a plain white outer garment worn over the cassock. To many radicals, however, any special priestly garb beyond the "grave Genevan gown" worn by the Reformed on the continent (which was really academic dress, and emphasized the minister's role as a learned expositor of the Word of God) was considered "rags of popery" and unwarranted interference of the monarch in matters which should be determined by the church itself. Led by returned exiles Laurence Humphrey and Thomas Sampson, some Puritans refused to wear the obnoxious garment, even if it meant deprivation from office. Others wore it under protest, convinced that it was better to work for change from within their positions than be deprived. Yet others, especially in the remoter areas, or those with sympathetic bishops, were never compelled to wear the surplice at all.

There were other matters which the Puritans wanted remedied in the constitution and fabric of the church. They objected to the sign of the cross in baptism, the use of wedding rings in marriage (reminiscent they thought of the Catholic doctrine of marriage as a sacrament), the use of the term "priest" in the rubrics of the *Book of Common Prayer*, bowing at the mention of the name of Jesus in the service, baptism by midwives, and much else.

Some of their desired changes related to the very structure of parish life and worship. They were concerned that such abuses as pluralism (the amassing of many offices and parishes by a single cleric) and nonresidence (not residing in the parish of which one was the incumbent) prevented many parishes from having a competent minister; their hope was that with the remedy of these abuses each parish would be supplied with a "godly, preaching" minister, trained at the universities. In lists of particulars drawn up to support petitions which they prepared for parliament they detailed the unworthiness of many clergy: some could not preach, being without any education, or neglected their pastoral duties, or in doctrine were "popishly affected", or were morally unfit, guilty of such things as adultery and "tippling" in the taverns. Clearly, to the Puritans such a state of things must be remedied.

In desiring these changes however they ran up against some very strong obstacles. In the first place, the Queen hardly wanted militant Puritans in every parish, preferring those who would do the royal bidding and make no trouble, though it was in her interest to place trained preachers in the more remote and still Catholic areas of her domain since they would be supporters of her Protestant establishment. But also there were not sufficient monetary resources available to the church to support such a complete turnover in personnel, and the abuses of pluralism and nonresidence were so widespread precisely for this reason, many parishes providing a stipend too small to support a university trained minister, especially as he was now likely to have a wife and children. Accumulation of benefices resulted from this poverty of the church, and in the course of the sixteenth century the situation was worsened by inflation. But the Puritans accurately saw that the generality of the clergy left much to be desired in their theological training and faithfulness to their duties. Many of these incumbent clergy at the beginning of Elizabeth's reign were men who had changed religion a number of times to keep their posts while monarchs and religions came and went: Catholics in 1530, the great majority became Henricians, then accepted the complete Protestantism of Edward's reign, then were Roman Catholic again under Mary and now had just recently become Protestants again by royal proclamation. That they should be theologically learned or conscientious in their duties was to ask too much—many who had been either of those had been weeded out long before.

Whatever the obstacles, the Puritan party was straightforward in demanding reform. Edward Dering, preaching before the Queen in 1570, called attention to a number of abuses, describing some of the clergy as "ruffians, some hawkers and hunters, some dicers and carders, some blind guides and cannot see, some dumb dogs and will not bark." Of Elizabeth's own chapel he declared "I need not seek far for offences whereat God's people are grieved, even round about this chapel I see a great many." He explained to the Queen that God appoints rulers to be "nurses" to his church and root out evils, "And yet you, in the meanwhile that all these whoredoms are committed, you at whose hands God will require it, you sit still and are careless."[5] We are not surprised to hear that the Queen was angry with this preacher. An *Admonition to the Parliament* appeared in 1572, frankly outlining Puritan demands, but parliament did not act upon its suggestions. Speaking in parliament in 1576 a Puritan member, Peter Wentworth, maintained that parliament could not wait for the Queen to act but must press ahead with reforms; for his outspokenness he spent the rest of the parliamentary session in prison, receiving the Queen's pardon only when it was over.

With the death of Elizabeth in 1603 the Puritans hoped for

better things from the Scottish James I, presenting him with their "Millenary Petition" requesting moderate changes; but they were to be disappointed, James telling them to "either conform yourselves or I will harry you out of the land." In 1618 James ordered the "Book of Sports," which urged the populace to Sunday recreations, to be read from pulpits, but since this violated their sabbatarianism many Puritans refused, some even suffering deprivation from office as a result.

In the reign of Charles I which began in 1625, the Puritans found themselves confronted by a monarch more hostile to them than Elizabeth or James. Charles I patronized the new group of "High Church" Anglican divines and appointed the anti-Calvinist and anti-Puritan William Laud to be bishop of London and then Archbishop of Canterbury. Laud not only enforced the strictest conformity to all the rules and rites of the church but promoted changes in the fabric and worship of the church which gave the Puritans additional matter for denunciation, such as the replacement of Holy Tables with Altars in the chancels of the parish churches. In a characteristic protest against this new ritualism, Peter Smart, a prebendary of Durham Cathedral, complained of the innovations made there by the "Laudian" John Cosin, whom he claimed had burnt candles to the Virgin, set a cross and candles on the altar and bowed before them, revived the wearing of eucharistic copes, enjoined the congregation to stand for the Nicene Creed, insisted that worshippers pray facing eastward, "scolding and brawling with them, even in time of Divine Service, which refuse to do it," and introduced into the service the playing of those musical instruments "which were used at the consecration of Nabuchadonozer's golden image."[6] To the Puritans with their insistence on plain biblical simplicity all this was intolerable.

Stymied so often in their attempts to reform the English church, many Puritans began to question the very structure of the church's government; thwarted by bishops who were the Queen's appointees, they began to question the legitimacy of the government of the church by bishops. There were several motives for questioning the episcopal system: they wanted to give greater freedom to the 'godly' laity in choosing their own pastors so that they could receive the spiritual nourishment for which they hungered; to put the power of excommunication into the hands of the congregation, so that it could be exercised for the maintenance of discipline within the parish; and they thought that the government of the church should be exercised by the whole body of faithful and conscientious ministers.

These motives were all involved in the "Presbyterianism" of Thomas Cartwright, a Cambridge scholar who in the 1570's argued that in the New Testament bishops and elders are the same office under different names and that consequently all the clergy should be on the same level, without any ruling over the others. The church should be governed by an eldership of equals which included lay elders and which carried out the business of the church through congregational consistories and higher regional synods. Cartwright found it necessary to go into exile on the continent, but his ideas were acceptable to many Puritans, and received wide dissemination through the writings of Walter Travers. Basically this "Presbyterianism" would have put authority in the church into the hands of the Puritan ministers themselves.

In the "prophesyings" of the later years of Elizabeth's reign there appeared a kind of "underground" Presbyterianism. These prophesyings were local meetings of clergy and sometimes their lay supporters who listened to sermons and discussed mutual problems, especially pastoral concerns. Such meetings were interpreted by many in authority, including the Queen, as potentially seditious and certainly unauthorized, and she ordered them to cease. However, her archbishop of Canterbury, Edmund Grindal, who had himself spent some years of exile in Zurich, refused to carry out this order, believing that the prophesyings were helpful in training the clergy. Deprived of much of the authority of his office thereafter, Grindal shows how sympathy for Puritanism could be found in the highest levels of the church. In spite of Grindal, the prophesyings were suppressed.

There were other Puritans unhappy with the government of the church who went farther than Cartwright, arguing that all authority in the church resided in the local congregation of "gathered" believers, which was the only real "church." Such "Congregationalism," going back to Robert Browne, often led right out of the Church of England altogether, but some Congregationalists, led by Henry Jacob, early in the seventeenth century sought to reconcile their views with acceptance of the established church. Both the Presbyterian and Congregationalist schemes represent dissatisfaction with the state's interference in religious matters and were important ideals for many Puritans, but it would be mistaken to think of them as anything like "denominations"—they represented tendencies present within Puritanism.

Preoccupation with the proper government of the church, central to Puritanism as it was, was not the most central element. For every Puritan who concerned himself with such things there were many more who were more interested in the preaching and pastoral duties of their parishes. William Haller in his classic *The Rise of Puritanism* focused on this aspect of Puritanism, viewing the movement as a "brotherhood of preachers" concerned primarily to be "physicians of the soul." Such men as John Dod, long active as a minister in Oxfordshire, or Richard Sibbes, a prominent preacher at London, were sometimes in trouble for their lack of conformity to the rites of the Church of England, but concentrated not on those things but on the care of souls. They proclaimed a message dealing with sin, salvation, and conversion. They themselves had had religious experiences in which they progressed through a consciousness of sinfulness and the need of grace to an experience of conversion leading to a gradual process of spiritual growth, and they tried to bring such experiences through their preaching and pastoral care to those placed in their charge, surrounding themselves especially with a body of 'godly' laity who listened intently to their sermons and avidly received their spiritual direction. These preachers were greatly concerned with the problem of assurance: how may one know and feel a gracious God, and experience the forgiveness of sins? In a typical sermon of assurance, Sibbes told his hearers that God "is a physician good at all diseases, especially at the binding up of a broken heart," and that "there is more mercy in Christ than sin in us."7 In addition to sermons, their piety can be seen in letters of spiritual advice written to friends, in which they provided warm solace for a devout following. Most commonly the letters and sermons portrayed the Christian life as a pilgrimage through sin to grace and as a struggle against the power of evil in oneself and the world. The Puritan classic *Pilgrim's Progress* can be looked upon as the distillation into symbol and story of thousands of Puritan sermons and treatises and above all of the religious experience which those sermons reflected.

With such an interest in the spiritual life of the individual it is not surprising that diaries and biographies were popular elements in Puritan piety. The diary was usually kept privately and to it one could confide the most profound yearnings and searching questions in the process of spiritual pilgrimage, probing existentially the mysteries of sin and grace. Puritans thrilled to the spiritual exploits of their heroes and saints as these were recounted in biography. Often these biographies took the form of funeral eulogies in which the piety of some notable figure of the "brotherhood of preachers" was celebrated; these biographies were often brought together in compilations and became important reading matter for the devout.

Sermon and spiritual biography enables us to see clearly what was really central to Puritanism. For at its heart Puritanism was a peculiarly intense piety, an "Augustinian piety" which magnified the grace of God and saw sinful man as helpless before Him, stressing the Christian life as a continual dependence on grace. This piety could be an ecstatic piety, in which the believer rejoiced in God's grace, and it could be an experience of agony, as one struggled to find signs of grace within. The other concerns of Puritanism were outcroppings of this very personal and intense version of the core of the Protestant Reformation.

This Puritan concern with grace and the spiritual life was enshrined in a theological system which was an English modification and systematization of the themes central to the Reformed theology of the continent, going back especially to Bucer and Calvin but dependent also on such other theologians as Peter Martyr and Heinrich Bullinger. This Puritan theology was written by men at the universities, and William Perkins of Cambridge, reputedly one of the most learned Protestants of his time, is a good example. In his *A Golden Chaine* he provided a summary of theology which was widely influential. Perkins sought to exalt God's grace in salvation through an emphasis upon such elements in the order of salvation as predestination (that so far was faith from being man's achievement that it was the result of God's eternal choice, thus guaranteeing that no man could claim that his salvation was through his own merit); justification by faith (that man was redeemed by Christ's merits imputed to him, and not by his own desserts, and must respond in trust to a gracious God); sanctification (that God through his Holy Spirit works in his chosen believers to make them a holy people who fulfill His will on earth); and glorification (that those who have trusted in God will be brought finally to his presence). The theology of Puritanism accordingly was closely related to its piety, but sometimes this is far from apparent because of the logical and scholastic manner in which it was presented and the growing preoccupation with predestination which often lost sight of that doctrine's original roots in piety and turned it into a complex and mysterious determinism. The Puritan interest in the biblical covenants tended to modify the harsher aspects of Puritan theology and refresh it with a livelier biblical imagery and greater recognition of human responsibility.

In the later years of Elizabeth's reign and into the next century many Anglican writers began to call in question this Reformed and Calvinist theology so dear to the Puritans, substituting for it a greater emphasis on the sacraments. To this the Puritans responded in alarm, fearing that the very essence of the Christian faith as they understood it was being undermined from within the Church of England. In the seventeenth century accordingly, Puritan came to be increasingly divided from Anglican over theological belief as well as over the fabric, ritual and government of the church. When under Laud an effort was made to silence all teaching on the subject of predestination the Puritans became far more alientated from the Church than ever before and called for the return of the church to its original theological moorings, attacking the new "Arminian" school of Anglican theology as a halfway house to "popery." John Davenport, who later went to New England, wrote to a friend that Puritans must join together against the new theological danger which was far more serious than earlier disputes over ceremonies. Bitterly assailing the English Church for apostasy, Puritans began to find relief in exile—either in the Netherlands or across an ocean in America.

Puritanism was a movement for the reform of the church, and a type of Christian piety and theology, but it was also a movement for the re-ordering of society and the state—"the Puritan thrust carried all Puritans into a determined effort to erect a holy community"[8] —and it was probably at this point that Puritanism had its most revolutionary impact.

Puritan concern with the building of a Christian society was first of all part of its continental Reformed heritage. The sanctification so emphasized in the Swiss Reformation involved not only the individual but the sanctification of the community as well, the creation of a disciplined Christian community. Bucer had written his *The Kingdom of Christ* in 1550 and presented it to the boy king Edward VI in the hope that he might lead England to be such a kingdom of Christ on earth. Beginning with the premise that it is the duty of Christian people and magistrates to erect the perfect Christian society, Bucer detailed the elements of such a society: there would be prosperity and work for everyone; the oppression of the poor by the rich would cease; no amusements not conducive to piety would be allowed; all who were qualified would have educational opportunity. More important than Bucer's book was the example of Calvin's Geneva, to Puritans a truly reformed city where matters of economic and social policy were under the influence of pastoral direction. Some earlier English religious leaders, most notably bishop Latimer, had advocated significant reforms in English society as consequences of religious reformation. The Reformed ideal to which Puritans looked was one which affirmed that religion was not to be narrowly confined to some "spiritual" realm but had ramifications for the whole corporate life of humanity.

Puritan theology was imbued with the idea of the biblical covenants. Such covenantal thinking carried over beyond the realm of theology proper: the concern with church government was often an application to the local congregation of certain implications of this idea, with the congregation formed by the members covenanting with one another to walk together in Christian fellowship and covenanting together with God to believe and obey. It carried over also to the whole nation: just as ancient Israel was in a special covenant relationship with God, so was England, with the demand made upon her by God that she fulfill the terms of the covenant, that England as a nation be holy. Such ideas about England's covenant were fostered by John Foxe's *Acts and Monuments*, or "Book of Martyrs." There the vicissitudes of England's religious history were explained as the result of a divine scheme of reward and punishment whereby God, just as in his dealings with ancient Israel, set before men the choice of blessing or cursing depending on their fulfillment of his commandments. And so England too must obey God; covenanted with Him as a people they must do His work in the world, shaping the nation into His Kingdom.

There was revolutionary potential in such ideas about the "holy commonwealth," especially when coupled with the enthusiasm of Puritanism. Puritans were proponents of an idealistic program for which they were willing to struggle and sacrifice. Like modern political zealots, they were alienated from customary ways of thinking and feeling and wedded to an ideology,. an intellectual scheme by which they would remake the traditional order. Such a way of thinking and acting about society was to have a freer hand in shaping New England than it ever had in old, though in old England too the force of the Puritan "holy commonwealth" was to be felt in the years of Cromwell's power.

The emergence of this new Puritan character had implications for the economic realm too. Much has been written about Protestantism, and more particularly Puritanism, and capitalism (Max Weber and R. H. Tawney are best known for this). Going back to Luther, Protestantism had felt that one's true Christian duty was to be worked out not in some special spiritual realm of withdrawal, but in the arena of everyday life and occupation and service to the neighbor. For Luther, the Christian shoemaker expressed his faith by making the best shoes he could through diligent labor and not by closing his shop and going on a pilgrimage. Protestantism as a whole emphasized the citizen's useful work, and with a "this-worldly asceticism" whereby there was little inclination to squander profit in the pursuit of frivolities, wealth accumulated and could be reinvested. Puritanism added to this the sense of being cut off from the time-worn patterns of the past and engaged in fulfilling one's destiny.

through sober and earnest application of talents. It is not surprising then that there was an affinity between Puritanism
and the developing middle class. But many discussions of the
subject have added that Puritans equated godliness and prosperity and believed that the predestined would grow rich. In
fact, it is very difficult to find any Puritan writer through the
end of the seventeenth-century saying any such thing: often
Puritan writers echoed the medieval theme which identified
piety and poverty, although not in the passive sense that little
could be done about one's lot in life, but because the Christian life is such a self-conscious struggle against the ways of
the world that the Christian warrior should expect adversity
from a hostile world and chastisement from the God with
whom he is covenanted, but the terms of whose covenant he
can never perfectly fulfill. "Puritans had much to say about
poverty but, certain modern writers to the contrary, they
knew better than to teach that the godly would invariably
prosper and that the poor were innately vicious."9 And as
long as Puritanism was a living religious force, it not only
thrust people towards hard work and prosperity but checked
their acquisitiveness with an idealism exalting sacrifice and
generosity.

For all its concern with the political, social and economic
life of this world, Puritanism was always informed by a
strong sense of God's grace being all important, and thus its
ideas about the Kingdom of God on earth were not only
beliefs about what humanity must be busy doing but also
about what God was in the process of accomplishing. This
was the "eschatology" of Puritanism, consisting of faith in
God's power to shape the future. Eschatological thinking was
prominent in Christianity from the beginning when the early
believers expected an imminent end of the present world
order. This enthusiasm waned, but Christians never
abandoned their hope that Christ would return to
consummate history. These beliefs were typically· other-
worldly, but in the later middle ages religious movements

arose which revived eschatology and gave it a more immediate meaning: a new age was about to dawn in which old oppressions would end and a new era of peace and justice arrive. At the beginning of the Reformation some Anabaptists proclaimed such views, and by the later sixteenth-century there was a growing Puritan interest in this. The focus of Puritan eschatology tended to be "this-worldly"—not the end of earthly existence but its reordering. This was a powerful motivating force for those striving to reform church and state, for they came to feel that in their struggles they were God's advance guard in bringing about His new day. In the excitement of the years of civil war in the 1640's hopes about the coming new age flourished, and Puritan eschatology became more apocalyptic, envisioning future events as a dramatic and cataclysmic divine intervention in history. In New England all this had its direct application: going to a new world and building there a new society were to Puritans actions related to the coming of God's kingdom.

With so much revolutionary potential built into its piety, it is no wonder that when civil war came to England in 1642 the Puritans were decidedly on the side of the Parliament against King Charles I. Historians since have sometimes termed it the Puritan Revolution. To be sure there were many grievances besides religious ones separating monarch and parliament, but not only had the Puritans long been alienated from the monarchy because of its ecclesiastical policy (and that alienation had become far worse in the 1630's with Laud's "high church" supremacy in the Church of England), but also the Puritans had generally sympathized with parliamentary defense of the common law and resistance to the arbitrary exercise of monarchical prerogative.

Puritan political thought became more radical as it first justified rebellion against the king and then the execution of the king, although some Puritans never supported either. In defending these actions the Puritans drew upon their continental Reformed heritage: Calvin had permitted resistance to tyrants when led by the "lesser magistrate" and not simply anarchical, and the French and Dutch Calvinists in their long struggles with Catholic authority had carried the argument much further. In their Reformation too the Scots had claimed the right to overthrow an ungodly government, so there was precedent for the Puritans. Anglicanism on the other hand had exalted monarchy and denied the right to resist even an unjust ruler whom God had appointed.

When however Puritans did come to power in England in the short period of Cromwellian rule before the Restoration of the monarchy in 1660, they had spent so many years in the wilderness awaiting the promised land that having arrived there they were unable to agree among themselves as to the right pattern for their new age. In the early years of parliamentary supremacy the more moderate "Presbyterian" Puritans had been in control: they wanted England to be a more "constitutional" monarchy, to reform the Church of England of its abuses, abolishing episcopacy, but maintaining it as a tightly controlled state church, firmly wedded to the strict Calvinism of their recently produced *Westminster Confession.* But Puritanism for many had moved far beyond such a stance, producing not only the desire for greater independence of Congregationalism, but also a welter of new sects. With the execution of the King and Cromwell's personal rule after 1649 a much wider and more tolerant church system obtained than the presbyterians desired, one in which individual parishes had considerable freedom to go their own way, with many having "Congregationalist" pastors, and the whole supervised by boards of clergy who removed incumbents who were either unfit or disloyal to the new government. Cromwell himself favored the "Independent" or "Congregationalist" party, but continually strove, with little success, to get most of the religious factions of the land to work together.

With Charles II on the throne in 1660 the days of Puritan triumph were over and thereafter Puritanism was to be a quite different movement. Expelled from the Church of England *en masse* in the St. Bartholomew's Day Ejection of clergy in 1662, Puritanism was on the way to becoming the "dissenting denominations" of the next century: denominations of Presbyterians, Congregationalists, Baptists and Quakers outside of the state church suffering from the various civil disabilities of dissenters from the Establishment and yet settling down to the quiet life of dissenting chapels and academies and the sober piety of leaders like the hymnwriter Isaac Watts.

But in the period before the Toleration Act of 1689 Puritans were to suffer another time of trial, with the Restoration government forbidding their meetings and harassing them through cruel penal laws. Two major figures of Puritanism in that era were Richard Baxter and John Owen, leaders of the Presbyterians and Congregationalists, respectively. Baxter had been offered a bishopric by Charles II if he would conform to the surplice and *Book of Common Prayer* (he had never supported Cromwell) but these compromises he was finally unable to make. He led scattered "Presbyterian" groups of moderate Puritans who still hoped for inclusion within the state church on terms more liberal than any yet offered them, only accepting their status as "dissenters" after 1689. As a theological writer Baxter had modified Calvinism, placing greater emphasis on freedom of the will; these Presbyterians as a whole minimized dogma, becoming a more theologically liberal element within Puritanism. Baxter's moderate school of Calvinism was to have considerable influence in New England at the end of the century.

It was far different with John Owen. Staunch revolutionary and religious adviser to Oliver Cromwell, he had preached before parliament in defense of the King's execution, and was in danger of his life at the Restoration, considering for a while removal to Massachusetts. Protected by influential friends among the gentry, he emerged as the leader of Congregationalists no longer interested in inclusion in the state church. The greatest English Calvinist theologian of his day, whose voluminous writings defended orthodoxy against all challengers, Owen's legacy was a strictly Calvinist Congregationalism which found it ever more difficult to cooperate with their Presbyterian brethren. Of tremendous reputation in New England, Owen's advice was several times sought concerning matters related to Harvard College, and he was dubbed by Cotton Mather "our great Owen."

Puritan Separatists

After the Restoration Separatism was the condition of Puritans as a whole, forced upon them whether they accepted the principle of it or not. This meant that differences which had earlier appeared to be of the greatest importance were no longer meaningful distinctions. But long before 1660 many Puritans had become impatient and withdrawn from the national church. These Separatists were usually inspired by some aspect of the piety and program of Puritanism and had chosen to pursue it outside of the established church. In many cases those who became Separatists were simply Puritans who lived in an area where an unusually severe suppression was experienced, or were pastors responding to the radical thrust of their own lay followers, or laity angered by the deprivation of their desired minister. In short, if Puritanism was the Protestant dissatisfaction with the Elizabethan church settlement, Separatism was dissatisfaction with that Puritan dissatisfaction.

There had been several early conventicles of radical Protestants before the reign of Elizabeth, perhaps with connections to the Anabaptist radicalism of the continent, and by the end of her reign convictions about the utter corruption of the Church of England and the character of the true church as "gathered" and voluntary appeared among those of Puritan inspiration. One of the earliest was Robert Browne who formed a separated congregation at Norwich in 1581 and published his *Reformation Without Tarrying for Anie* the next year. For Browne the only true church was a local body of gathered believers, subject to discipline from each other and "walking together" in a covenant relationship. Indeed, the exercise of discipline and the "owning of the covenant" within a small fellowship was of the very essence of the Separatist mentality—unlike the mainstream of Puritanism they abandoned larger schemes for church and nation and concentrated on the spiritual purity of the few. Browne was arrested for holding an illegal meeting, released, fled to the Netherlands, and by 1585 had conformed again to the Church of England. But others had taken up the ideal, and two of these, Henry Barrowe and John Greenwood, were executed in 1593 for denying the Queen's supremacy in matters of religion. Francis Johnson had been associated with Greenwood, but released from prison he led some Separatists to the Netherlands where, by 1597, he was their pastor. A similar group was led to the Netherlands a little later by John Robinson from Scrooby, England, and they later moved to Plymouth in New England—to them we shall later return.

Some of the Separatists resident in the Netherlands took a further step under the leadership of John Smyth who, educated at Cambridge and ordained in the Church of England, gathered a Separatist following at Gainsborough in 1606 from whence they moved to the Netherlands. There he concluded from scripture that there was no warrant for the baptism of infants and that the true gathered church was to be made up of adult believers only, baptized as adults. He therefore proceeded to rebaptize himself by affusion and then rebaptized those of his followers who could take this further step towards congregational purity with him. Later he contacted the Dutch Anabaptists and abandoned Calvinist theology, thus becoming the founder of the General Baptists, or those who believed in a general or universal offer of salvation rather than in predestination.

One of Smyth's followers who had followed him from Gainsborough and become a Baptist with him, Thomas Helwys, could not take this final step of theological change, and so became a leader of a faction of Baptists who remained Calvinists, considering themselves therefore quite distinct from the Dutch Anabaptists. They came to be known as the Particular Baptists because of their belief in God's predestination of particular persons and were in the long run the most important of the English Baptists.

Puritanism thus had a kind of "splintering" dynamism within it: urging persons to the most intense kind of religious experience, making that experience deeply personal, and insisting that the Bible was an absolute guide to the true form of the church, it produced many highly individualistic figures who pushed to the limit their own biblical interpretations. Such persons were often lonely individuals, suppressed for heresy by the authorities, without even their erstwhile Puritan friends to help them; and with the advent of civil war and the execution of the king, religious and social radicalism of Puritan ambience began to luxuriate, nourished both by the new freedom and by heightened eschatalogical hopes, capitalizing on "a breakdown of confidence in established forms of religion" which was "conspicuously prevalent in London and the Army, especially among the young."[10] The "Presbyterian" Puritans, who had hoped to control the revolution, were horrified by this development and strove to impose greater religious uniformity; one of them, Thomas Edwards, declared in his *Gangraena; or A Catalogue and Discovery of many of the Errours, Heresies, Blasphemies and pernicious Practices of the Sectaries of this time*, that the tolerance of the day was "the cause and fountain of all kinde of damnable Heresies and Blasphemies, loose and ungodly practices" and "would destroy all Religion."[11]

Included among these sectarians were not only Separatists and Baptists but also "Seekers," Separatists who denied that there was any truly constituted church yet on earth and awaited Christ's future action to establish it; "Levellers," who maintained that the Kingdom of Christ levelled all social distinctions; "Diggers," to whom all earthly things were to be held and used in common since at creation there had been no establishment of property; "Ranters," a vague term which covered anticlerical scoffers and even sceptics; and many other individual heretics who taught such things as did John Overton, who denied the immortality of the soul, holding that the soul sleeps until the last resurrection, or John Biddle, who denied the divinity of Christ. Thomas Edwards included in his list of current heresies such opinions as "the Scriptures no where speak of Sacraments," "there ought to be no distinct order of ministers," "'tis lawful for women to preach," and "That using of set forms of prayer prescribed is Idolatry."[12]

Eschatological enthusiasm about the end of the age was often important as inspiration for new "heresies." Bizarre eschatological beliefs had long flourished on the edges of Puritanism, like the claim of Francis Kett in the 1580's that true believers should gather in Jerusalem to await the Second Coming of Christ. Certainly the Seeker inspiration was eschatological, that God would establish a new church. Most eschatological of all were the Fifth Monarchy Men, who opposed existing human government because they expected an imminent rule of the saints on earth, along with the returning Christ, which would last a thousand years and be the fifth monarchy of Daniel's prophecy. This enthusiasm was opposed to Cromwell and inspired abortive revolts. The Fifth Monarchists were greatly feared by their contemporaries, one heresiographer reporting that they taught "That all the ungodly must be killed" and "that the wicked have no property."[13]

The mixture of eschatological enthusiasm and extreme individualism in radical Puritan piety had its most significant fruition in the appearance of the Society of Friends or "Quakers." Hopes about a new age of purely spiritual religion went back to the later middle ages and the thought of Joachim of Fiore who had predicted a new age of the Holy Spirit; these hopes were revived by radical spiritualists at the Reformation. The new spiritual age would be one in which persons would have direct unmediated experience of the divine presence. George Fox and his followers, derisively called "Quakers," revived such expectations in Cromwellian England. Fox, proclaiming the light of Christ within each individual and the coming of the new age of the Holy Spirit, gathered a considerable following from among the spiritually dissatisfied of his time. Although the Friends were an off-shoot of Puritanism ("characteristically Quaker teachings were often Puritan attitudes pushed to severe conclusions"[14]), developing especially out of the Puritan belief in the indwelling of the Holy Spirit in the believer, which to them meant the superiority of inner "spirit" even to the outer "letter" of scripture, they abandoned many elements of traditional belief retained in Puritanism such as the practice of the sacraments and the professional ministry. They also rejected the Calvinism of the Puritans. Quakerism was considered by the authorities a dangerous aberration, disruptive of all legitimate authority and a menace to public order—Quakers frequently interrupted church services, denouncing the places of worship as "steeple-houses" and the ministers as "hireling dogs." They were frequently imprisoned, and their suppression was especially severe after the episode of James Naylor. Naylor led a band of followers into Bristol seated on a donkey with the crowd waving branches and crying out "hosanna." To the Friends this was a dramatic recognition of the Christ who is within all; to the authorities it was a blasphemous parody of the triumphal entry of Christ into Jerusalem and met with the sternest punishment—Naylor himself was imprisoned and died there. With the Restoration government of Charles II the suppression of Quakerism was to be especially cruel, large numbers suffering imprisonment; Cromwell earlier had felt some affinity with them and in the case of Naylor had sought to save them from the excesses of their enthusiasm.

All of these Separatist groups at the "left" of Puritanism represent dissatisfaction with the Puritan dissatisfaction with the insufficiently reformed Church of England. They also represent a withdrawal from the official religion of the state, and the best of them represent the attempt, in freedom, to realize in a small band of like-minded individuals the true experience of a disciplined Christian fellowship and of heart-felt personal faith. The mainstream of Puritanism, however, continued to consider such separation wrong, for it meant abandoning the very possibility of reforming the church from within which was the center of their hopes. Nonetheless Separatism had appeal and power precisely because it built upon all the points of Puritan discontent, and then concluded that the only honest response was to leave the Church of England as a false church, upbraiding the non-separatist Puritan for inconsistency and the failure to act his convictions.

Roman Catholicism in England

There was also a totally different kind of dissatisfaction with the Church of England from that of Puritans and Separatists, the dissatisfaction of those who could not be reconciled to the established church because it was a Protestant church which had forbidden the old religion. Thus we turn to the continued presence in England of those loyal to mass and papacy.

There was some resistance from the beginning to Henry VIII's changes, but even with the suppression of the monasteries protest was minimal—most of the former monks and nuns accepted government pensions and the royal supremacy, only a very few emigrating to the continent to continue the religious life there. Before that some Carthusian monks had been executed for not accepting the King's supremacy in religion, and of course there were the more famous martyrs

Sir Thomas More and Bishop John Fisher. There were several local peasant risings, often as much economic as religious in inspiration, in which a hearkening back to the old religion was echoed among the grievances felt, such as the revolt in 1549 in Cornwall and Devon, which called for the restoration of the mass. Even in Elizabeth's reign there was still a good deal of conservative feeling which longed for the religious satisfactions which had been provided through the mass, the confessional, the various local shrines and church festivals. Late in her reign the Puritan writer George Gifford represents the "simple sort" as nostalgically remembering "the merry world when there was lesse preaching, and when all things were so cheape, that they might have xx eggs for a penny." 15. No doubt this kind of residual folk Catholicism long lingered in many areas of England, having much to do not only with the acceptance of an Anglicanism with a more traditional outer fabric and resistance to the inroads of a more strenuous Puritanism, but also with the later revival of Roman Catholicism in such areas as the remoter north.

After the short interlude of the restoration of Catholic worship under Queen Mary, the 1559 Act of Uniformity abolished the mass again, the Roman Catholic bishops were ousted from office for refusing the oath of supremacy, something over two hundred papalist clergy were removed, and the renewed monastic communities were dissolved. Then a series of penal laws were enacted to crush the profession of the religion of the Church of Rome: the oath of supremacy was required for public office, thus excluding Catholics who could not acknowledge the monarch as "supreme governor" of the church; clergy who refused the use of the *Book of Common Prayer* were subject to fines and imprisonment; laity were fined for absences from parish churches on the Sabbath. At first many of Catholic opinion continued to attend the parish churches, although the mass was sometimes said privately, but Pope Pius V in 1566 advised them that it was unlawful to attend the parish services; those who withdrew and made themselves subject to the penal laws were now called "recusants."

Meanwhile English Catholic exiles were regrouping on the continent to carry out an attack upon the new religion of England. Among these exiles were a number of former scholars of the University of Oxford, which had been something of a Catholic stronghold, and whose Catholicism had been strengthened by Queen Mary's appointments. William Allen, later to be made a cardinal, established at Douay in Flanders in 1568 an "English College" as a center for the exiles and a launching-pad for a "mission" to England. Two former Oxford men, Thomas Harding and Thomas Stapleton, attacked the Church of England in print, stigmatizing it as schismatic and heretical. From this group came a new translation of the Bible for the use of Catholic Englishmen, the Douay-Rheims version. There developed also among these English Catholic exiles a school of devotional writing, typified by such a figure as Robert Southwell, martyred in 1595, the author of baroque devotions and mystical poetry.

Catholic hopes were reawakened with the coming to England of Mary Queen of Scots in 1568; but her presence also revived the monarchy's fear of Catholic plotting and rebellion, confirmed in the next year by a revolt of some of the northern nobility; planned to coincide with this rebellion was an invasion by a Spanish Catholic army from the Netherlands, but it never came. Buttressing both rebellion and invasion was to be the definitive decree of the pope concerning Elizabeth: in his bull of 1570 Pius V called Elizabeth a heretic and "abettor of heretics," who had incurred the sentence of anathema. Moreover this anathema had a political consequence, declaring the Queen to be deprived "of her pretended right to the aforesaid realm" and declaring her subjects to be freed of all obligations of loyalty to her. Even assassination of the Queen received papal approval in 1580 if it was done with the intention of serving God. A few years later the papal blessing was given to the attempt of the Spanish Armada to crush England. All this further drove a wedge between English nationalism and loyalty to the monarch on the one hand and the Roman Catholic faith on the other, forcing English Catholics with a cruel choice between nation and religion; nor was the papacy sympathetic to their dilemma, Pope Clement VIII responding to the pleas of English Catholics with "Do you wish to live among thorns and yet not be pricked?"16

In the meantime "seminary priests" trained at Douay were secreting themselves into England, saying mass and hearing confessions in the private homes of the Catholic gentry and nobility of the north country. The story of this English Catholicism is a dramatic one, as fugitive priests moved furtively from place to place, finding refuge in the "priest-holes" or special secret passages of country manors, with discovery meaning imprisonment, torture and possibly death. Steadily the priests poured in: before the removal of the Douay academy to Rheims in 1578 some fifty-two had found their way into England. Three Jesuits arrived as part of the English mission in 1580, and many more were to come; William Allen had long desired the participation of the militant and able Jesuits in this effort. Robert Parsons, who had fled England under suspicion of Romanism and joined the Jesuits became the leader of this phase of the mission.

Against this Catholic offensive the authorities in England acted. It was declared treason to call the Queen heretic or obey the papal excommunication of 1570; in 1581 a law enacted by parliament made it treason to convert to Roman Catholicism or to convert someone else; in 1585 another Act decreed that any Catholic priest ordained abroad since 1559 must depart England within forty days or else take the oath of supremacy—after that "grace" period to remain or even to harbor a remaining priest was punishable by death. And thus the bloody story of the execution of these priests began. None however was executed for specifically religious reasons, their crime (and punishment) being that of treason.

Elizabeth had said she had no desire to make windows into men's souls, but she was surely concerned for their outward conformity to her church and loyalty to her rule. Her government did all it could to implicate Catholics in treasonable plots to make the suppression of the priests all the more political. Before Elizabeth's reign was over, nearly two hundred priests had suffered death in England. To Catholics they were martyrs, but to the English government traitors; as A. G. Dickens comments, "Seen as individuals, these missionaries are true heroes and martyrs, yet the fact remains that they were sent by superiors and rulers with every intention of using their work as a basis for the forcible imposition of a foreign Catholic monarch upon England."[17].

In the midst of persecution, Catholics found occasion for an internal conflict of their own over the extent of the independence of English Catholicism and the implications of their religious loyalty. Essentially what emerged was one party gathered around the secular priests who were more English in their outlook and hopeful of reconciling their Catholicism with national loyalty and another oriented to the leadership of the Jesuits, who were more willing to engage in anti-government plotting. The Jesuit leader Robert Parsons advocated the claims of pretenders to the English throne, but was opposed in this by the others, called "Appellants" because of their appeals to Rome against Jesuit activities, some of whom even blamed the Jesuits for their troubles with the government.

With the death of Elizabeth, the Protestant succession was secured through James I from whom, as the son of Mary Queen of Scots, the English Catholics at first had high hopes (as did the Puritans for quite different reasons). He released some Catholic prisoners and paid less attention to the activities of the priests than his predecessor had, but after the implication of Catholics in the gunpowder plot of 1604 persecution flared up again. The Stuart monarchs felt less need to act against the Catholics, and even recognized in them supporters against their other opponents the Puritans. Sometimes Catholics were utilized in the government, and Charles II because of his Catholic Queen Henrietta Maria allowed mass to be said privately in her chapel, and some English sympathizers as well as foreign ambassadors attended. Preferring himself the "High-Church" Anglicanism of the Laudians, he lacked the hostility to Rome of his predecessors. This of course was one of the things which his Puritan enemies held against him, and in the civil wars he could count on Catholic support against Parliament. The civil war years experienced a rise in the persecution of Catholicism, but the years of Cromwell's rule were relatively peaceful for English Catholics (if not for Irish) who were allowed to pursue their faith so long as there were no overtones of political disloyalty. At the end of the century with the coming to the throne of the Catholic James II there was a new opportunity for the revival of the Roman allegiance in England, but by then it was much too late for such a change, with James' clumsy efforts in that direction only leading to his own deposition in the Glorious Revolution in 1688 and his replacement by the staunchly Protestant Dutchman William of Orange who ascended the throne, with his Stuart wife and Queen, Mary, as William II. Henceforth Roman Catholicism was to exist on the barely tolerated margins of English life, retreating into the religious ethos of the north where priests privately said mass and led their followers in a life of quiet devotion. Still liable to fines and penal laws, like the Protestant dissenters outside the established church they lost some of their civil rights by virtue of their religious profession, and were subject also to the occasional rising of the mob when the virulence of "no-popery" agitation revived. A small percentage of the English population, they lived a withdrawn life until their legal emancipation in the nineteenth century.

It was from this situation that some English Catholic gentry sought escape when under the leadership of Lord

Baltimore they sailed across the atlantic to Maryland, named in honor both of Henrietta Maria and the Virgin Mary.

The Scottish Reformation and Presbyterianism

While all the religious conflicts of England were transpiring, events were far from stable in the Kingdom of Scotland to its north, into which the currents of Reformation faith had also penetrated. There had been early "Lutheran" martyrs there, but the growth and spread of Protestantism in Scotland really got underway in the 1550's with a large faction among the ever unruly nobility adopting the new faith. Although Scotland had strong ties to France and the French monarchy supported the cause of the Roman Church there, English support for Scottish Protestantism in the first years of Elizabeth's reign, coupled with the strong leadership of John Knox, whom we have already encountered as an important figure of the English Reformation, proved more effective. In 1560 the Scottish Parliament repudiated papal authority and abolished the mass, in spite of the Catholic faith of the ruler, Mary Queen of Scots, who was eventually driven from her throne.

The form of Protestantism adopted in Scotland was of a less compromising sort than that of the Church of England, much more attuned to the pattern of continental Protestantism and especially to Geneva, where Knox had been an exile. A markedly Calvinist confession of faith written by Knox was adopted; the *Book of Common Order* provided a simplified Protestant liturgy. The form of government and discipline adopted, although by a fairly gradual process, was Presbyterian, with lay elders chosen in the parishes and the parishes in turn united together in presbyteries with the whole joined by a national Assembly. When James VI of Scotland became James I of England in 1603 the destiny of the two nations was more closely intertwined than it had formerly been: thereafter the religious struggles of England were also religious struggles in Scotland too, with the attempt being made under King Charles I to force bishops and the use of the *Book of Common Prayer* upon Scotland. Meeting with fierce resistance, turmoil in Scotland precipitated the civil war which was to bring down Charles I. It was out of the conflicts of the seventeenth century that Scotland's church and people became so loyally Presbyterian and adamantly opposed to episcopacy, with the Scottish "Episcopalians" reduced to the status of a dissenting minority outside of the established Church of Scotland.

PART TWO

The First Settlements

2

The Puritan
Holy Commonwealth
in New England

As we have seen, Puritanism bore within itself many
tensions; as it unfolded in its New England environment these
were to cause frequent disruption. One of the most disruptive of these tensions, illustrated in the conflicts over
Separatism, was that between its ideal of the Holy Commonwealth—the pure church and rightly-ordered state—and its
insistence that each individual appropriate for himself and
experience within himself the piety of conversion and spiritual growth so central to the whole Puritan movement. The
Puritans wanted both a state church which included within
its care every member of society and congregations in which
a standard far beyond that of merely nominal Christianity
would apply—a church which would include all and yet in
which all would be saints! Previously Christianity had
known the small devout group of those withdrawn from the
world for the practice of a higher conception of the demands
of Christian faith and life; this had characterized earliest
Christianity itself, as well as many movements of sectarian
withdrawal thereafter, right down to the Anabaptists and
other radicals of the Protestant Reformation. The Puritans
likewise wanted the spirituality and fellowship of such
withdrawal but for everyone within an established church,
without withdrawing apart at all. They tried to hold together
those religious impulses demanding an especially devoted

and committed life which had previously resulted in withdrawal, with impulses towards creating a whole, ordered Christian society which they shared with the majority of Christians since the time of Constantine and the union of Christianity with the Roman Empire. In the Reformation these two approaches were notably present: Lutherans, Anglicans and Calvinists shared with Roman Catholics a sense of the unity of religion and society, seeing the state as the instrument through which Christianity would come to permeate all of life; the Anabaptists on the other hand withdrew from the larger social whole to reproduce pure and disciplined "gathered churches". The Puritans tried to hold both of these things together, and it was the tension resulting from that attempt which caused controversies that distressed the religious life of New England from the beginning of its settlement. First one individual and then another would challenge the viability of this delicate balance of ideals and disrupt the colony.

Distinctions need to be made between the various Puritan groups who came to New England with reference to where they belonged on that line which runs from the one pole of the state church to the other pole of the pure church. The first of the Puritans to come, the Pilgrims who made their settlement at Plymouth in 1620, had a Separatist background which had been gradually modified both in the Netherlands and in the new world, but which meant that they were primarily concerned with the pure church. This was probably true to a lesser degree for that group which settled at Salem, farther up the Massachusetts coast, in 1628. But the largest group of all, that which settled Massachusetts Bay in the next few years, saw itself above all as creating an ideal holy commonwealth as a whole society, and it was they who in the long run absorbed the earlier settlements of Salem and Plymouth into their more ambitious idealism.

Plymouth Colony
The small band of settlers who came to Plymouth derived

from a Separatist congregation which had formed in Scrooby, England, under the leadership of William Brewster and John Robinson. They believed it was necessary to withdraw from the Church of England and form a church of gathered saints walking together in Christian fellowship and discipline, following the precedent of Browne, Greenwood, Francis Johnson and the other Separatists met in the first chapter. John Robinson was a Cambridge educated clergyman who had been deprived of his parish in the Church of England in 1606 because he objected both to bishops and ceremonies; he came to Scrooby to be pastor to a secret congregation already meeting at the house of Elder William Brewster. In the next several years the members of this group made their way to the Netherlands, settling in 1609 in Leyden. There they remained a considerable time, with Robinson taking hesitant steps away from his earlier extreme Separatism through his contacts with other English exiles including the "congregationalist" but not separatist Henry Jacob and William Ames. Ames was an English theologian of considerable reputation who commanded the respect of the Dutch Church. The result of Robinson's contact with these men was a modification of his earlier Separatism so that he "came backe indeed the one halfe of the way: Acknowledging the lawfulnesse of communicating with the Church of England, in the Word and Prayer: but not in the Sacraments and Discipline."[1] They also came as a group to grant legitimacy to the settling of religious affairs by the government.

Dissatisfied with their life in Holland, "Not out of any newfangledness, or other such like giddie humor" Bradford tells us, but because of such solid reasons as the difficulty of making a living in a strange land and of holding together as a group,[2] they began to consider removal to America, applying to the Virginia Company of London for a patent to settle in Virginia but finally leaving for the new world under the auspices of a joint stock company formed by London merchants. Some of the Leyden congregation, but not pastor Robinson, then returned to England and set sail from Plymouth in September, 1620, in the "Mayflower", with one hundred and two persons aboard, about forty of whom came from the original congregation. Their spiritual leader was now William Brewster, "elder" of the congregation, and their political leader William Bradford, whom they chose as governor of their colony thirty times. Still aboard ship, but having found their way to Cape Cod Harbor, they drew up the famous "Mayflower Compact" to serve as a constitution and provide some measure of social control for their incipient colony. Because they settled in Massachusetts they had to get a patent from the New England Company to justify their settlement.

The story of the early hardships of that first winter at Plymouth is familiar. Less familiar is the story of their attempt to maintain the original religious purpose for which they had come, the free exercise of their faith in the gathered and disciplined church for which they had sacrificed so much. From the beginning they were concerned about the 'non-congregationalist' majority of the settlers, and through the Compact and limitations in the franchise sought to preserve their control over the whole population of the colony. Having no pastor, they had to be content with the ministrations of Elder Brewster, but he, upon consultation with Dutch ministers in New Netherland, chose not to administer any sacraments—thus there was the need for a pastor as well as elder. The London financial backers were not eager for Robinson to join the colony since they feared he might be a source of trouble for non-separatist settlers, but meanwhile Robinson died in Holland, where he had remained until his death as pastor of what was still the majority of the original congregation who had either chosen not to emigrate or had delayed their leaving. In 1624 John Lyford, an Anglican minister, was sent to the colony, in the hopes that he could minister to the whole body of settlers, Separatist and non-Separatist, but the Plymouth leaders soon sent him on his way. Buying out the London Company's interest in their plantation, they made themselves independent of such unwonted interference. In 1629 Ralph Smith, an English Separatist of fairly strict persuasion, became their pastor.

With the peopling of Massachusetts Bay to their north, the Plymouth colony was more and more absorbed into the pattern of Puritan life characteristic of that larger settlement. Although they had a tendency to go their own relatively quiet way in comparison with that other colony, their later history is increasingly that of Puritan New England as a whole.

Massachusetts Bay Colony

A much larger group of Puritan emigrants was soon establishing itself at various places around Massachusetts Bay. This settlement began with the efforts of some merchants of Dorchester, England, to form a company which would maintain outposts on the Massachusetts coast and engage in fishing. Such a post was created in 1623 at Cape Ann but not until the Dorchester Puritan minister John White convinced some wealthy Puritan laymen to create a new company did the settling of Massachusetts Bay begin in earnest. Under the sponsorship of this Massachusetts Bay Company John Endicott came to the Bay in 1628 and pulled some earlier scattered settlements together at Salem. A charter obtained from King Charles I in 1629 granted the right of self-government to the company and its colonies and this charter itself was soon brought to Massachusetts, as the emigrating Puritans themselves came to control the company. In 1630 seventeen ships bearing a thousand colonists arrived and the new towns of Boston, Charlestown and Newtown (later Cambridge) were added to Salem; by 1640 the Bay colony had a population of twenty thousand. Nor did the population restrict itself to the bay area; in the course of the 1630's settlements had been made at Hartford under the leadership of the Puritan minister Thomas Hooker and at New Haven under the leadership of another minister, John Davenport. These and other scattered towns were formed together as Connecticut in 1662. Outposts in what are now Maine and New Hampshire were also founded. In all of these places the same Puritan values soon prevailed.

That this emigration should occur on such a large scale in such a short time by so homogeneous a group was the result of the combination of Puritan fervor with the harsh measures being put into effect by Archbishop Laud and others to enforce uniformity in the Church of England. William Laud, who had become Archbishop of Canterbury in 1633, represented, as we have seen, new emphases in ritual, sacrament and theology offensive to the Puritans. As these matters were forced upon them, the Puritan clergy in the Church of England had fewer alternatives open to them than before. To carry on their usual kind of preaching and pastoral care in defiance of the authorities was becoming too difficult. There were open to them the paths of Separatism and/or exile in the Netherlands, but neither of these was attractive to most Puritans, the first because of their reluctance to abandon the hope of capturing and reforming the state church and the second because long experience had shown the difficulty of maintaining in the Netherlands the specific usages and traditions being nourished for eventual use in a fully reformed Church of England. Many did however go to the Netherlands, and under the leadership of Hugh Peter, John Forbes and others experimented with various patterns for the ideal church.

Emigration to New England offered a more satisfactory solution to the Puritan dilemma: there in freedom they could carry out the construction of their ideal church and state, and do so in a new and vacant land, in the hope that some day their turn would come to reshape the mother country. Removal to America could not be construed as Separatism, for they would be the Church of England in New England, the Church of England rightly reformed according to the Word of God; not as it was in old England, still filled with compromises with an old order which stood in the way of the realization of the true holy commonwealth. Massachusetts offered Puritans the opportunity to shape the Church as their dreams wanted it to be, without threat or interference from a hostile monarchy or hierarchy, and yet without being forced clearly and explicitly to tread the path of separatism.

Among the earliest emigrants were Puritan leaders and ministers with long experience in the Puritan cause. It is doubtful if any group of colonists anywhere ever had in their midst such a high percentage of well-educated persons—by 1646 some one hundred and thirty university alumni had migrated to Massachusetts. Among the most important of the early ministers was John Cotton: educated at Emmanuel College, Cambridge, he became rector in 1612 of St. Botolph's, Boston, in Lincolnshire. A convert as a result of the sermons of Perkins and Sibbes, he was renowned for his pulpit eloquence. Summoned to appear before the court of high commission in London in 1633 for refusing to kneel at the Lord's Supper, he fled to Massachusetts where he was soon one of the ministers in the Boston church. Like Cotton, Thomas Hooker had been educated at Emmanuel, and remained there as a Fellow, coming into conflict with the church authorities in 1629 for nonconformity. He too came to Massachusetts, and not in agreement in all things with Cotton and others he moved on to found Hartford, Connecticut. Another early leader eventually to settle in Connecticut was John Davenport, educated at Oxford unlike Cotton and Hooker, who rose to prominence as a London preacher until running afoul of Laud. He first went to the Netherlands, from there coming to New England and establishing himself at New Haven, Connecticut. Long before coming he had been involved with the group who launched the Massachusetts venture. Also prominent among the early ministers was Thomas Shepard, educated at Emmanuel and chaplain in various noble houses of Puritan sympathy. Charged with illegal preaching, he was brought before Laud, who "after many railing speeches against me, forbàde me to preach;" then he began to think of emigration, "most of the godly in England were awakened and intended much to go to New England," to which he added sadly "I saw the Lord departing from England when Mr. Hooker and Mr. Cotton were gone."[3] He arrived in the Bay colony in 1635 and became pastor at Cambridge, eventually authoring many works of theology and devotion.

Other prominent leaders were laymen, such as John Winthrop, who came in 1630 and was many times chosen governor of Massachusetts Bay. Of a prominent family, and educated at Cambridge, Winthrop was a prosperous lawyer of Puritan outlook. Associated with the Dorchester merchants who had formed the Bay Company, he chose to accompany the charter to the new colony. Similarly prominent was Thomas Dudley, who, like Winthrop, came in 1630. Often Winthrop's rival for the governorship, he was to spend his life in public service to the colony.

Other layfolk came who were not leaders but conscientious souls who sometimes even preceded their pastors to the new land. In the nature of the case less articulate, and yet important as a group for the success of the colony, we know much less about them than we would like. An obscure settler named Thomas Tillam left a poem about his feelings, entitled "Upon the First Sight of New England, June 29, 1638," which begins:

> Hail holy land wherein our holy Lord
> hath planted his most true and holy word;
> Hail happy people who have dispossessed
> yourselves of friends, and means, to find some rest
> for your poor wearied souls, oppressed of late
> for Jesus' sake, with envy, spite and hate...[4]

The Puritans came to the new world with a consciousness of mission: in their self-understanding they were engaged in a venture of world significance as they pioneered in the creation of the ideal church and society and became an example to Christendom. Insight into how they felt about their mission is provided by Edward Johnson, one of the emigrants of 1630 who later wrote an account of their coming in his *Wonder-Working Providence of Sions Saviour in New England.* He portrays the migrating Puritans as saying "I am now prest for the service of our Lord Christ, to re-build the most glorious Edifice of Mount Sion in a Wildernesse;" mocked by the world God will use these small beginnings for his greater purposes: "...now the Scorne and Derision of those times, and for this their great enterprise counted as so many crackt-braines; but Christ will make all the earth know the wisdome he hath indued them with...." To Johnson God's providential hand is to be traced in one incident after another as His people prevail in spite of dangers of voyage and settlement. It was with a vivid sense of expectation that Johnson looked to the future; their first churches were "but the beginnings of Christs glorious Reformation, and Restoration of his Churches to a more glorious splendor than ever."5.

The churches which the New England settlers founded were congregational, although not Separatist. That is, they argued that while the Church of England needed much reform it was not a totally false church. Francis Higginson, later "teacher" of the Salem congregation, declared when leaving England:

> We will not say as the Separatists were wont to say at their leaving of England, 'Farewel, Babylon! Farewel, Rome! but we will say Farewel, dear England! Farewel the Church of God in England, and all Christian friends there. We do not go to New England as Separatists from the Church of England; though we cannot but separate from the corruptions in it, but we go to practice the positive part of church reformation and propagate the gospel in America.6

For them there were in England the nuclei of true churches in those parishes of the established church where godly persons gathered under the tutelage of faithful preaching ministers. Their non-Separatist congregationalism enabled them to see the seed of the true church in the Church of England. In New England, though, the difference between Separatists and non-Separatists was not so easily perceived, especially since at Plymouth practices of a semi-Separatist sort had come to prevail. In New England it was more a difference over the level of concern felt for the need to create a whole Christian society, and for the Bay colony non-separatism was related to their need to see themselves as not broken totally from the Church of England but as reformers of it.

But whether in Plymouth, Salem or Boston, the form of the church was congregational. It was once thought that the larger Puritan migration to the Bay was made up of those not finally committed to any one form of church government but vaguely "Presbyterian" and that they were converted to congregationalism by the example of Plymouth, mediated especially through the Plymouth physician Deacon Fuller who had aided the colonists at Salem and elsewhere in the early years and dispensed congregationalism along with his medicines. More recent scholarship has suggested that the Puritans who came to Massachusetts Bay were already committed, at least in broad outline, to congregationalist church government. The earlier Puritan thought about church government associated with Cartwright and usually called "presbyterian" had within it many of the elements of congregationalism. Later there was a whole school of non-separatist congregationalist teachers, led by Henry Jacob and William Ames, and it was with these men that the group who came to New England had the closest contact: Cotton had come to congregationalist views through reading Ames; Davenport through his contact with John Lathrop, Jacob's successor in the Southwerk congregation; and Hooker through his experience with such congregationalism in the Netherlands.

To be sure, the full congregationalist system of New England only took shape after considerable experience and in that process no doubt Plymouth's example had some influence, but more important were internal discussions and problems within the Bay colony's own early history. A later minister, John Norton, felt that it was this experience which finally clarified the proper form of the church: "...the people in a short time clearly understanding that truth in practice, which by dispute they could not in a long time attain unto."[7] A similar process went on among exiles in the Netherlands from which non-separating Congregationalists were to return to England during the civil wars to influence events there.

Congregationalism meant first that the local congregation was formed, or "gathered" by a covenanting act in which its prospective members pledged to walk with one another in Christian fellowship and the way of Christ. This in itself could prove to be a long and complicated task, as the example of the Dedham congregation shows: there were many meetings before six men seemed to show sufficient evidence of grace to covenant themselves together and form the nucleus of a congregation and then they spent months searching the scriptures to confirm the right form of their church.[8] The covenant of a gathered church however could be quite simple, as was the 1629 covenant of the Salem fellowship: "We Covenant with the Lord and one with an other; and doe bynd our selves in the presence of God, to walke together in all his waies, according as he is pleased to reveale himself unto us in his Blessed word of truth."[9] This gathered fellowship chose its own officers and pastor and exercised discipline over its membership. For problems which a congregation could not solve or which involved more than one church synods were convened, attended by representatives from the various churches.

Independent though the churches were, they were not separate from the state. The government of the colony was charged with the responsibility of providing for church and ministry by taxation and public funds and also had the power to interfere in the churches when necessary to enforce the decision of a synod. Sometimes the Bay colony is termed a "theocracy" but this is misleading, for although the ministers exerted considerable influence as advisers to the magistrates, and were certainly important in shaping public opinion, they could not hold political office, unlike England or France where bishops and cardinals served as ministers of state. On the other hand, the magistrates had considerable authority in church affairs. One way in which church and state were united was the limitation of the franchise to church members, which was done to keep the control of the colony in the hands of its Puritan leadership, but even this represented a more democratic practice than that of England where the franchise was limited to those of wealth and property. And in both Plymouth and Connecticut some were allowed to vote who were not church members.

The government had, as in England, the right and duty to supress heresy and blasphemy and insist upon religious uniformity. Believing that it was "the duty of the Christian magistrate to take care that his people be fed with wholesome and sound doctrine," no congregation could be formed without the approval of the magistrates and the advice of elders from existing churches. Unauthorized preaching was forbidden, and an "Act Against Heresy" of 1646 provided penalties for the denial of the fundamental doctrines of Christianity. Even as late as 1697 a law established whipping and imprisonment as the punishment for blasphemy and atheism. All of this echoed the common attitudes and practices of the Christian world at the time, in which religion and society were so closely intertwined that it was thought inconceivable that public order could be maintained without religious uniformity. Indeed, when Nathaniel Ward, minister at Ipswich, Massachusetts and one who had been deprived of his parish in England by Laud, defended the colony's intolerance it was to insist upon the colony's respectability, denying that they were, as "We have been reputed," a Colluvies of wild Opinionists, swarmed into a remote wilderness to find elbow-roome for our phanatick Doctrines and practices," but that like the Christian world as a whole they suppressed dangerous heresies. All who disagreed with the New England way in religion, he added, had full "liberty" to stay away from the colony![10] John Cotton gave the definitive statement of the New England position in his *The Controversy Concerning Liberty of Conscience in Matters of Religion,...,* printed in London in 1646, where he employed the ancient and at the time widely accepted argument that liberty of conscience meant the freedom to respond to the truth; to hold a false opinion was not freedom, but bondage to error. And while it is true that a person in error cannot be forced to believe what he does not believe, he may be restrained from "blaspheming the truth" and leading others into error. The argument of course depends upon the assumption that you know the truth!

It is sometimes claimed that the Puritans were inconsistent in fleeing England because of religious persecution and then becoming persecutors themselves, but however deplorable to the modern mind their behavior may seem, it was not inconsistent: they had not even when persecuted in England maintained that the established church ought not to suppress heresy but only that it was mistaken in persecuting them since they were not in error. Nor did the Puritans ever say that in power they would not persecute heretics—only that they would not have persecuted the truth. Much later in New England Samuel Willard, a Boston minister, when confronted with the argument of some Baptists that the Puritans were inconsistent in fleeing persecution and then persecuting the Baptists replied

> I perceive they are mistaken in the design of our first Planters, whose business was not Toleration; but were professed Enemies of it, and could leave the World professing they died no Libertines. Their business was to settle, and (as much as in them lay) secure Religion to Posterity, according to that way which they believed was of God.[11]

After the Bay colony had been settled, congregations es-

tablished, and the government given responsibility for the
maintenance of order in church and state, the colonists
turned their attention to a school for the training of ministers
who would perpetuate the high standards of piety and learning which the founders envisaged as essential to their Zion,
"dreading to leave an illiterate Ministry to the Churches,
when our present Ministers shall lie in the dust." Through the
benefaction of John Harvard, one of the early New England
ministers, who gave his library and half his estate for the
purpose, an infant college was founded in 1636. The college
was named after its benefactor and soon had a building and a
president in Cambridge-educated Henry Dunster. The curriculum presupposed that the entering student had already
mastered latin grammar and instructed him in the liberal arts
of the traditional European university: Grammar, Logic,
Rhetoric, Arithmetic, Geometry and Astronomy, as well as
in Metaphysics, Ethics, Natural Science, Ancient History and
Hebrew. Much of the instruction was conducted in Latin,
and of course some of the ancient writings studied were in
Greek. It was the typical education of the medieval university modified by newer elements of Renaissance humanist
learning. Theological learning came through the reading of
the Bible and the standard handbooks of Protestant theology. Most important however was the student's spiritual
development; an early sketch of the college declares "Let
every Student be plainly instructed, and earnestly pressed to
consider well, the maine end of his life and studies is, to
know God and Jesus Christ which is eternall life." Strict
discipline was maintained, the rules enjoining that the pupils
would "studiously redeeme the time; observe the generall
houres appointed for all the Students, and the speciall houres
for their owne Classis: and then dilligently attend the Lectures without any disturbance by word or gesture."12

Harvard College was not only the only sign of intellectual
life in early New England. Many towns established elementary schools where children learned to read and memorized

the catechism. The alphabet was learned through the famous New England Primer, with each letter given a moral or biblical significance: for "A", "in Adam's fall, we sinned all," or "F", "The idle Fool is whipped at school." Beyond these elementary schools were grammar schools for learning latin in preparation for college. The publishing of books was another sign of intellectual life, with the first printed in New England in 1639. By 1700 more English books were printed in Boston than anywhere else except London. And by that year there were also seven booksellers in Boston. A very high proportion of books printed and sold in Boston were religious in content.

Challenges to the Puritan Zion

Within a few years the experiment of an ideal Puritan commonwealth in the wilderness could be considered well under way, and the hopes of the founders were high. But events were to lower those hopes, as one problem after another arose which challenged the Puritan Zion—what was so especially difficult in the situation was that usually these problems arose right out of that tension in Puritanism between the pure church and the established church. A series of episodes in the early history of New England religion will illustrate the dissolving powers of that tension.

The first episode revolved around Roger Williams. His early career paralleled that of many of the first ministers of the colony: educated at Cambridge, in trouble for his nonconformity in the Church of England, he came to Boston in 1631, where he was invited to take the office of pastor, but he refused because he considered the Boston church "unseparated" since it did not sufficiently renounce the Church of England as a false church. Feeling that Plymouth would be more congenial, he went there and remained for about two years as their "teacher." There too he had difficulties: according to William Bradford, Williams was "godly & zealous," "but very unsettled in judgmente," and ministered ably among them until he "begane to fall into some strang opinions, and from opinion to practise; which caused some controversie between the church & him, and in the end some discontente on his parte, by occasion wherof he left them some thing abruptly."[13] He was granted dismissal by the Plymouth church, however, to go to Salem where he became the unofficial assistant to the pastor Samuel Skelton and after the latter's death, the pastor. The Massachusetts authorities objected to this, brought him to trial for irregularities of opinion and practice, and banished him in October, 1635. Only some months after that did he leave, staying for a while among the Indians and then going to Rhode Island, a story which will be told later. The issues debated by Williams and the Bay authorities reveal him to have been consistently Separatist and his Separatism was interpreted by the government of the colony as inimical to the colony's survival. For Williams it was not enough to separate from the Church of England but one must continually denounce it: when some members of the Plymouth church who had gone to England and participated in the worship of the church there returned Williams felt that they should not be readmitted to the Plymouth congregation until acknowledging their fellowship with the Church of England as sin. But to the authorities in Massachusetts to avow Separatism and denounce the Church of England was to ask for trouble as well as to run counter to the very purpose of their effort which was by a temporary withdrawal from England to eventually reform its church through their example. Williams also objected to the colony's requirement of a loyalty oath because an oath naming God was an act of worship and it would be blasphemous for an unregenerate person to take such an oath; indeed his Separatism led Williams to reject finally any public prayer or worship which mixed the regenerate and unregenerate together. To so deny the use of an oath, however, was to call in question an element of legal practice regarded as a bulwark of social order, and so to threaten one of the major bonds of human society. Williams also criticized the charter of the colony because in it the king granted land to the colonists which in truth belonged to the Indians. Obviously the Bay government was not prepared to seek a revised charter from the king on those grounds!

Coming out into the open through the writings of Roger Williams was an even more important presupposition which put him at odds with the Puritans of Massachusetts Bay: his denial altogether of the magistrate's authority in religious affairs. Williams' Separatism had led him to believe outright in a freedom of religious choice so that the necessarily "unchristian" state (he rejected any reference to a whole land or people as "Christian" since true Christians were but a scattered remnant within the whole population) would never compromise the purity of the churches of believers by its interference. In taking this momentous step, Williams was not so much a proponent of abstract notions of personal liberty like those of a later age as he was an extreme Separatist and Calvinist concerned for the absolute freedom of conscience which ought to be enjoyed by God's elect, who would inevitably be a small withdrawn group. Williams also denied the necessity of religious uniformity for social stability and order.

Unfortunate as the conflict may have been, it is possible to appreciate the position taken on each side: the proprieters of a fragile colony fearing royal hostility should they prove to be too singular and feeling that this "disturber of Israel" jeopardized the integrity of their whole enterprise, and Williams, daring to stand against all for his own principles. It was a classic conflict between those who feel keenly the need to preserve established order and the individual who feels equally keenly the necessity of dissent from that order.

No sooner had the disruption begotten by Roger Williams' search for the pure church on earth been settled than a new cause of disturbance arose with Anne Hutchinson. She represented more of the vagaries of radical and extremist Puritan teaching than Williams had, and announced conclusions later adopted by radical Puritans in England. Anne Hutchinson was an example in New England of the kind of lay-oriented, individualistic and biblicist Puritan radicalism which so beset England in the years of the civil war and commonwealth.

In 1634 Anne Hutchinson came to Boston in New England from Boston in old England that she might continue, with her family, to receive the spiritual ministrations of her pastor John Cotton. Within a few years she was joined by her brother-in-law John Wheelwright, a Cambridge graduate who began preaching in Massachusetts. Anne Hutchinson was a midwife and folkhealer, and had access to many homes and was soon on familiar terms with many of Boston's families. To her services she began to add religious teaching, and eventually held meetings for the women of the parish in her home in which she commented upon the sermon of the preceding Sunday, whether by Cotton or John Wilson, the pastor of the Boston church (Cotton was the "teacher"). In these sessions, and increasingly as larger groups gathered for them, she criticized Wilson's theology and that of the other clergy of the colony for being too centered on good works and for minimizing divine grace. It was her opinion that all the ministers of the colony except for Cotton and her brother-in-law Wheelwright preached what she dubbed a "covenant of works" rather than the covenant of grace. Her basis for this claim was that the other ministers insisted upon sanctification, or the good works of the believer, as the necessary evidence of true regeneration whereas for her the new birth in Christ was an immediately self-authenticating experience in which you were conscious of the indwelling spirit of God and simply "knew" that you were one of God's chosen. As many who heard her adopted her opinion the colony was soon in turmoil, and in the Boston congregation the majority supported her, bringing pastor Wilson into considerable disfavor. According to Winthrop, "it began to be as common here to distinguish between men, by being under a covenant of grace or a covenant of works, as in other countries between Protestants and papists."14 Her position was supported by the young and recently arrived Henry Vane, chosen governor of the colony in 1636, and later executed in England as a regicide. Public fasts were decreed to restore harmony, and that failing, on August 30, 1637, a synod to resolve the matter began to sit. The synod condemned a number of doctrines associated with Anne Hutchinson (eighty erroneous opinions plus many more "unwholesome expressions" and "scriptures abused") and when this failed to bring peace she and a group of supporters were banished; others were disenfranchised. Meanwhile Vane had lost the governorship to Winthrop and returned to England; Anne Hutchinson, Wheelwright and some others migrated to Narragansett Bay, later part of Rhode Island. Later she moved to Long Island where she was killed by Indians.

The major errors with which Anne Hutchinson was charged were those of antinomianism and enthusiasm. By antinomianism ("against law") was intended her denial of the necessity of good works as evidence of regeneration and the new birth. To her opponents this denied the connection between justification and sanctification which was so central in Reformed theology, and it also placed the determination of whether or not someone was converted outside of the realm of concrete testing, making it purely a matter of private inspiration. The process of admitting individuals to full church membership included inquiry into the "Christian conversation" of the prospective member as a touchstone of the genuineness of conversion. But to the Hutchinsonians that was "works-righteousness." The other charge, enthusiasm, was the result of the pressure of events, when in the process of being questioned (she was very skillful in bandying theology with her accusers) she was pressed repeatedly as to how she knew the truth of what she taught and finally responded that it was by the Spirit of God within her. To the Puritan leaders such a claim to private inspiration was very dangerous, for it could become the basis for all kinds of religious novelties. Enthusiasm ("filled with God") was the theologians' name for the heresy of claiming as an individual to have access to special revelations from God beyond the word of the Bible and its interpretation in the church. Some of her followers were reputed to be saying that "the letter of the scripture holds forth nothing but a covenant of works; and that the covenant of grace was the spirit of the scripture, which was known only to believers."[15]

Both of these supposed heresies of Anne Hutchinson were to the Puritan leaders dangerously individualistic notions which if not checked would lead to the dissolution of the whole colony. Pastor Wilson argued at her trial that her ideas would breed such separations and alienations as would destroy Massachusetts; her opponents were fond of citing the example of the Anabaptists at Münster where a holy commonwealth had been taken over by unbalanced fanatics and eventuated in horrible disorder. Once again, as in the case of Roger Williams, events had occurred which illustrated the tension in Puritanism between individualistic religious intensity and the needs of orderly church life, and once again the effort to restore balance tilted the colony further in the direction of order.

The later incident of Dr. Robert Child forced the colony to take a step in the opposite direction. Child and his fellow petitioners asked the General Court in 1646 for the widening of the franchise and of church membership so that "divers sober, righteous, and godly men, members of the Church of England," might participate in the sacraments, charging that the rights of Englishmen were being violated in some of the practices of the colony. Child and his associates were charged with seditious contempt of the government and fined; when Child tried to personally take an appeal to England he was held in the colony under virtual "house-arrest." What Child represented was not so much the opening of the churches to Anglican practice as the adoption of more "Presbyterian"

Puritan standards for membership and admission to the sacraments. Among Puritans, "Presbyterian" usage came to mean not only a stronger synodal government but a more inclusive church membership and the administration of baptism and the Lord's Supper to a wider Christian public in which only the openly "scandalous" were excluded. To follow the path of Child's request would have made the church in Massachusetts Bay more truly a "national" church, and in resisting this the Bay colony indicated that it had not abandoned its ideal of the pure church.

Because of a longer experience and so many unsettling incidents, the New England churches felt the need for a general synod which would tie up the loose ends of congregationalist practice. The General Court of Massachusetts Bay convoked a synod for December, 1646 which would include ministers and lay delegates from the churches of Plymouth and the Connecticut colonies as well as the Bay colony. After several delays and aborted meetings the synod finally met at Cambridge, Massachusetts, in September of 1648 and produced the *Cambridge Platform*, intended as a definitive statement of congregationalist belief and practice.

According to the Platform the visible church (as opposed to the purely spiritual church of the elect, known only to God) consisted only of actual individual congregations, brought together by covenant for worship and fellowship. The members of such churches should be persons who are not only free from "gros & open scandals" but able to make a profession of their faith and repentance and who "walk in blameles obedience to the word." Their children may receive baptism as infants. The only officers of the church pertain to congregations, nor is there any "church" larger than a congregation or above congregations, except for the spiritual church. There are two offices in the church, deacons and elders; of the latter, "some attend chiefly to the ministry of the word, as the Pastors and Teachers," while others attend to the government and discipline of the church and are called ruling elders. The functions of teachers and pastors were distinguished as those of concern with "doctrine" and "exhortation," respectively. The ruling elders are to join pastors and teachers in "acts of spiritual rule" but not participate in preaching or administration of sacraments. Ruling elders were responsible for the admission of members upon profession of faith and conversion, the ordination of officers chosen by the church, the admonition and excommunication of offenders, visiting and praying with the ill, and calling the church together for its business. The deacons were to receive the offerings of the church and keep its "treasury" as well as to provide for the Lord's Table at the sacrament of the supper. In addition to these officers, widows were to assist the deacons.

The choice of officers, the Cambridge Platform says, belongs to the congregation. Once chosen, they received authority to rule, and the congregation must "willingly submit to their Ministry in the Lord, whom they have so chosen." In cases of "manifest unworthyness & delinquincy" officers may be removed by the congregation. A minister chosen to officiate in one congregation cannot perform any act of his office in another unless called to do so by that congregation. Excommunication, as the power to expel unworthy members from congregations, is to be exercised as a prerogative of the individual churches, but it does not carry any civil penalties or consequences, nor does it touch "princes, or other magistrates, in point of their civil dignity or authority." No congregation has authority over any other, as John Cotton, whose writings were crucial in the development of congregational polity argued, "no particular church standeth in subjection to another...all the churches enjoy mutuall brotherly communion amongst themselves."16 But congregations are to seek one another's advice, especially in such matters as the calling of a new minister or the founding of a new congregation. Such advice can be sought more formally by the convening of a synod of representatives of the congregations, and synods will be needed for times of trouble and to "debate and determine controversies of faith." Synods are advisory to congregations but if they conclude something which a congregation refuses, the synod and other congregations may withdraw fellowship from the offending church. The magistracy, which has the responsibility of maintaining true religion and suppressing heresy, may not interfere in functions belonging purely to church officers nor may church officers "meddle with the sword of the Magistrate," that is, usurp purely political roles.

The Cambridge synod also adopted the *Westminster Confession of Faith* and the Westminster catechisms which had recently been drawn up by the English Puritans as the theological standards of the Church of England, in their control with the coming of civil war. Later, after English Congregationalists had modified the *Westminster Confession* at their Savoy Synod of 1658, chiefly under the leadership of their theological giant John Owen, that revised version of the work of the Assembly of Divines was adopted by the New England churches. Its differences from the thoroughly Calvinist *Westminster Confession* are few, consisting mainly of verbal changes, except that the *Savoy Confession* states more explicit hopes for the coming of God's kingdom on earth and has a stronger insistence upon the need for a very personal experience of conversion.

The work of the Cambridge synod was intended to preclude future problems by clear definition of the polity of the New England churches. But it proved impossible to control the future: the succeeding generation was to witness more disorders. Again, the problems arose because of that taut balance New England Puritanism was striving to maintain between the ideal of the pure church and the need for an established church.

One problem with dissenters came from the Baptists. Sharing much of the theology and spirituality of the Puritans, the English Baptists emerged as a more "extreme" party within Separatist Puritanism, who pushed the search for the pure church to the point of denying the baptism of infants. Denial of infant baptism appeared among some of Anne Hutchinson's followers, especially in their later careers, and from time to time there were reports like that of John Winthrop who described "A poor man of Hingham" who "was now on the sudden turned Anabaptist, and having a child born, he would not suffer his wife to bring it to the ordinance of Baptism."[17]

Among the early Baptist disrupters of Massachusetts was John Clarke, an English Separatist educated both in medicine and theology. Coming to Boston in 1637, he sympathized with the Hutchinsonians and soon departed for Rhode Island. In 1651, at the request of an aged Baptist in Lynn, Massachusetts, Clarke and two fellow Baptists journeyed there to provide spiritual solace to their co-religionist. While he was speaking to a small gathering in the home of this Lynn Baptist, by Clarke's own account, "two Constables, who with their clamorous tongues made an interruption in my Discourse, and more uncivilly disturbed us, than the Pursuivants of the old English Bishops were wont to doe; telling us, that they were come with Authority from the Magistrate to apprehend us."[18] The meeting being unauthorized, they were seized and fined, and one of those who had come with Clarke, refusing to pay the fine, was whipped. Clarke got his revenge later by publishing in England an account of this persecution, *Ill Newes from New England*, in which he concluded that there is no authority from Christ to force the consciences of others.

There were other scattered attempts at Baptist meetings in Massachusetts which met with the ire of the established order, but by 1686 the Boston Baptists had built a small meetinghouse and harassment of Baptists declined. To the Puritans the most shocking inroad of the Baptists was the defection to Baptist views of Henry Dunster, the president of Harvard College. At first refusing to present a child for baptism, in 1654 he publicly spoke against the baptism of infants. Under pressure he resigned the presidency of the college and relocated in the more flexible Plymouth colony where he was soon pastor of a congregation. But the old rigor passed, and by 1718 two leading ministers of Massachusetts, Increase and Cotton Mather, assisted at the ordination of a Baptist minister!

After the Baptists came the more difficult Quakers. They too, like the Baptists, had pushed to an extreme point an element of Puritan faith and piety, the emphasis on the work of the Holy Spirit in the believer, and had come to see the pure church as consisting only of those to whom the Spirit had come. The Quaker danger was felt to be much more acute than that of the Baptists: the authorities saw Quaker "enthusiasm" as conducive to all kinds of bizarre revelations which would disrupt a stable social order and bring anarchy. The Quakers were reminiscent of the worst features of the Hutchinsonian rebellion which had so agitated the colony. Thus Massachusetts reacted to them with ferocity. In 1656 two Quaker women arrived from Barbados and were immediately imprisoned and then banished; no sooner were they gone than eight others arrived from England and received the same treatment. The authorities clearly feared the infection of their colony from these "errorists" and destroyed Quaker books in the possession of these missionaries and forbade anyone from speaking with them before they could be expelled from the colony. Laws were enacted to keep Quakers away which called for imprisonment, whipping and even their execution if they would not stay away from the colony. Under that law four Quakers who refused to stay out of the colony were hanged between 1659 and 1661. In spite of such persecution the Quakers continued to provoke the magistrates, refusing to remove their hats before them in court, reviling them and otherwise testifying: one appeared naked in public as a "sign" against the evil of the colony, another interrupted an act of worship by breaking bottles, and a third entered a church meeting in Boston with blackened face and clothed in sackcloth, making "an horrible Disturbance, and affrighting the People." Persecuted and despised, the Society of Friends nonetheless made converts in New England and by the end of the century they, like the Baptists, were meeting unmolested in Boston.

In spite of efforts to the contrary, religious uniformity in Massachusetts was breaking down and at least this part of the founders' intentions seemed to be failing. The severest blow came not with the sectarian Baptists and Quakers but when Massachusetts had to abandon the claim to be the Church of England in New England, which came with the loss of their charter, the coming of a royal governor, and the beginning in the colony of worship according to the Anglican *Book of Common Prayer*.

After the Restoration King Charles II wanted Anglican worship allowed, but the colonists evaded his wishes. Commissioners from the king came to Massachusetts in 1664 to press the matter, "it being very scandalous that any man should be debarred the exercise of his religion, according to ye laws and customs of England, by those who by ye indulgences granted have liberty left to be of what profession in religion they please."[19] In an effort to have his will in this and other matters, the king revoked the charter of the colony in 1684, and in 1686 the new king, James II, sent Sir Edmund Andros to Boston as royal governor over the Dominion of New England, a new administrative unity which included New York and New Jersey. Disliked in Massachusetts because of his policies regarding taxation and local government, Andros sought to borrow a congregational church for use as his chapel where Anglican worship could take place. Andros' rule, however, was short lived because of the English Revolution of 1688: then while Connecticut resumed its life under its old charter Massachusetts received a new charter which provided for a royal governor. Under this charter, freedom of religion was granted to all orthodox Protestants, and the religious test for the franchise abolished. Anglican worship now had to be allowed in Massachusetts, and soon King's Chapel was founded for that purpose.

Sacraments and Church

In addition to these challenges to New England's religious practice, there were internal matters as well which arose out of the attempt to bridge the gulf between the pure church and the inclusive church. The inclusiveness or exclusiveness of the congregations was above all focused in the sacramental actions of the worshipping community—just who were fit subjects for the reception of baptism and the Supper of the Lord? And although Puritanism had simplified the ceremonial of worship and emphasized the preaching of the word the two sacraments were still of great importance. Baptism was in their view a sign of inclusion in God's covenant which had replaced the sign of circumcision in the Old Testament. The Lord's Supper, following Calvin, was viewed as the means by which the elect people of God were sealed with the promises of God, as by the power of the Holy Spirit those who partook of the bread and wine in faith had applied to them the redemptive benefits of Christ's sacrifice.

The first dispute concerned the qualifications for baptism. Religious ardor had cooled with the coming of age of a second New England generation, and the number of people who presented themselves for full membership in the congregations on the basis of their ability to offer a testimonial to their personal faith and conversion was declining. The original population was being scattered out into new farms and settlements, and Boston was becoming a commercial town of significant numbers—the preoccupation with religious matters was waning. Many who had been baptized themselves when infants because, their parents being full members of the church, they were considered within the covenant, were now adults with families of their own, but had never themselves fully owned the covenant as adult believers. Should their children receive baptism? They attended the services of the church, and believed in its doctrines (that is, they had "historical faith") but they could not testify to the reality of "saving faith" within themselves. Often they wanted their children baptized, and this was sometimes true of the grandparents, full church members, as well. Such people were dubbed "half-way covenanters," for they were half-way church members—baptized but not eligible for the Lord's Supper. At the Cambridge synod of 1648 the question of the baptism of their children had been raised, but opponents of change, led by Increase Mather, had argued that baptism could only be given to infants at least one of whose parents was a full church member. In the next decade there was much debate on the subject as pressure built up for the modification of this practice, and in 1657 some ministers of Massachusetts and Connecticut proclaimed that the children of such half-way members should be baptized. Jonathan Mitchell, prominent among the younger New England clergy, in defending this position later wrote:

> The Lord hath not set up Churches onely that a few old Christians may keep one another warm while they live, and then carry away the Church into the cold grave with them when they dye: no, but that they might, with all the care, and with all the Obligations, and Advantages to that care that may be, nurse up still successively another Generation of Subjects to Christ that may stand up in his Kingdome when they are gone...[20]

In response to agitation over the matter, the General Court of Massachusetts Bay summoned a synod, which met in Boston in March of 1662 and adopted the more liberal practice, sanctioning the baptism of the children of half-way members, which was thereafter called the Half-Way Covenant. This conclusion considered any baptized person who had historical faith and was of good character enough of a member of the visible church to warrant his or her children being in turn baptized. In spite of this resolution of the matter, the practice of the New England churches continued to vary. Before the decision of 1662 some congregations had already administered baptism more inclusively, and after that decision many continued to follow the more restrictive practice. By 1670 most Massachusetts churches had still not adopted the newer practice, though by 1692 most had. Opposition to the newer practice came from the laity more than the clergy, and surprisingly, more from the churches of the larger towns than from the remoter villages. But whatever the practice followed by an individual church, the raising of the problem showed the tension involved in setting up a pure, gathered church which was also theoretically a church for the whole community with even the franchise tied to membership in it. The decision of 1662, like the decisions with respect to Anne Hutchinson and Roger Williams, shows the New England way alert to danger from tendencies which would have pulled it toward a more individualistic and sectarian piety. Nor did the adoption of the Half-Way Covenant necessarily mean a decline of piety; the newer practice can be seen as "a reaffirmation of the Puritan Mission."[21]

Not receiving so decisive a conclusion was the controversy concerning qualifications for receiving the bread and wine of the Lord's Supper. This sacrament was in New England restricted to those in full church membership, who as adults had made a profession of their faith. But as in the preceding case, some now argued for a more inclusive practice for this sacrament too, claiming English Puritan precedent. The more inclusive administration of the sacraments within Puritanism was called "presbyterianism" since the "presbyterians" were those Puritans who favored a more inclusive national church. In New England by the 1670's a more inclusive practice with respect to the Supper was gaining ground, led by Solomon Stoddard, the pastor of the frontier settlement of Northampton, Massachusetts. There Stoddard, a Harvard graduate, had instituted a more liberal policy because, as he argued, echoing "presbyterian" Puritans in England, the

Lord's Supper was a "converting ordinance" as well as a seal of grace. And in the interests of a ministry which would reach out to enlarge the membership of the church, he accordingly "lowered the bar" to this Sacrament. Stoddard would include within the church all those who make profession of believing Christian truth, leaving it to God alone to know which of these really had the full experience of conversion—and perhaps the Supper would be the instrument of that conversion. He met with vigorous opposition from Increase Mather who argued that it was not primarily a matter of whether you have to be totally certain of someone's conversion prior to admitting him to the sacrament but of the identity of full church membership with those who may receive the sacrament, since God has appointed it as a means for the sealing of his grace in those who are his elect. To Mather it was therefore ridiculous to speak of the Supper as a "converting ordinance" since conversion was its prerequisite.

Practice continued to differ on this matter as with baptism, with congregations following their own preferences, though the older practice probably continued in most places; nor was there any decision of a synod to resolve the matter. In the tension between pure church and inclusive church this step of wider admission to the Supper was to many too great a concession to the latter and an abandonment of the ideal of the pure church.

At the end of the century a new congregation was founded in Boston which adopted wider admission to the sacraments as well as other modifications of the usual New England practice. Behind this effort was a group associated with Harvard College which was attuned to the more liberal practices of the English Presbyterians. Prominent in this group were John Leverett, tutor at the college and later its president, William Brattle, also a tutor and pastor in Cambridge, and his older brother Thomas Brattle, a person of substance who donated the land for the new church, which became known as the Brattle Street Church. This church also abandoned the public account of religious experience by the prospective member and made such innovations in worship as the liturgical use of the Lord's Prayer. They chose as their first minister Benjamin Colman who had been educated at Harvard but had meanwhile gone to England where he associated with the English Presbyterians, adopting their more liberal attitudes. Colman received ordination in England, and thus he and the Brattle Street Church violated the congregationalist practice of ordination being within the church to which one was called. For this reason and also because it was formed without the permission and advice of the other congregational churches those other churches did not at first enter into fellowship with the Brattle Street Church. But as in the case of other changes in religious practice, the whole episode does not necessarily represent religious decline but the adjustment of the New England Way in the direction of a more inclusive church even if some of the elements of the pure church ideal were compromised.

Benjamin Colman in time took his place among the leading clergy of Boston. He gained a reputation for preaching sermons characterized by the more "rational", moderate, and moralistic tone of the early eighteenth century English Presbyterians who were the disciples of Richard Baxter. Colman did not abandon any of the essential points of Calvinist theology but the tone of his teaching reflected a new spirit.

Another move in the "presbyterian" direction was taken by the churches of Connecticut in their adoption of the "Saybrook Platform" of 1708. At the behest of the colony's legislature and in order to resolve problems which had arisen in the Connecticut churches, elders and messengers of the Congregational churches met in Saybrook in September, 1708 and drew up a statement of church order. The major innovations of this assembly were that it set up a system of regularly meeting consociations which would bring the churches closer together in dealing with mutual problems and created ministerial associations for the oversight and ordination of ministerial candidates and for the resolution of controversial questions propounded to them. In addition there would be an annual association of the clergy of the whole colony. Individual churches were not required to participate, but otherwise would not receive the benefits of establishment as the articles were approved by the legislature. With these measures Connecticut Congregationalism took a significant step in the direction of "presbyterianism" and in its subsequent history was to have close relations with the Presbyterian churches of New York and New Jersey. Similar measures had earlier been contemplated for Massachusetts by Cotton Mather and others, and brought forward in the "Proposals of 1705," but with vigorous opposition directed against such consociation were never put into effect. Notable among the opponents was John Wise, pastor at Ipswich, who saw the proposals as an attempt to overthrow the "democracy" of Congregationalism.

Connecticut Congregationalism also showed independence in the founding of its own college in 1701. The new college was eventually located at New Haven and in 1718 in response to the benefactions of Elihu Yale took his name. The founders of Yale were sympathetic to the more conservative Massachusetts ministers such as Cotton Mather, and were motivated not only by the desire to have their own college nearer to their churches but also by suspicion concerning the newer religious ideas current at Harvard.

The Sense of Decline

The tensions of New England religion had led to one conflict after another in the attempt to maintain an established church which would also be a realization of the ideal of the pure church. By the last generation of the seventeenth-century there was in New England a widespread sense of failure that the brave attempts at a new and ideal order made by their fathers had foundered on the shoals of innumerable difficulties. How would that attempt be carried on by the sons in a different age? Becoming frequent in the later part of the century was what Perry Miller identified as the tradition of the "Jeremiad"—a lamentation concerning past failures coupled with a call to take up again the original task. William Stoughton, born in New England in 1631 and educated both at Harvard and Oxford, preached a sermon in 1668 in which he highlighted the theme to be so frequently developed thereafter, that the New England experiment was God's special work in and through a chosen people and that if they failed, they would be judged unsparingly: "Divine Expectations frustrated will issue dreadfully, when the Lord shall make us know his breach of promise, Numb. 14. 34. This we must know, that the Lords promises, and expectations of great things, have singled out New-England, and all sorts and ranks of men amongst us, above any Nation or people in the world; and this hath been and is a time and season of eminent trial to us."[22]

A number of ministers concerned about the failures in their mission and alarmed by recent disasters such as the war with the Indians, a fire in Boston, and an epidemic of small-pox, urged the General Court of Massachusetts to summon a synod to deal with the shortcomings of the colony. In September, 1679 the synod began to meet; Increase Mather was its dominant leader. This "Reforming Synod" presented a statement of the evils then current in New England with a call for repentance and renewal of their covenant with God. Beginning with the memorable words that "God hath a Controversy with his New-England People" and has "written his displeasure in dismal Characters against us," the synod interpreted recent disasters in "deuteronomic" terms as signs of God's displeasure with their failure to fulfill their mission. Specifically the synod enumerated as the sins of the colony the decay of godliness in the churches, sabbath-breaking, quarrelsomeness, "Pride in respect of Apparel," "hearing and telling tales," intemperance in drinking, "unlawful gaming," idleness, lack of public spirit, "an insatiable desire after Land,

and worldly Accomodations," and selling of merchandise at excessive prices. [23]

Related to the discouraging sense of failure which beset New England by the end of the century was the tragic story of the plague of witches. The witchcraft panic of 1692 is more understandable in the light of the malaise of fear and uncertainty about the future which pervaded the colony of Massachusetts Bay at the time. This episode, however, was far from unprecedented in the contemporary Christian world, though New England earlier had known only isolated incidents of witchcraft. There had been in the whole Christian world an upsurge in the persecution of witches since the fifteenth century which lasted well into the seventeenth century. Thousands had been executed for witchcraft in Protestant and Roman Catholic lands alike, witches being considered dangerous persons who might blight the crops, cast a spell on a child or otherwise wreak havoc. The populace feared witches and the more they feared them the more effective their witchcraft became, a correspondence which was not accidental. And it is important to recognize that there actually were those who practiced witchcraft in the Christian world of that time and that the whole matter was not simply a delusion. As modern anthropological studies in witchcraft have shown, such individuals can cause considerable harm in communities which believe in their powers. In the Christian world witches were thought to have pacted with Satan in order to gain certain powers from him, which they exercised through magical rites and the keeping of familiars such as cats or toads.

In 1692 in Salem Village one accusation led to another and in an overcharged atmosphere panic ensued; before the whole occurence came to an end some twenty persons had been hanged for witchcraft, the Bible itself declaring "Thou shalt not suffer a witch to live" (Exodus 22:18). Many of those put to death were apparently innocent persons and refused to confess to witchcraft even though it might have meant lighter punishment.

Witchcraft at Salem inevitably turns attention to Cotton Mather, who has often, and quite unfairly, been blamed along with other ministers for the tragedy. He was the grandson of Richard Mather, one of the major clerical leaders in the first years of the colony, and the son of Increase Mather who had been both president of Harvard and pastor in Boston. Cotton succeeded to his father's congregation and through his indefatigible labors as pastor and writer became the foremost minister in the colony by the time of his death in 1728. Cotton Mather took great interest in the subject of witchcraft, and wrote about it in his *Wonders of the Invisible World*, in which he defended the witchcraft trials and interpreted the events as the invasion of the colony by an "Army of devils." But earlier he had warned against the too casual acceptance by the court of evidence which was "spectral," that is, evidence provided by those who were or were accused of being witches or by those possessed by demons. Such evidence was by its very nature unacceptable since Satan was the "father of lies" and his minions would be expected to follow his example. Instead Mather had recommended the use of more objective forms of evidence drawn from the knowledge of witchcraft which had developed over the years for use in court proceedings: for example, the bodies of witches could be tested for numbness, a characteristic of witches, or examined for the presence of the devil's bite on the back of the neck or for supernumerary teats, used, it was thought, in the suckling of familiars. Witches were also supposed to be unable to repeat the Lord's Prayer or read the words of scripture. Cotton Mather, with his rather scientific interest in the subject (he was a fellow of the Royal Society of London for Improving Natural Knowledge and later experimented with smallpox vaccination) tested this matter of what a witch could read quite carefully and found them while unable to read books of Puritan theology quite able to read Roman Catholic or Quaker writings. In some of the trials objects used in the acts of witchcraft were introduced as evidence; in an earlier case of witchcraft reported by Mather four children began to have "fits" of demon possession which he described as involving deafness and dumbness and strange contortions of the body. When medical efforts proved fruitless a complaint of witchcraft was lodged against Goodwife Glover, "a scandalous old woman" who was brought into court. Mather's account of her trial continues:

Order was given to search the old woman's house, from whence there were brought into the court several small images, or puppets, or babies, made of rags and stuffed with goat's hair and other such ingredients. When these were produced the vile woman acknowledged that her way to torment the objects of her malice was by wetting of her finger with her spittle and stroking of those little images....But one of the images being brought unto her, immediately she started up after an odd manner and took it into her hand. But she had no sooner taken it than one of the children fell into sad fits before the whole assembly. This the judges had their just apprehensions at, and carefully causing the repetition of the experiment found again the same event of it.[24]

Granted the beliefs of the day, there were more objective procedures than the simple acceptance of someone's accusation as to who was a witch, and Mather had at first cautioned about this. But because he later defended the trials and wrote so much on the subject he has been held up as an example of the whipping up of excitement over witchcraft.

The witchcraft panic aside, Mather's career was a remarkable one, and yet ever clouded over by his sense of failure in living up to the standards of the fathers, a failure he felt most keenly being himself descended from so many of them—not only were his father and grandfather prominent leaders but on his mother's side he was descended from John Cotton, from whom he received his first name. He strove to keep the New England way pure, resisting the wider admission to the Lord's Supper and the newer religious currents present at Harvard, but he accepted the Half-Way Covenant and in many ways foreshadowed the new outlook of the eighteenth-century, with his interest in nature, his moralism as exemplified in his *Essays to do Good*, and his concern for practical Christian work in the world, such as missions. As a writer he is probably best known for the florid prose of his *Magnalia Christi Americana; or the Ecclesiastical History of New England*, which begins with the phrase "I write the Wonders of the Christian Religion, flying from the Depravations of Europe, to the American Strand...", and in which he celebrates the deeds of the founders, but always with a lurking sense of the failures of the sons.

Everyday Religion in Colonial New England

Up to this point the story of religion in New England has concentrated upon problems arising out of the tension between the disparate ideals of the pure church and the established church. But of course the meaningfulness of religious faith in the everyday lives of the colonists was more closely related to the institutions and practices of worship and teaching with which they had continual contact than it was with the complex problems of Puritan theology, and thus attention must be given to the everyday religious life of the colony.

The setting for the religion of New England was the "Meeting-House," a name consciously chosen, and in continuous use to the nineteenth-century. It made clear that the "church" named a community of believers and not a building, and indicated that the building was a place for other purposes as well, such as the town meeting. The building itself was not sacred, but merely the gathering place of the church. It was built in plain style, at first square, then larger and in rectangular shape, with an interior that would admit as much light as possible. It was a place for hearing the word of God explained, designed for hearing and not for the celebration of arcane mysteries. The architectural style thus said something about the type of worship—clear, instructional, auditory—every bit as much as a gothic cathedral tells of medieval spirituality. Within it had high-backed pews, often with pew doors and the pews were sometimes assigned by the dignity of the members with a notable figure in the community given a pew near the pulpit. At the back might be a bench for those who were not regular attenders or who for one reason or another did not qualify for a pew. At the front, often the long side in a rectangular building, stood the pulpit, raised high above the hearers, often with as many as three decks. In front of the pulpit stood the holy table (never called an altar) for the administration of the Lord's Supper. There was little symbolism in the building and its arrangements except its stark simplicity and the centrality of the pulpit, which proclaimed it a place for the hearing of God's Word.

Into this setting came the minister, in early New England a man of exalted position and towering dignity. His position and dignity did not derive from a priestly function but from his authority as preacher of the gospel, an office which was "a mark of the true church, a perpetual institution that rested on the will of God."[25] Criticism of a minister was considered a serious offense, and many were those disciplined for it. When request was made of the dying Boston pastor John Wilson for his last words of exhortation, he singled out his fear of God's displeasure with the colonists for the sin of "Corahism," "when people rise up as Corah, against their ministers or elders,"[26] alluding to the story of Korah's rebellion against Moses in the Old Testament. Once established in a congregation, ministers seldom moved, and some ministries lasted over fifty years in the same town. At the tolling of the hour of worship by the church bell the minister would walk solemnly across the town square, enter the church door and proceed to the pulpit while the congregation stood in respect. Then he would lead a simple service of worship: there would be a long prayer by the minister, the reading, with commentary, of a chapter of the Bible, the singing of psalms, and the sermon. No hymns except Psalms were acceptable, for songs of "human composure" could not compare to the singing of God's own word. The singing was laborious, for there were no songbooks nor instrumental accompaniment; the "clerk" of the congregation, a layman chosen for this honor, would stand at the lowest deck of the pulpit and "line-out" the paraphrase of a psalm, with the congregation singing each line after he read it.

The climax of the sabbath-day worship was the sermon, based on a biblical text of which it was the exposition. The sermon was to be informed by the learning of the preacher, but this learning must not be paraded but rather used to explain in as simple and practical a manner as possible the meaning of the passage, drawing out of it its "doctrines" and applying it in its "uses." The sermon while not to be ornately declaimed was to be given with feeling or "godly affection," and we hear of preachers shedding copious tears in the course of a sermon. The modern reader of New England sermons is struck by their length; sermons were expected to last one hour and often took two, nor did ministers preach from notes until later in the century. One sermon in a week was not deemed sufficient: the congregation returned on Sabbath afternoons for another and often gathered during the week for a third, typically the "Thursday Lecture."

There were no special days for worship besides the Sabbath or Sunday, a day made holy by Christ's resurrection and to which the Puritans applied the Old Testament Sabbath legislation, beginning it on sundown Saturday and continuing it until the next sundown. John Norton described the routine of the Sabbath in the ministry of John Cotton:

> He began the Sabbath at evening; therefore then performed Family-duty after supper, being larger than ordinary in Exposition, after which he catechised his children and servants, and then returned into his Study. The morning following, Family-worship being ended, he retired into his Study, until the Bell called him away. Upon his return from Meeting, he returned again into

his Study (the place of his labour and prayer) unto his private devotion: where (having a small repast carried him up for his dinner) he continued till the tolling of the bell. The publick service being over, he withdrew for a space to his prementioned Oratory for his sacred addresses unto God, as in the forenoon; then came down, repeated the Sermon in the family, prayed, after supper sung a Psalm, and towards bed-time betaking himself again to his Study, he closed the day with prayer.[27]

Not even Christmas received attention as a holy day. The Puritans knew that it had its origins in a pagan festival and to their minds there was no scriptural warrant for such days beyond the Sabbath itself. There is a well-known story of Governor Bradford who allowed some laborers of the colony to take Christmas day as a holiday from work because of their consciences, but when he found them engaged in recreation stopped it telling them that it "was against his conscience, that they should play & others worke."[28]

The only special Sabbath days were those when the Lord's Supper was celebrated. This was usually once each month, frequently with special weekday services of preparation leading up to it so that no one would partake unworthily of the bread and wine. The sacrament itself was administered plainly as this contemporary account attests:

...they receive the sacrament, the ministers and ruling elders sitting at the table, the rest in their seats, or upon forms.... The one of the teaching elders prays before and blesseth and consecrates the bread and wine, according to the words of institution; the other prays after the receiving of all the members...And the ministers deliver the bread in a charger to some of the chief, and peradventure gives to a few the bread into their hands, and they deliver the charger from one to another till all have eaten; in like manner the cup, till all have drank, goes from one to another. Then a psalm is sung, and with a short blessing the congregation is dismissed.[29]

How did the laity react to this spiritual regimen? They seemed eager for sermons, which to them provided news and intellectual stimulation as well as edification. Although the social pressures and authoritarian structures of New England life compelled people to go to church, there is plenty of evidence that they went willingly, in spite of hardships of freezing weather and long distances. But there were other reactions as well: the synod of 1679 denounced the evil of sleeping during sermons and Increase Mather preached against the practice, complaining that "such is the woful corruption and desperate hardness of the hearts of the Children of men" that "some will sit and sleep under the best Preaching in the World," adding that "Some woful Creatures, have been so wicked as to profess they have gone to hear Sermons on purpose, that so they might sleep, finding themselves at such times much disposed that way."[30] Upon such sinners God promises judgment according to Mather, citing the story of Eutyches in the New Testament. But even a minister could tire of long sermons, Michael Wigglesworth confiding to his diary that "I found my vile heart apt to be weary beforehand of the feared length of the publick ordinances."[31]

Moral and spiritual discipline was exercised by church and community over the laity. In some towns "tithing-men," so called because each was to have supervision over ten families, were to report to the magistrates families who neglected public worship or failed to keep the sabbath. When offences by church members were reported to the church, the officers of the church (which of course included lay officers) were to decide upon the proper disciplinary steps. Such discipline had a double purpose: it was an extension of their belief that one of the marks of the true church was disciplined Christian living, and thus its aim was to purify the church; but it was also part of the Puritan impulse to create the ideal community of the Kingdom of Christ on earth. If found guilty of a charge a person might be publicly rebuked or suspended from the sacrament; if of sufficient seriousness the sentence was excommunication. But discipline always had in mind the reclamation of the offender, who by this means was to be brought to repentance and restoration. The record book of the first church of Boston provides examples of the offenses for which members were disciplined: Robert Parker was excommunicated "for scandalous oppression of his wives children in selling away their inheritance from ym, & other hard usage both of her & ym;" Anne Walker for "Sundry Scandalls, as of Drunkenish, Intemperate, & uncleane or wantonish behaviours, & likewise of cruelty towards her children;" Captain John Underhill for "Comitting Adultery...Revyling ye Governor;"[32] others were admonished publicly for selling wares at excessive prices, quarreling and lying.

In Puritan New England even the layout of communal life reflected the ideal of a disciplined Christian society. The form of settlement was the agricultural village in which the houses were close together so that most were reasonably near the meeting-house, compacted together as a congregational fellowship instead of so scattered that they were removed from the disciplinary reach of the church. The Reforming Synod of 1679 complained that many who moved in search of more land were thereby forsaking the ministry of their churches.

In Puritan New England part of the godly discipline so necessary for Christian society was exercised by the family. So important was this institution that individuals without family were often assigned to one that they might be under its discipline, and this could even be true of older unmarried persons. Celibacy was not preferred to marriage, although to the Puritans marriage was a civil and not sacramental act and therefore performed by public magistrates rather than ministers. The father was indisputably head of the family and had an almost priestly role in his responsibility for the spiritual as well as physical well-being of wife, children, servants and others included in the household. Christopher Hill aptly comments that "The Reformation by reducing the authority of the priest in society, simultaneously elevated the authority of lay heads of households."[33] The father as head of the household was to lead family prayers and provide religious instruction as well as mete out discipline.

The ideal wife was the pious and dutiful helpmate of the man—John Norton said of his predecessor John Cotton that "He was blessed above many in his marriages, both his Wives being pious Matrons, grave, sober, faithful...."[34] Like Cotton, when widowed Puritan men remarried and kept the family unit intact. Puritan marriage theory introduced some new elements: the wife's task was not just to bear children, but also to provide companionship for her husband and he for her, and thus unlike some earlier forms of Christian thought concerning marriage, the Puritans regarded companionship as one of its purposes and could discuss human sexuality in that framework as well as in relation to procreation. This ideal of companionate marriage, with the significant corrolaries it bears about the role and capacity of women is an important Puritan contribution to modern thinking about human relationships. The woman who could be a companion to her husband was thought of as capable of piety and education, and many Puritan women were quite remarkable in their own right as Anne Hutchinson or Anne Bradstreet show.

The place of the child was naturally subordinate and disobedience to parents was considered a grave sin and many of the evils of society were blamed upon it. But children too had rights, and parents were frequently disciplined by the magistrates or churches for their mistreatment. Cotton Mather, who commented of the punishment of children "Better whipt, than Damn'd," also advised parents against "The slavish way of Education, carried on with raving and kicking and scourging (in Schools as well as Families) 'tis abominable...."[35] The family was responsible for the formation of the piety and character of the child. Sometimes it was felt that a child would receive better character formation in another home, and children were temporarily exchanged by relatives or neighbours that they might receive discipline less tainted by partiality. Servants too were under the tutelage of the family, and defined as having an inferior status accordingly; if minors they were considered so much a part of the family that they might receive baptism if their superiors were full church members, just like the children of members.

In order to make concrete this discussion of Puritan piety in New England two persons who were both spiritually sensitive and articulate as poets will serve as examples, Anne Bradstreet and Edward Taylor. Anne Bradstreet came to Massachusetts in 1630 with her husband who rose to prominence in the political leadership of the colony. Her life was occupied by the busy work of a large family but also by the poetry which she wrote and some of which was published in London in 1650 under the title *The Tenth Muse Lately sprung up in America. or Severall Poems, compiled with great variety of Wit and Learning, full of delight*. Called "the first important book of poems written in America," it and a later edition of her poems contained verses on the events of everyday life as well as more theological meditations. Her poetry shows a close observation and enjoyment of nature: in a poem on the seasons she describes April:

> This is the month whose fruitful showrs produces
> All set and sown for all delights and uses:
> The Pear the Plum, and Apple tree now flourish
> The grass grows long the hungry beast to nourish.

In that same month

> The fearfull bird his little house now builds
> In trees and walls, in Cities and in fields.
> The outside strong, the inside warm and neat;
> A natural Artificer compleat:

But the examination of nature leads to contemplation of nature's author:

> If so much excellence abide below;
> How excellent is he that dwells on high?
> Whose power and beauty by his works we know.

> *Sure he is goodness, wisdome, glory, light,*
> *That hath this under world so richly dight:*

Much of her poetry, like the spirituality of the Puritans as a whole, finds a lesson of piety in the experiences of life, even harsh ones; sorrowing over the loss of treasured possessions in a fire, "My pleasant things in ashes lye," she concludes "And did thy wealth on earth abide?/ Didst fix thy hope on mouldring dust...." The vanity of earthly things is often her theme:

> *O Time the fatal wrack of mortal things,*
> *That draws oblivions curtain over kings,*
> *Their sumptuous monuments, men know them not,*
> *Their names without a Record are forgot...*

But for those who trust in God there is a glorious hope

> *Then soule and body shall unite*
> *and of their maker have the sight* 36

Edward Taylor was the minister of the congregational church of Westfield, Massachusetts from 1671 to 1725. Influenced by nonconformists in England, he had left there in 1668 and became a student at Harvard. A strict Calvinist, he opposed the wider admission to the Lord's Supper begun by Stoddard. His poetry was not for publication but was rather a record of his own spiritual life, much of it written as meditation on the sacrament of the supper as he prepared himself to administer and receive it. In style his poems use the "metaphysical conceits" associated with the poetry of John Donne or George Herbert, and are often striking and bold:

> *Be thou Musician, Lord, Let me be made*
> *The well tun'de Instrument thou dost assume.*
> *And let thy Glory be my Musick plaide.*
> *Then let thy Spirit keepe my Strings in tune,*
> *Whilst thou art here on Earth below with mee*
> *Till I sing Praise in Heaven above with thee.*
>
> *Oh! Graft me in this Tree of Life within*
> *The Paradise of God, that I may live.*

Thy Life make live in mee; I'le then begin
To bear thy Living Fruits, and them forth give.

Most vivid is his eucharistic imagery:

...And he to end all strife
The Purest Wheate in Heaven, his deare-dear Son
Grinds, and kneads up into this Bread of Life.
Which Bread of Life from Heaven down came and
stands
Disht on thy Table up by Angells Hands. 37

In spite of their own oft-voiced sense of failure, the New England Puritans succeeded in planting their faith in a new land where it flowered not only in theological systems and ecclesiastical institutions but also in the heartfelt piety of those like Anne Bradstreet and Edward Taylor.

The Church of England in the English Colonies

In the age of the Reformation, as we have seen, most Christian groups thought that the natural and proper form of the church was one in which it was established by the state. Therefore it is not surprising that wherever English colonies were founded it was assumed that the Church of England established by law in old England would enjoy the same monopoly and privileges in the new world. In New England, for reasons described in the last chapter, the established church was quite different from the Church of England but in the English colonies to the south of that region the story of religion is first of all the story of the extension of the established Church of England into new areas. In places where the English came first Anglicanism was relatively easily established; where others had first come as in New York the process could be more complicated. But everywhere in the English colonies, and sometimes against considerable opposition, the Church of England insisted upon special prerogatives.

Anglicanism in Virginia
In Virginia, the Anglican, or Episcopal church was the first. Long before the settlement at Jamestown, Anglican rites had been performed in the ill-fated Roanoke Island colony of Sir Walter Raleigh, but the permanent establishment of An-

glicanism in the New World dates from the landing at Jamestown in 1607, when Robert Hunt, a minister educated at
Oxford, and one of the petitioners for the trading company
charter under which the colony was founded, celebrated the
Holy Communion on the fourteenth of May. Hunt distinguished himself by his piety and fidelity to duty, tending the
ill and dying, reconciling quarrels, and according to Captain
John Smith, never repining at the loss of his books and possessions in a fire. Overcome himself by the sickness which
plagued the infant colony, Hunt died within less than two
years of his coming. John Smith provides us with an account
of early worship in Virginia:

> When I went first to Virginia, I well remember wee did
> hang an awning (which is an olde saile) to three or foure
> trees to shadow us from the Sunne, our walles were rales
> of wood, our seats unhewed trees till we cut plankes, our
> Pulpit a bar of wood nailed to two neighboring trees. In
> foule weather we shifted into an old rotten tent; for we
> had few better, ... Yet wee had daily Common Prayer
> morning and evening, every Sunday two Sermons and
> every three moneths the holy Communion, till our
> Minister died: but our Prayers daily, with an Homily on
> Sundaies, [these would be sermons read by a layman
> out of the Book of Homlies] we continued two or three
> years after till more Preachers came...1

From the beginning the laws and directives concerning the
colony assumed an Anglican church establishment. In
chartering the Virginia Company James I declared that its
colonies should conform to the doctrine and practices of the
established Church of England. The Virginia charter of 1606
instructed the prospective settlers to plant the Christian religion in the new land to which they were going. After 1609
greater power was given to the governors and they ruled with
a sternly-worded body of regulations named "Dale's Laws"
after one of the early governors. These laws required church
attendance:

Everie man and woman duly twice a day upon the first towling of the Bell shall upon the working daies repaire unto the Church, to hear divine Service upon pain of losing his or her dayes allowance for the first omission, for the second to be whipt, and for the third to be condemned to the Gallies for six Moneths. Likewise no man or woman shall dare to violate or breake the Sabboth by any gaming, . . . but duly sanctifie and observe the same, both himselfe and his familie, by preparing themselves at home with private prayer . . . as also every man and woman shall repaire in the morning to the divine service, and Sermons preached upon the Saboth day, and in the afternoon to divine service, and Catechising, upon paine of the first fault to lose their provision, and allowance for the whole weeke following, for the second to lose the said allowance, and also to be whipt, and for the third to suffer death. [2]

By these draconian statutes everyone was also required to give an account to the minister of his religious knowledge, and if deficient, to go to the minister for additional catechising; if instruction was refused, it would be reported to the governor and the offender whipped daily until willing to learn! There were penalties for ministers who failed in the fulfillment of their duties. Furthermore it was enacted that anyone who spoke "impiously or maliciously" of the Trinity or against the articles of the Christian faith or blasphemed God would be put to death. The severity of these laws is to be accounted for by the fragile status of the colony and its need for law and order, especially with much of its population drawn from the dregs of English society. These strict laws were used by the Company in advertising for new settlers— no doubt before responsible people were willing to set out for such a place as Virginia they wanted to be assured that lawless conditions did not prevail there! The more extreme penalties however were not employed.

Later laws of colonial Virginia continued the public support of religion. In 1618 the Company instructed the governor to set aside one hundred acres of glebe land for the support of each minister active in a parish of the colony (the glebe was a unit of cultivable land which accompanied a parish incumbency in England). When the colonial Assembly first met in 1619 it declared that ministers should conduct their duties according to the ecclesiastical laws of the Church of England and also sought to control behavior by restricting idleness, gaming, swearing and drunkenness.

The Company lost control of the colony in 1624 when it became a royal colony with a royal governor. The code of laws was revised in 1632 and now included the provision that "there be a uniformitie throughout this colony both in substance and circumstance to the cannons [sic] and constitutions of the church of England as neere as may bee." Ministers were required to preach a sermon every Sunday and were to be presented to the governor and council in case of failure. The minister was also required to catechise weekly "the youth and ignorant persons of his parish in the ten commandments, the articles of the beliefe and the Lords prayer."[3]

In 1643, in reaction to Puritan dissenters within the colony and their attempt to invite ministers from New England, the Assembly passed an act which asserted that:

Ffor [sic] the preservation of the puritie of doctrine & unitie of the church, It is enacted that all ministers whatsoever which shall reside in the collony are to be conformable to the orders and constitutions of the church of England, and the laws therein established, and not otherwise to be admitted to teach or preach publickly or privately, And that the Govr and Counsel do take care that all non-Conformists upon notice of them shall be compelled to depart the collony with all conveniencie.[4]

In the 1660's other laws were passed by the Assembly directed against dissenters. There appeared in 1660 an act against "an unreasonable and turbulent sort of people commonly called Quakers" which made it illegal for ships to bring them into the colony and provided for the apprehension of all known Quakers within the colony who are to be "imprisoned without baile . . . till they do adjure this country or putt in security with all speed to depart the collonie and not to returne again." A later law levied fines for granting hospitality to Quakers. Another statute declared that all who refused to have their children baptized were to be fined, half of the fine going to the informer. These acts show the governor and Assembly of Virginia hostile to the type of nonconformity repressed both in England and New England, Quakers and Baptists.

As we have seen, the Anglican or Episcopal church was promoted and established in Virginia by the colony's sponsors. But what is also to be noticed is that this early Anglicanism of Virginia had within it a strongly Puritan component; nor ought that to appear strange when it is recalled that the largest group of Puritans in 1607 were still a party within the Church of England, dissatisfied to be sure with much which characterized that church, but nonetheless not Separatists outside of it. Thus it is not surprising that Puritans would be represented in the early years of the Church of England in Virginia.

The world-view and self-understanding expressed in the writings of the first Virginia colonists were remarkably like those of the New England Puritans. There was the same rhetoric about God's providence and about establishing an outpost of the kingdom of God on foreign soil: Sir Thomas Dale, one of the early governors, wrote to a friend in London that he was engaged in a "religious Warfare" in which he was looking to God "in whose vineyard I labor, whose Church with greedy appetite I desire to erect." As in New England, they spoke enthusiastically about converting the native heathen: John Smith said that the purpose of the colony was "the erecting of true religion among the Infidells, to the overthrow of superstition and idolatrie."[5] Not only the language, but also the intensity of the religious practice of the infant colony remind one of New England. The point is not that religion was the primary motive of the colony's settlement nor that Virginia was no different from New England but that its inhabitants shared much of the mental universe of their fellow colonists to the north. Certainly the line between Puritan and Anglican in 1607 was less clear than later; the Church of England in 1607 was still predominantly Calvinistic in its theology. The religious ideals of Virginia and New England were not so different as some who have sought to depict Virginia as a worldly society far different from New England have supposed.

The company which was chartered to settle Virginia included many persons of Puritan sympathies, and Sir Edwyn Sandys, the leading member of the company, was a prominent supporter of Puritanism in Parliament. Just before the charter of the company was revoked, King James sent him to the tower and accused him of trying to build a Puritan state in America, dubbing the Virginia Company a "seminary of a seditious parliament."6 Sir Robert Rich, the Earl of Warwick, another member of the company, had aided many distressed Puritans. It was this company which had given the right to the Leyden Separatists to settle in Virginia, although they had ended up at Plymouth. John Pierce, who had helped the Leyden Separatists, came to the colony in 1620 with a group of settlers, and some members of Francis Johnson's Separatist congregation came to Virginia under the leadership of their elder Edward Bennett. In 1622 some of these radical Puritans started a settlement south of the James river. No less a Puritan leader than Henry Jacob, one of the founders of non-separatist Congregationalism, emigrated to Virginia in 1624, but apparently he died shortly after his arrival.

Even many of the ministers who came out under the company's sponsorship, if not nonconformists like Bennett and Jacob, were of markedly Puritan outlook. After the death of the first minister, Hunt, two other ministers came in 1610, Richard Buck and William Mease; Alexander Whitaker, Nicholas Glover and a Mr. Poole came the next year. Glover and Poole died within a few months of arrival; for several years the three parishes of Jamestown, Henrico, and Kecoughtan were under the spiritual leadership of Buck, Whitaker, and Mease respectively. Richard Buck, who performed the marriage ceremony for John Rolfe and Pocahontas, was described in good Puritan fashion as "an able and painful preacher." Mease stayed ten years and returned to England; little is known of him. Alexander Whitaker was an able clergyman who wrote an important early book about Virginia, *Good Newes from Virginia*, published at London in 1613, in which he called attention to the need of the Indians and pled for efforts to convert "these naked slaves of the divell."[7] It was he who baptized Pocahontas upon her conversion. He was the son of the noted Cambridge theologian William Whitaker, an important defender of Calvinist theology. He had graduated from the university of his father and had come to Virginia with Governor Dale. Sympathetic to the Puritans, he expressed surprise that so few of the nonconforming clergy who "were so hot against the Surplis and subscription" came to Virginia, "where neither are spoken of."[8] There is considerable evidence from later times too that Virginia Anglicans omitted the use of the surplice which had been so rigorously enforced in England: a later Virginia minister declared that surplices had been "disused" for "a long time in most churches."[9] Due to the scarcity of ministers, Whitaker also served two other churches in addition to his own; he tragically died by drowning in 1617, thus ending the career of one of Virginia's ablest and most faithful ministers.

Other early Virginia clergymen showed Puritan leanings. William Wickham, who first assisted Whitaker and then replaced him (although it is unclear whether he celebrated the sacraments) was probably of Presbyterian rather than Episcopal ordination. George Keith, a Scotsman, came the year of Whitaker's death; he wrote of the *Book of Common Prayer* service "I use it not at all. I have, by the help of God, begun a Church government by ministers and elders...."[10] Patrick Copland who came to Henrico as the prospective leader of an Indian college corresponded with John Winthrop in New England and with Hugh Peter, later notorious as a Puritan regicide. Copland himself ended his days as a radical Puritan in the British island colonies. Hawte Wyatt, who served as pastor at Jamestown for three years, was later in trouble in England for nonconformity. Samuel Maycocke, active in Virginia for only a few years, may be identical with a Puritan preacher of the same name of Southwark, England.

After 1624 Virginia was a royal colony, and greater Anglican strictness began to prevail, with the Puritanism of the colony no longer so marked. As we have seen, conformity to the Church of England was required by law and an act of 1643 struck at Puritan dissenters. Nonetheless, several New Englanders preached for short periods in the colony, and the settlements south of the James continued to be served, albeit irregularly, by men of Puritan outlook. One Puritan in Virginia, Thomas Harrison, was presented in 1645 for not reading the *Book of Common Prayer* nor baptizing according to the rules of the church; by 1648 he had gone to New England.

When Virginia acknowledged the authority of Cromwell's government in England, Puritanism had a renewed opportunity to flourish in the colony. In 1652 Parliamentary Commissioners appeared in Virginia and took control; but they made few changes and allowed the colony more self-government than it had had before. The use of the *Book of Common Prayer* was ordered to cease after one year, but this order was not enforced and no doubt many parishes continued to use it. A number of Puritan and non-conformist clergy came to the colony during the Cromwellian years, both from England and New England, and although these men were seldom episcopally ordained, most remained in Virginia long after the restoration of the King in 1660. One of these, Francis Doughty, had earlier been active in New England and New York and later in Virginia criticized the king and admitted only those of proven piety to the Holy Communion, a Puritan practice. Clergy of Presbyterian rather than Episcopal ordination continued to come long after 1660: usually they were either Scotsmen or French Protestant exiles.

In the second half of the seventeenth-century, however, Anglicanism in Virginia was less tainted with Puritanism as a more "mainstream" Anglicanism grew up. But many difficulties besides nonconformity and dissent troubled it.

However much the church in Virginia benefited from public support and the earnestness of some of its first ministers, that which most characterized its history in the early colonial period was its ineffectiveness as a religious system in a new land with a scattered and often indifferent population. Foremost among its difficulties was the large size of parishes. With the population widely scattered in plantations spread along the riverways and not compacted into towns as in New England, it was almost impossible to maintain a normal parish life except in the coastal regions of earliest settlement. Some parishes were strips of land fifty miles long; in new areas, a whole county would be but a single parish. Even when parishes were smaller, a ride of nearly ten miles to the parish church was not uncommon. Frequently large parishes would have "chapels of ease" built in outlying places with the minister occasionally holding services there. Many remained without the regular ministrations of religion or received them but infrequently. *Virginia's Cure*, written in 1662, probably by the Reverend Roger Green, said that it was impossible for many to go to church, "the more remote Families being discouraged, by the length or tediousness of the way, through extremities of heat in Summer, frost and Snow in Winter, and tempestuous weather in both, ..."[11] The same author also represents the Indians asking the colonists why they have not built their homes nearer the parish church so that they might worship their God. Morgan Godwyn, a young minister who spent only a few years in Virginia and who had a very jaundiced view of conditions there, claimed in 1667 that "It is most Certain that there are many Families, who have never been present at any public Exercise of Religion since their Importation into that Colony."[12]

Still the parish was the only existing unit of ecclesiastical life in Virginia. It was responsible for maintaining a minister, erecting buildings as needed and providing for public worship and religious instruction. In time many more or less civil functions accrued to the parish: it was responsible for taking care of aged persons, the sick poor, and orphaned and illegitimate children, for whom it was both to provide homes and later bind out as servants or apprentices. Gradually the parishes accumulated endowed wealth from gifts to the needy within their care. The parish even had responsibility for the maintainence of boundary lines between property units and sometimes for the clearing of roads and building of bridges. For its various tasks the parish collected a levy or tax.

The government of the parish was in the hands of the vestry. At first the laws simply spoke of the minister and officers being assisted in their responsibilities by the "chiefe of the parish" but soon the term "vestry" came into use to designate these lay leaders, and the law code of 1643 provided that "the most sufficient" men of the parish "be chosen and joyned to the minister and churchwardens to be of that Vestrie" which will in each parish levy the money needed for parish business. A few years later the election of the vestry was given to the voters of the parish, and thenceforth it grew in influence. Eventually the number of vestrymen was fixed at twelve. After their election, vestrymen remained in office for life, and the practice developed of their choosing others to fill up such vacancies as occurred, the vestry thereby becoming a self-perpetuating oligarchy in each parish. During Bacon's rebellion one of the demands of the rebels was a triennial election of vestrymen. The only recourse which either ministers or aggrieved lay people had against the vestry was appeal to the General Court or the Assembly, which would carry out an investigation of the charges and sometimes order the election of a new vestry. Under this procedure the Reverend John Munro complained that the vestry of his church had nailed the church doors shut to keep him out; another merely complained that the vestry when displeased with his work locked him out.

This very extensive power of the vestry meant that the parish was virtually congregationalist, especially since there were no bishops in colonial Virginia. But their congregationalism was unlike that of New England in the lack of religious earnestness with which vestries often acted: not freely elected by the congregations, except at first, as were New England elders, they had also never been examined for their piety, and consequently thought of their duties less as a spiritual responsibility than as an opportunity for political influence.

One of the major duties of the vestry was the appointment of the officers of the church, including the ministers. This right was given them in legislation of 1643; previously the Company and the governors had appointed ministers—the appointment of the minister at Jamestown continued to be in the hands of the governor. The vestries often assured themselves of complete control over their ministers by refusing to present them to the governor for legal induction into the rectorship of the parish and instead simply hired them by contract from year to year. Otherwise the vestries feared they could never remove an incumbent once inducted, for to do so required an ecclesiastical trial in a bishop's court, which was not possible in Virginia. Perhaps as few as one-tenth of the ministers of the parishes of the colony were ever inducted into office. One consequence of this practice was that ministers had little sense of security: if they displeased the leading vestrymen they would lose their position. Morgan Godwyn condemned the vestries for treating the ministers as "hirelings:" they "use them how they please, pay them what they list, and...discard them whensoever they have a mind to it."[13] With such a system those clergy who could do better in England were reluctant to come to Virginia and the colony therefore attracted many who were inadequately educated or morally unfit. Complaints that ministers neglected their duties and passed their time in the taverns were common. In response to this situation the Assembly in 1676 decreed that "such ministers as shall become notoriously scandulous by drunkingnesse, swearing, fornication or other haynous and crying sins" shall upon first conviction forfeit to their parish one half of a year's salary and for the third be declared incapable of holding further ministerial office in the colony.

But as William H. Seiler remarks, "the most significant fact about the clergy at this time is their scarcity; to debate their character is to obscure the major issue."[14] The supply of Puritan clergy was cut off by the insistence on conformity; some royalist exiles came during the Interregnum, but not many. *Virginia's Cure* stated in 1662 that no more than one-fifth of the parishes had ministers; even in 1702 there were only thirty-seven ministers for fifty-one parishes.

Difficulties of parish size, contentious vestries and unworthy ministers notwithstanding, some Virginia clergy served their churches ably. They travelled great distances to preach in different parts of their parish, in spite of frequent discouragements; as one complained "Sometimes after I have travell'd Fifty Miles to Preach at a Private House, the Weather happening to prove bad, on the day of our meeting, so that very few or none have met; or else hindered by Rivers & Swamps rendered impassible with much rain, I have returned with doing of nothing."[15] Many ministers during the week held schools to teach reading and writing to the children of the parish. There were also duties of catechising the young. The law required them to preach one sermon in their parish every Sunday and to administer the Holy Communion three times in the year. Like the ministers in New England they were protected by law from the contumely of the populace with punishments provided for any who disparaged their minister.

The minister was assisted by other officers in the fulfillment of his duties. The Assembly called for deacons to assist the ministers in the large parishes, by reading the service in those parts of the parish from which the minister was absent. Few deacons came to Virginia (in Anglican practice a deacon was a person in "minor orders," ordained by a bishop preliminary to ordination to the presbyterate) and the effect of this enactment was to appoint "lay readers" to assist in the parish. Eventually the vestries of every parish chose such a person, who was usually called a "clerk", and would lead the prayer-book responses of the congregation when not leading the service in some chapel of ease. The clerks also kept parish records, registering births and deaths. The system however led to quarrels between minister and clerk and the division of parishes into factions. The vestries were also to appoint and pay a sexton to take care of the church property.

In 1643 each vestry was required to choose two churchwardens. They were to be responsible for discipline in the parish, and their activities were similar to the tithingmen in New England. They were to report regularly to the county courts the names and particulars of all within the parish who had been guilty of swearing, adultery, drunkenness, profanation of the Sabbath, or contempt of public worship. The churchwardens were also required to provide for the "ornaments" of worship: a "greate bible" for reading the lessons, two folio sized prayer books, one for the clerk and one for the minister, the pulpit cushion upon which the sermon was placed, and the communion cloth and vessels.

The worship of Virginia Anglicanism would be considered quite plain and simple in comparison to more modern Anglican practice: the Holy Communion was celebrated only three or four times in the year and the emphasis, as in New

England, fell upon the sermon. Instead of an altar with cross and candles the interior of the church was dominated by a large pulpit, often with three decks, the first for the clerk, the second for the minister's reading of the prayers, and the third for the sermon. The communion table was usually a plain table kept at one side though sometimes a larger one was brought in for the Eucharist with the worshippers sitting around it. The minister might wear a surplice for the first part of the service and for the communion but he usually preached in a "Genevan gown," the black robe of Puritan usage. The interior walls of the church might have the ten commandments, Lord's Prayer and Apostle's Creed written on the otherwise bare walls—this had a practical use where there were few prayerbooks. The buildings themselves were often of the plain meeting-house style, with the pulpit on the long side of the rectangle, though they became more elegant and "Georgian" in the eighteenth-century.

The parishes and vestries preceded the formation of a diocese, and the absence of a bishop accounted for much that was special about Virginia Anglicanism. Several abortive attempts at providing a bishop for Virginia were made, and theoretically the colony was under the authority of the bishop of London since the company which had settled it had been chartered in London. But little interest was shown in the colony by the bishop of London until Henry Compton came to that office in 1675; he sought a better regulation of the church in Virginia and finally established a system of commissaries. In the meantime, without a bishop, it was not possible to fulfill many functions in a proper way: confirmation required a bishop, but in Virginia people were admitted to the Lord's Supper without that rite; nor could churches be properly consecrated, with the result as reported by a Virginia minister that "The Churches being not consecrated are not entered with such reverent Demeanour, as ought to be used in God's holy Tabernacle."[16] Most important, there was no way to ordain clergy in Virginia.

As the temporal head of the church in Virginia, the governor had many powers and functions which would otherwise have belonged to a bishop. New parishes were formed by vote of the House of Burgesses and the approval of the governor; he inducted ministers into their parish rectorships when presented by the vestries; later he had to approve and license all ministers who would serve in the colony. In 1680 Bishop Compton delegated his authority to the governor to see that the clergy conformed to the discipline and liturgy of the Church of England. Eventually too the governor exercised the role of a bishop in punishing offending ministers.

The problems of the church in Virginia came closer to solution than ever before with the leadership of James Blair, the first commissary. Blair, a Scotsman, had been educated at Edinburgh and came to Virginia in 1685 as minister at Henrico; four years later he was appointed commissary by Bishop Compton. Blair had delegated to him the episcopal powers of supervision and administration, though not the authority to confirm or ordain; in the words of his biographer "It was a half-step between absentee administration by the bishop of London and creation of a new bishopric."[17] As commissary, Blair announced by "An Order for the more convenient Execution of Ecclesiastical discipline" that he intended to put into effect the ecclesiastical laws as they pertained to both lay and clergy against immorality and ecclesiastical irregularity, including Sabbath-breaking and contempt of the sacraments. To that end he summoned a convention of all the clergy of Virginia and carried out a visitation of its parishes, trying to reform the church by raising clerical salaries, encouraging vestries to induct their ministers into rectorships, securing the appointment of a representative of the ministers of the colony to the governor's council, purging the colony of unfit ministers, and founding a college for the training of an indigenous clergy. The reforming of vestries and removal of "scandalous" ministers proved nearly impossible, but Blair had some success with his other schemes, of which the most important was the chartering in 1693 of the College of William and Mary at Williamsburg. But when the school opened under Blair's presidency it attracted few advanced students and was long more of a preparatory academy than college. Blair was a strong leader and excellent preacher, but could never draw the support from the ministers of the colony which he needed to carry out his reforms. Yet he proved to have influence in other ways: his quarrel with Governor Andros had much to do with the latter's removal from office. He soon quarreled with Andros' successor too, accusing him of oppressing the clergy and the infant college. There was clearly a conflict between governor and commissary over the extent to which each ruled in the church as the representative of the bishop. Rector of Williamsburg from 1710 until his death in 1743, Blair continued to act energetically as commissary.

The Anglican or Episcopal church grew in less than a century into an important institution in colonial Virginia. Not only did it provide worship for the colonists but it became an important institution in other ways: the parish and vestry were units of local government and taxation, public announcements were made through the churches, and it was a place for meeting and making friends and for the informal transaction of all kinds of business. Because of its role in government and the character of the vestries it was associated with social privilege, and dissent from it, like that of the Quakers, could have within it an element of social as well as religious protest. But all of its privileges and high social status could never, in the face of the serious difficulties it encountered, render it a really effective church in directing and controlling the colony's population. Nor did it in the long run, as did the churches of New England, create an atmosphere of intense religiosity and moral earnestness: as Seiler comments "The views of colonial Virginians were liberal in regard to moderate pleasures, and an extremely emotional approach to religion was not countenanced. Low church attitudes prevailed; the moderate Puritanism of the company period developed into a tolerant latitudinarian approach in theological matters, and the more severe injunctions against immorality were directed in support of a stabilized class system."[18]

Anglicanism Elsewhere in the Southern Colonies

The story of the Anglican or Episcopal church elsewhere in the southern colonies is similar to that of Virginia, except that the problems of scattered population, oversized parishes and clerical shortage were greater and the efforts made to overcome them less.

Anglicanism in Maryland came closest to the Virginia pattern, at least after the early Roman Catholic period of the colony's history. The earliest Anglicanism there resulted from the spilling over of the population of Virginia into this area to their north: a small settlement on Kent Island in the Chesapeake, not far from the present Annapolis, was founded by William Claiborne and had Anglican services and the ministrations of a clergyman prior to the coming of Lord Baltimore's settlers in 1634. The area was then incorporated into Calvert's domains, but even in the early Catholic settlement of St. Mary's Anglican services were held, led by laymen using the *Book of Common Prayer.* The first Anglican minister to remain in the colony for long was William Wilkinson, who arrived in 1650, but unable to find support for his ministry he turned to a secular calling.

An early document giving us a picture of Anglicanism in Maryland comes from the Reverend John Yeo, an Anglican minister at Patuxent who wrote to the Archbishop of Canterbury in 1676 to inform him of conditions in the colony and urge him to take steps towards an Anglican establishment. Yeo reported that there were "but three Protestant ministers of us that are conformable to the doctrine and discipline of the Church of England" although he speaks of others who "pretend they are ministers of the Gospell" but are unqualified. He appealed for the sending of ministers who could refute the claims of "Popish Priests" and others. In the absence of such sound clergy, many "dayly fall away either to Popery, Quakerisme, or Phanaticisme," the last probably a reference to Puritans. He was also concerned about the "notorious vices" of the colony, including the profanation of the Lord's Day, which made the colony "a Sodom of uncleannesse."[19]

As a few Anglican churches grew up in Maryland, they suffered from some of the same problems as the churches in Virginia. In Maryland too population was widely scattered on farms and plantations, making parish life difficult, and, as in Virginia, parishes were sometimes of unmanageable size. Nor were such ministers as were available always worthy: we hear of one who conducted a service while inebriated, threatened the governor with a duel, and apparently was a receiver of stolen goods!

After the Glorious Revolution in England, a smaller revolution in Maryland took power away from the Calverts and in 1691 Maryland became a royal colony with a governor appointed by the crown. Sir Francis Nicholson, governor for several years after 1694, promoted the Anglican church, brought over several ministers and encouraged the building of many churches, including a large brick one in Annapolis. By an act of 1702 the Church of England became the established church of the colony. The colony was divided into thirty parishes, and the election of a vestry which would employ a minister was required in each parish. When a convention of the Maryland clergy was called in 1700 fourteen were present, and this did not include all of the Anglican ministers of the colony. While supporting only Anglican worship, the act of 1702 granted toleration to Quakers and dissenting Puritans, but excluded Roman Catholics. Indeed the act establishing Anglicanism in the colony had been delayed by the strength and influence of Puritans and Quakers and could only pass when it granted them toleration. With establishment, the Anglican Church in Maryland grew stronger, especially among the landowning class, and came to fulfill a social role similar to that of the Anglican church in Virginia. Many of the families of previous Catholic faith converted to the Anglican church, including the Calverts, when in 1713 Benedict Leonard Calvert conformed to it and received back his family's charter for the colony.

The story of Anglicanism in colonial Maryland would be incomplete without inclusion of Thomas Bray, who became the bishop of London's commissary in that colony in 1696. Educated at Oxford and a parish priest in England, he was unable to go to Maryland and fulfill his commission until 1699 and then he remained there only a few months, returning to London in order to further the cause of the establishment of the church in the colony; but his life after his appointment was devoted to the welfare of the church in the colonies. His major achievement was in founding two societies of missionary purpose, the Society for the Promotion of Christian Knowledge, which established theological libraries in the colonies, and the Society for the Propogation of the Gospel in Foreign Parts, which recruited and sent missionaries to the colonies, eventually providing a steady supply of able men. Missionaries of the S.P.G. (as it was called) were soon in Maryland and the other colonies and had enormous effect in rooting Anglicanism in the new world. It was supported by private contributions collected in England as well as from wealthy colonials.

The Church of England was never so firmly established in the other southern colonies as it came to be in Virginia and Maryland, though the others had at least a nominal Anglican establishment. The original Carolina charter of 1663 allowed for the toleration of dissenters in the colony and a promotional pamphlet of a few years later declared that "There is full and free Liberty of Conscience granted to all, so that no man is to be molested or called in question for matters of Religious Concern; but every one to be obedient to the Civil

Government, worshipping God after their own way."[20] The promoters of the colony wanted settlers and knew that religious dissenters made likely candidates; nonetheless, the official constitution of the colony, drawn up in 1669 possibly with some help from the philosopher John Locke, provided public support only for the Church of England though it allowed other persons to maintain their own religious fellowships and forbade the disturbance of any for their religious convictions. A revision of this constitution in 1682 exempted dissenters from taxation for the support of the Anglican churches.

The population of Carolina from the first included many dissenters (including Quakers) and Anglican churches were late in getting started: Governor Sayle and his council wrote the proprietors from Albemarle Point in 1670 that "Wee are in great want of an able minister, by whose meanes corrupted youth might be very much reclaimed and the people instructed in the true religion, and that the Sabbaoth and service of Almighty God be not neglected."[21] An S.P.G. missionary who travelled through North Carolina in 1704 reported that he found only three small Anglican churches, each with a lay reader; he preached and administered the sacraments but found most of the people to be either Quakers or "something like Presbyterians." In 1711 the Assembly of North Carolina voted the establishment of the Church of England there.

Meanwhile a much more compact society centering around Charleston had grown up in South Carolina and had its own assembly. An Anglican church had been completed in Charleston in 1682 and served by Atkin Williamson until 1696 when Samuel Marshall, recommended by Bishop Compton, took over. In 1698 the South Carolina Assembly provided for his support. In 1704 the assembly enacted a statute setting up an Anglican establishment with parishes and vestries to be created in the areas outside of Charleston and excluding dissenters from holding office in the colony.

After protest this latter provision was dropped in 1706. After 1707 South Carolina had a commissary of the Bishop of London, resident at Charleston; yet even by the next year there were only five Anglican ministers in the colony. In 1719 South Carolina became a royal colony and a few years after that had thirteen active parishes of the Church of England.

Further to the south the colony of Georgia was founded in 1732 as an experiment in Christian philanthropy. It was chartered to a board of trustees to be administered on behalf of persons imprisoned for debt for whom it would be a haven. But the founders also hoped it would be a refuge for religious exiles and in addition provide a bulwark against Spanish and Catholic expansion from Florida. Nominally Anglican, the trustees of the colony admitted dissenters from the Church of England, although they supported an Anglican chaplain for the colony. When Georgia became a royal colony in 1752 efforts were begun to establish the Church of England there which bore fruit in 1758. Several missionaries of the S.P.G. were active for varying lengths of time in Georgia, including both John and Charles Wesley, prior to their activities in the founding of the Methodist movement. In spite of establishment, there were never more than two ministers in the colony at one time, and the Anglican church failed to flourish there.

Anglicanism in the Middle Colonies

If the story of Anglicanism in the southern colonies as a whole follows the pattern of Virginia, that of the extension of Anglicanism into the middle colonies and New England is similar to Anglicanism in Maryland in at least the one point that it was not established at first but had to struggle to gain special prerogatives if it gained them at all.

Anglicanism in New York was the second church established there, the first being the Dutch Reformed. The English seized control of the colony in 1664 and held it thereafter except for a brief return of the Dutch a few years later.

During the first years of English rule, the only Anglican worship was that conducted by the chaplain who accompanied the royal governor and it took place in the Dutch church at an hour different from their worship. The earliest date for which there is any certainty of the presence of an Anglican chaplain is 1678, when Charles Wolley held that post. The Dutch and English apparently amicably shared the same church until 1697 when the latter founded Trinity parish; aided by bequests of land, this parish grew in wealth and influence and founded chapels in outlying areas. Many English-speaking children of the Dutch joined the Anglican church as did many French Protestants who had come to New York.

The first English laws for the colony in 1665 granted toleration to the Dutch and required towns to build and support a church and minister of their choice. Later, when there were more English in the colony, Governor Benjamin Fletcher sought special privileges for the Church of England in New York which led the colonial assembly to pass in 1693 a New York Ministry Act which enjoined that money be raised by taxation for the maintenance of a "good sufficient Protestant Minister" for the city of New York and for the counties of Richmond, Westchester, and Queens, the latter two counties to have two ministers each—the act was restricted to the areas where the English were numerous. The Act also provided for the selection of ten vestrymen and two churchwardens in each parish. Governor Fletcher intended the act to aid only conformists to the Church of England, but the Dutch supported it because of the ambiguity of the phrase "good sufficient Protestant Minister" and there was no mention of conformity to the liturgy or canons of the English church in the law. Under its provisions some nonconformists received support.

The first minister called to Trinity parish was William Vesey, a graduate of Harvard who had earlier been active as a preacher on Long Island. Invited to Trinity, he first went to

England to receive episcopal ordination. Vesey encouraged the S.P.G. to send more ministers to New York and in 1712 was appointed the commissary of the bishop of London for New York.

In New Jersey and Pennsylvania (including Delaware) the presence of the Church of England in the early years was slight. In the Quaker colony of Pennsylvania there were some members of the Church of England from its beginning, and they formed into a congregation in Philadelphia, with a building, the precursor of the present Christ Church, completed in 1695; a schoolmaster, presumably in deacon's orders, was leading services there in 1698 when he reported to the governor of Virginia that "We have a full congregation and some very desirous to receive the sacrament."[22] They were occasionally visited by a minister from Maryland who celebrated holy communion there. By the end of the century they had a regular minister, who reported five hundred members in his parish. Evan Evans, sent by the S.P.G., introduced Anglican worship into a number of places surrounding Philadelphia, including Chester, which had its own minister after 1704. Soon there was also regular Anglican worship in Dover and New Castle, Delaware.

The founding of the Episcopal Church in New Jersey is bound up with the career of George Keith. A scottish Presbyterian educated at Aberdeen, he came to Monmouth, New Jersey as a convert to Quakerism. He was distressed, however, by the subjectivism of the Society of Friends, concluding that they placed too little emphasis upon the historical revelation of Christ in the Bible. Rebuffed by the Friends in Philadelphia, for a while he led a party of "Christian Friends" but eventually returned to England and left Quakerism altogether. In 1702 he was ordained to the ministry in the Church of England and was back in the colonies as an agent of the S.P.G., commissioned to travel and gather information about the status of the Church there. Wherever he went he engaged in theological dispute with his former correligionists "to endeavour to reduce the Quakers from their errors,"[23] and by his own report won a number of them to his new church. He was especially active in New Jersey, where he was accompanied by John Talbot, also sent by the S.P.G., and he and Talbot sought to strengthen the small Anglican groups they found in such places as Amboy and Burlington. Talbot eventually settled as minister at Burlington while Keith returned to England for the remainder of his life. What was to become another important Anglican church in New Jersey was begun in 1705 at Elizabethtown. Although the first royal governor of New Jersey, Lord Cornbury, had received instructions to promote Anglican worship in the colony, no act establishing the Church of England there was ever passed.

Anglicanism in New England

The main story of the Anglican struggle for recognition and position in New England belongs to the eighteenth-century and is bound up with the attempt to bring a bishop to the colonies. But the previous century did witness the first planting of Anglicanism in that Puritan bastion.

There was slight Anglican presence in the first generation of New England settlement. Anglicans, including several conformist ministers, were scattered around Massachusetts Bay in some of the early settlements which preceded the great Puritan migration: Thomas Morton's group which was expelled by John Endicott because of their maypole would be a celebrated but not very typical example and the layman Samuel Maverick another. To the north of Massachusetts in the grant of land given to Sir Fernando Gorges Anglican worship was begun: Portsmouth, New Hampshire, had a church, parsonage, and minister in the 1640's, and the Reverend Robert Jordan was active in Maine until his death in 1672.

The first Anglican worship intruded into the Puritan Zion of Massachusetts came with Robert Ratcliffe who arrived along with a new governor in 1686, equipped with *Book of Common Prayer* and surplice. Worshipping at first at the Old South Meeting House, in spite of Puritan protests, an Anglican congregation, with vestry and churchwardens, was formed and in 1689 had a house of worship in King's Chapel. Later the S.P.G. became most active in New England, and second and third Anglican churches were founded in Boston in 1722 and 1740. An Anglican church was also formed at Newport, Rhode Island, with a building completed in 1702. Anglicanism in Connecticut came a little later, with the first permanent congregation founded at Stratford in 1718 and the second at Fairfield in 1727.

Anglicanism in the American colonies presents the picture of the extension of the established Church of England into the new world, expecting and sometimes gaining there the same kind of favored treatment it was accorded at home. With establishment in six colonies it had many advantages over other groups. But even where establishments were created, they were beset with so many problems that their effectiveness was greatly impaired, and where no establishment was forthcoming Anglicans had to fit into the role of dissenter from another kind of state church or else of member of an independent church in a pluralist society. In fact, the attempt to transplant to the new world the traditional pattern of Christendom in which one church had a monopoly in the state was at best a very limited success, leaving the path open for some new approach. Something of that new approach is represented by the Society for the Propagation of the Gospel, which, without waiting for legal enactments to smooth its path (though hardly adverse to them if they came) engaged in an essentially voluntary effort of missionary expansion. Many notable successes of colonial Anglicanism came through the society, which in the course of the eighteenth century was the major factor in the growth of a revitalized Anglicanism.

4

Roman Catholics in Colonial America

As we saw in the first chapter, Roman Catholicism was forbidden in the mother country, so that it is not surprising that it failed to flourish in the English colonies. Indeed, by the time of the American Revolution the Roman Catholic population was probably less than one percent of the entire number of the inhabitants of the English colonies. Protestant attitudes in the colonies paralleled those of England: fervent hostility towards the Church of Rome could always be assumed. Virginia had a law, dating from 1642, which prevented any Roman Catholic from holding public office in the colony, and which forbade "popish priests" from remaining there. Massachusetts Bay, despite the absence of Roman Catholics there, had a law by 1647 which made it illegal for any "ecclesiastical person" under papal authority to come into the colony; if such persons were cast ashore by shipwreck or other accident, they were to leave as soon as possible. The reason given for this law was the fear that Jesuits might secretly enter the province and create disorders. A later Massachusetts law made it a crime punishable by fine to receive, conceal or aid any person of the "Romish clergy." And as late as 1732 when Georgia was founded as a colony, its charter granted religious freedom to all "except papists."

The basis for this proscription of Roman Catholicism is to be found in the religious disputes of the preceding century and the fear of all things "Roman" which had grown up in the English consciousness, nourished from the time of "Bloody Mary" to the gunpowder plot. Later in the seventeenth century when broader notions of toleration began to appear, this still did not benefit Roman Catholics. John Locke, for example, arguing in behalf of greater religious freedom, did not think Catholics worthy of inclusion in a toleration as he considered them to be politically dangerous; since they did not themselves grant toleration or believe in it, he said, it ought not to be extended to them. The Toleration Act of 1689 followed this attitude, excluding Catholics from the general religious toleration it offered to dissenters of orthodox Protestant outlook, and leaving them, with the Protestant dissenters, without full civil and political rights.

To the objections against Catholics generally felt in England were added others that applied especially to the colonies. The colonies were intended to be outposts of the mother country in a new land which would extend Protestant strength abroad and foil the expansionist programs of Spain and France. Any Roman Catholics accepted into the midst of such outposts represented a potentially dangerous "fifth-column" which could be expected to cast its lot with Spain or France. Anti-Catholic feeling in the colonies flared up at times of conflict with France's expanding colonial empire in North America. Abetting such anxiety was another factor: Protestants feared that missionary efforts of Catholics among the Indians was designed to raise up forces hostile to Protestantism on the western and northern frontiers of the English colonies, and this fear was nourished by accounts like that of John Williams, a Massachusetts minister who was captured by Indian converts of French missionaries and described their efforts by torture to bring him to the Roman faith.

With such attitudes prevalent, it was only under special conditions that Roman Catholicism gained entry into the English colonies and was allowed to exist there at all, and such special conditions applied only in Maryland, in New

York for a short period of time, and in Pennsylvania as a Quaker colony giving religious freedom to everyone. Otherwise there were only a few scattered individuals and families of Catholic background who were in most cases lost to the Church through the absence of any continuing nurture in their faith: an Anglican minister of early South Carolina reported that "...two Strangers that were Papists come of their own accord to our Church and another who is reputed also a Papist and has been long settled here is very desirous to do better than he has done. I am in a few days to baptise four of his Children."[1]. The first Jesuits in Maryland reported to their superiors that they, "going out of the colony, found two Frenchmen, one of whom had been without the sacraments of the Catholic Church for three entire years; the other, who was already near death, having spent fifteen whole years among Heretics, had lived just as they do."[2]

English Catholics in Maryland

The colony of Maryland became a place of Roman Catholic emigration because it was chartered to a Roman Catholic proprieter, George Calvert. Calvert, created by the King the first Lord Baltimore, had pursued a successful career as statesman, sitting in parliament and acting as one of the principal secretaries of state for James I; but in 1625 he converted to Roman Catholicism and had to resign his offices. He had long been interested in colonization in the new world, having helped found a small but unsuccessful settlement in New-foundland in 1621 and having served in the commercial company which established Virginia. As a Catholic, he became interested, along with other English catholics of the gentry, in founding a colony which would provide refuge for their co-religionists. To that end he had been in Virginia in 1629 to pursue the possibilities of Roman Catholics finding relief there, but to no avail. His son Caecilius was married to the Lady Anne Arundel, whose family had given leadership to English Catholics and had long been interested in founding a refuge abroad for them. Thus Lord Baltimore petitioned Charles I for a grant of land north of Virginia, but having died in the meantime, his son Caecilius Calvert, the second Lord Baltimore, was the recipient of the grant. He raised money and gathered prospective colonists for the venture, but did not go himself, sending instead his younger brother Leonard Calvert to be the first governor of the colony.

Two ships, the "Ark" and the "Dove," landed the first settlers in the Spring of 1634, and they soon established themselves at St. Mary's City, not far from the confluence of the Potomac River and the Chesapeake Bay. The colony was named after the Queen, the wife of Charles I, Henrietta Maria, who was herself Catholic, and in honor of the Virgin Mary. Among the first band of settlers were a number of Roman Catholic gentlemen (a few less than twenty) and several hundred persons of the working class, many of whom came as indentured servants and most of whom were Protestant. The charter set up the new colony as a "feudal barony" with the proprietor having absolute ownership of all land but parcelling it out to the "gentlemen-adventurers" who had come with him for their separate "manors;" they in turn owed to the proprietor the various obligations due to a medieval baron. In the course of the first century of the colony's history this system was to break down, but it left behind a legacy of large manors and plantations and a rigid distinction between classes—Maryland was the most aristocratic of the colonies. Later dissidence in the colony was caused not only by religion but also by opposition to a government controlled by a small privileged class.

The majority of the first settlers was not Roman Catholic, and in succeeding years Catholics became an increasingly smaller part of the population, although the ruling class was Catholic. Three English Jesuits (one a lay-brother) had come in the first group, surreptitiously boarding the ships as they passed the Isle of Wight, and these Jesuits were the religious leadership of the infant colony. The outstanding figure

among them was Andrew White, an Englishman educated
and ordained at the Douay seminary who was recruited by
Lord Baltimore for this venture. He wrote an account of the
voyage and arrival, in which, like Puritan and Virginian en-
thusiasts, he spoke of the providential acts which accompanied the voyagers and of the high purpose of the colony in
converting the Indians and raising up a "kingdom for the
Saviour" in the new world. He described their first act of
worship when they landed on St. Clement's Island:

> On the day of the Annunciation of the Most Holy Virgin
> Mary in the year 1634, we celebrated the mass for the
> first time, on this island. This had never been done be-
> fore in this part of the world. After we had completed
> the sacrifice, we took upon our shoulders a great cross,
> which we had hewn out of a tree, and advancing in
> order to the appointed place, with the assistance of the
> Governor and his associates and the other Catholics, we
> erected a trophy to Christ the Saviour, humbly reciting,
> on our bended knees, the Litanies of the Sacred Cross,
> with great emotion.[3]

As the land was parcelled out into manors, chapels were built
on the various estates and Roman Catholic worship held
there. A chapel was built at St. Mary's and was shared by
both Catholics and Protestants—although there were no
Protestant clergy in the colony for a long time, services were
held by laymen reading from the Book of Common Prayer.

Roman Catholicism in the early seventeenth century did
not believe in principle in religious freedom any more than
did Protestantism, but nonetheless Maryland from the beginning had considerable religious liberty. Lord Baltimore
was himself a man of broad sympathies who was quite conscious of the distresses which religious persecution entailed.
And it was obvious that if the colony were to succeed there
could be no compulsion in matters of religion: seeking permission from a Protestant king to found a colony as a haven
for persecuted Catholics, there was no alternative but to

tolerate Protestants. Furthermore, only by means of a general religious toleration could religious freedom be exercised by Roman Catholics. Also, to be a financial success, the colony depended on Protestant workers, who could scarcely be induced to come on any other terms.

Lord Baltimore was very anxious lest any act of intolerance or even any flaunting of Catholicism jeopardize his venture. Though the charter was vague about religious matters, with nothing in it suggesting a general toleration, the proprietor instructed the rulers of his colony "that they suffer no scandal nor offence to be given to any of the Protestants, whereby any just complaint may heerafter [sic] be made," and added that "they cause all Acts of Roman Catholique Religion to be done as privately as may be, and that they instruct all the Roman Catholiques to be silent upon all occasions of discourse concerning matters of Religion."[4] There were several incidents in which Catholics were fined for violations of the Proprietor's instructions: in one case when a master reprimanded two servants for reading an anti-Catholic book, and in another when one of the Catholics prevented the Protestants from using the chapel at St. Mary's. And Lord Baltimore was annoyed when he learned that the Jesuits were laboring, with much success, for the conversion of the Protestants of the colony.

Maryland's famous Act of Religious Toleration came later, in 1649, and really represented a step backward from the early toleration of the colony. The law was passed at a time of impending turmoil when because of Cromwell's rule in England there was fear of the loss of the charter and of the abridgement of Catholic liberties in the colony; it was passed by a colonial assembly in which there were almost as many Protestants as Catholics, many of whom were sympathetic to Puritanism and were dubious about too extensive a religious freedom. The law provided that:

> ... whereas the inforceing of the conscience in matters of Religion hath frequently fallen out to be of dangerous

Consequence in those Commonwealthes where it hath
been practised, And for the more quiett and peaceable
government of this Province, and the better to pserve
[preserve] mutuall Love and amity amongst the Inhabitants thereof. Be it Therefore...enacted...that noe person or psons whatsoever within this Province...profes-
sing to beleive in Jesus Christ, shall from henceforth bee
any waies troubled, Molested or discountenanced for or
in respect of his or her religion nor in the free exercise
thereof within this Province or the Islands thereunto belonging nor any way compelled to the beleife or exercise
of any other Religion against his or her consent, soe as
they be not unfaithfull to the Lord Proprietary, or
molest or conspire against the civill Governemt [sic]
established or to be established in this Province under
him or his heires.

But there were other, less generous stipulations in this law,
for it decreed that

...whatsoever pson or psons within this Province...
shall from henceforth blaspheme God...or deny our
Saviour Jesus Christ to bee the sonne of God, or shall
deny the holy Trinity...shalbe punished with death and
confiscation or forfeiture of all his or her lands and
goods....5

Although such a provision was really "window-dressing"
intended to assure others that the colony was "mainstream"
in its attitude towards heresy, it certainly excluded Jews or
Unitarians from toleration, and later a Jew in Maryland was
charged under the act though soon released. The act also forbade the use of terms of reproach applied to members of
religious groups, specifically prohibiting calling others by
such names as "heretick, Scismatick, Idolator, puritan,
Independent, Prespiterian, popish priest, Jesuite, Jesuited
papist, Lutheran, Calvenist, Anabaptist, Brownist, Antinomian, Barrowist, Roundhead, Separatist...." The act also
forbade the profanation of the Sabbath.

The English Jesuits who had the care of religion in the colony soon were at odds with the proprietor. It had been made clear to them from the beginning that they would get no special support, but must come as others, receiving lands from which they could support themselves and their missions. The first three Jesuits were gradually joined by others, some of whom stayed only a short time. These Jesuits ministered to the spiritual needs of the Catholic colonists as well as undertaking missionary efforts directed to the conversion of the Indians and the Protestants. They reported to their superiors that they had had considerable success among the latter, who had no clergy of their own, describing many dramatic stories of conversion, including one of a Protestant who had long resisted their appeals but on his deathbed was reconciled to the Church of Rome. The Jesuit lands were worked by indentured servants, and as their plantations grew larger, by slaves. The Jesuits engaged in the management of their own lands: an account by a travelling French Jesuit in 1674 said that he found in Maryland two Jesuit fathers dressed like gentlemen and a brother dressed like a farmer and managing a farm, through which support "They labor successfully for the reduction of the heretics of the country."

The Jesuits in Maryland sought special privileges such as their order had received in colonies of the French and Spanish, and it was because of this that they came into conflict with Lord Baltimore. The Jesuits received lands directly by treaty with the Indians, without first seeking the proprietor's approval and they also claimed to be under the authority of the canon law of the church and that this gave them certain special considerations, including the exemption of their servants from military duty and of their lands from taxation. Lord Baltimore in response sought to replace the Jesuits with secular priests, thus importing into North America the English Catholic dispute between Jesuits and seculars. When two secular priests arrived in 1642, however, they soon took the side of the Jesuits. The dispute lasted until Lord

Baltimore appealed to the English provincial who had authority over the Maryland Jesuits and got an agreement that the Jesuit order would neither take more land from the Indians nor send new missionaries without the proprietor's approval. Later, probably beginning in 1673, some Franciscans founded a mission in Maryland, and they and the Jesuits got along together amicably. But at no time were there more than a few Franciscans in the colony, and their effort came to an end with the death of their last missionary in 1720.

Trouble for Maryland Catholics

Meanwhile Maryland was much disrupted by a series of political upheavals in which not only the feudal character of the colony but religion was at issue—the historian John Pomfret claiming that "If there was a single underlying cause of Maryland's unrest, it was the religious issue."[6] From the beginning of the colony's history there had been conflicts with William Claiborne who had started a settlement on Kent Island in the Chesapeake prior to the coming of Lord Baltimore's colonists; the number of Protestant dissidents was later increased when the proprietor offered a refuge in his colony to some Puritan nonconformists from Virginia.

With the coming of civil war in England there was a period of disorder in the colony in which Protestants claiming support for parliament against the king in England seized control, Leonard Calvert, the governor, fleeing to Virginia. Led by Claiborne, such a group seized the property of the Jesuits and sent two of them to England in chains to be tried under the penal laws. They were tried there for entering England in violation of the law against priests coming into that country, but acquitted on their defense that they had been taken there under compulsion! Regaining control of his colony, Lord Baltimore placed over it a Protestant governor, William Stone, and encouraged the enactment of the statute on religious liberty. In 1654 the Protestants of the colony, claiming grievances both economic and religious, formed an assembly of their own in which they rejected the proprietary government and amended the law on religion to exclude "popery" from toleration. A band of Protestants defeated the supporters of Lord Baltimore in a skirmish at the Severn River in 1655; they seized the property of their enemies, drove out the Jesuits, and hanged four of the Catholic leaders. These actions were defended and Protestant grievances aired in a pamphlet printed in London entitled *Babylon's Fall in Maryland* which purported to describe "a Relation of an Assault made by divers Papists, and Popish officers of the Lord Baltamore's against the Protestants of Maryland; to whom God gave a great victory...."7

Oliver Cromwell restored the colony to the Calvert family, although at first with a Protestant governor, but in 1660 Philip Calvert, half-brother of the proprietor, became governor. When Caecilius Calvert died in 1675, the proprietorship passed on to his son Charles. In 1689, following news of the Glorious Revolution in England which ousted the Catholic King James II after a short reign, Protestants seized the colony again. In 1691 it was made a royal colony and the Protestant town of Annapolis became the capital; in the next few years the Church of England became the established religion of Maryland as we saw in chapter three and the colony only reverted to its proprietary family in 1715 when a Calvert heir converted to Protestantism.

Now began a penal age for Maryland Catholics in which they suffered many of the disabilities of their English brethren. A test oath was passed which required all holders of public office to abjure the mass and the doctrine of transubstantiation. This removed Catholic office-holders and prevented their holding office in the future. Other laws forbade public Catholic religious services, awarded sums of money to informers who reported priests saying mass, prevented Catholics from practicing law and prohibited their purchasing additional land. Regulations which would have required church attendance and compelled everyone to worship according to the Episcopal *Book of Common Prayer* were defeated because of opposition from Puritans and Quakers who were numerous by then in the colony.

Until the eve of the American Revolution, most religious acts of worship by Catholics in Maryland had to be performed privately in homes. The Jesuits moved the center of their operations to Bohemia, in Cecil County near the Pennsylvania border, where they had acquired extensive lands, and were soon conducting there an informal school for children of the Catholic manorial class. From there they also rode into neighboring areas to conduct mass privately. In spite of these adversities, the Catholic landowning class continued to prosper, with some amassing large fortunes, although others of that group converted to the Church of England.

Roman Catholics Elsewhere in the English Colonies

Bohemia Manor had become the new center of Jesuit activities because of its proximity to the Quaker colony of Pennsylvania which enjoyed religious liberty. To Pennsylvania a number of Maryland Catholics moved, since there they could practice their faith in peace. There William Penn and his fellow Quakers insisted that religious liberty be extended to Roman Catholicism even if it brought criticism upon the colony. In fact, Penn himself, because of his friendship with the Duke of York who was later to be King James II, was suspected of being inclined to Rome, and at one point there were widespread rumors that he was secretly a Jesuit! A colonial Anglican complained that Quakerism was providing an open-door to "popery." In 1705, bowing to pressures from England, Pennsylvania did exclude Roman Catholics from voting or holding office.

Apparently Catholic worship first appeared in Pennsylvania in Philadelphia early in the eighteenth-century as Jesuits from Bohemia Manor travelled there to say Mass to a congregation including some who had departed from Maryland. There were also a few Catholics among the German immigrants who were arriving in Pennsylvania, and later in the century two German Jesuits arrived in order to minister to them. In 1733 a Catholic church building was finished in Philadelphia.

The appearance of Roman Catholics in New York preceded their coming to Pennsylvania, but their presence there was eventually proscribed. The proprietor of that colony after it came into English hands was the Duke of York, brother of Charles II who himself became king in 1685 as James II. In 1672 he had converted to Roman Catholicism (which was of course why he was driven from the English throne in 1688 after a short reign) and by the introduction of religious toleration into his proprietary colony he sought to ensure the well-being of his fellow Catholics there. He instructed his resident governor in 1674 that he was to allow persons of all religions to live in the colony, and in 1683, with Thomas Dongan, a Roman Catholic, as governor, it was declared that no one who believed in Christ should be molested for his religious opinions so long as they did not disturb the peace. During Dongan's term as governor there were other Roman Catholic officials in the colony as well, and a few Jesuits arrived who opened a chapel for worship at Fort James and for a short period conducted a school. With the Glorious Revolution in England, a local New York revolt was led by Jacob Leisler, a German soldier who had come to the colony with the Dutch long before. Raising fears of attack by Catholic French and Indians, Catholics were removed from all offices, their right to vote was taken away, and an order issued for the arrest of many of them. The Jesuits fled, some to Maryland, and order was not restored in New York until the arrival of a royal governor in 1691. At least one of the Jesuits returned and ministered to the remaining Catholics for a few years until his death, but before long various penal measures directed against Catholics came to prevail, including a prohibition against any Catholic priest entering the colony and the levying of fines against anyone who harbored such a person. A clergyman of the Episcopal church could later say that "There is not in New York the least face of Popery."[8]

The story of Roman Catholicism in the English colonies, in spite of short periods of prosperity in Maryland and New York and the exception of Pennsylvania, is remarkably like that of Roman Catholicism in England, with members of this church being feared and distrusted as dangerous by their Protestant neighbors. Far from the colonies providing them with a haven from persecution they met there the persecution to which they were so often subjected in the mother-country. Their story further illustrates the fact that the settlement of religion in the English colonies was not so much the experience of religious freedom in a new land as it was the history of the extension into a new area of the various religious establishments of the old world.

Spanish Catholicism in North America

While English Roman Catholics struggled against nearly overwhelming odds to gain small footholds in the British colonies, elsewhere in those portions of North America which were to become part of the United States Roman Catholic life and missions flourished under the support of Spanish and French rule. In both colonial empires there was the same assumption as in most of the English colonies that there would be religious uniformity, and thus Catholics in those colonies received the sponsorship they lacked in British North America.

Spain had preceded England in the building of an overseas empire, and her colonial expansion had coincided with a powerful religious revival in the homeland so that wherever the Conquistadores went they were naturally accompanied by representatives of the Roman Catholic Church. Spanish Catholicism had grown militant through centuries of conflict with the Moors, but it also knew the softer religious moods of mystics and saints. The Church in Spain was thus strong on the eve of the Reformation; the revival of Roman Catholicism at the beginning of the sixteenth century, which enabled the Roman Church to mount the offensives of the Counter-Reformation against Protestantism, had important roots in Spain. One such root was the scholarly and administrative advances of Cardinal Ximenes, and another the career of Ignatius of Loyola, founder of the Jesuits, and one of Spain's greatest religious heroes.

The Roman Catholic Church in Spanish America was an imposing institution by the end of the sixteenth-century: an episcopate had been established, magnificent churches built, universities founded, and even the Inquisition put into operation. But expansion into areas eventually to be incorporated into the United States came late in that century and mostly in the next, as these were "borderlands," frontier areas which remained tangential to the main centers of the Spanish American empire.

Important however to the Borderlands were missions, for it was by this means along with military outposts, that it was hoped to hold these areas, which eventually became important buffer zones against French and British imperialism. Presidio and mission thus marched together in pacifying the native population and spearheading colonization, but they did not always march in harmony: one of the major conflicts of Spanish America was between church and state over the treatment and control of the Indian. The missionaries usually desired the insulation of natives from soldiers and adventurers, lest the recent converts be corrupted by them; those with less churchly outlook saw the native population as a workforce to be exploited and resented church policy. It was in the border-land frontiers too that the early religious enthusiasm of New Spain was kept alive.

Florida was such a borderland. Explored early in the sixteenth century, permanent Spanish settlement there did not come until 1565, as a reaction to a small French Protestant colony there which the Spaniards destroyed, massacring the inhabitants. Thus was founded St. Augustine, and Jesuits were sent to the colony to begin missionary work among the Indians, some of them adventuring as far north as the Chesapeake Bay, only to be killed by Indians. The Jesuits were soon withdrawn, however, and missionary efforts were begun again in 1573 with the coming of several Franciscan friars. Their numbers were augmented by others in 1595, and in spite of an Indian rebellion of 1597 which took the lives of five Franciscans, the mission propsered. By the middle of the next century there were forty missions with 26,000 Indians under their charge. But thereafter the colony declined, subjected to pressure from the English to the north and from increasing Indian attack. Within a few generations the Indian missions in Florida had all but disappeared.

Far to the west, Spanish exploration, spurred on by the reports of gold and Indian treasure, penetrated into what is now New Mexico, Coronado reaching as far as Kansas. Coronado was accompanied by three Franciscans who remained to labor among the Indians when the great explorer turned back. At least one of them, Juan de Padilla, was slain by the Indians, somewhere in southwestern Kansas, and became to Roman Catholics the "Protomartyr of the United States." Later the Franciscan Augustine Rodriguez pioneered in the area. New Mexico was first colonized under the leadership of Juan de Oñate in 1598, and Santa Fe, founded in 1610, was soon the capital. To the Franciscans was assigned the spiritual leadership of New Mexico, and they scattered out among the Indian pueblos to begin their work. Within a decade of their coming, the Franciscans had made thousands of converts; there were eleven missions in 1626. Impressive adobe churches were constructed in some of these missions, those at Acoma, Isleta, and Jemez all being built in the 1620's and still standing.

In spite of the outward apparent success of these missions,

however, there were serious problems lying just underneath the surface. The conversion of the Indians had often been accomplished by a show of force, Spanish troops, for example, having taken the pueblo of Acoma by storm, massacring many of its inhabitants, and only then providing it with church and priest. Everywhere the Indians were forced to labor for the benefit of the missions, and many of their customs were disrupted by the friars as not consonant with Christian practice. Later in the century the area of Spanish control contracted under Apache attacks, the missions of Gran Quivira and Quarai being abandoned in 1675, with their large mission churches falling into ruin. Although the Pueblo Indians feared and suffered from the Apaches along with the Spaniards, they learned from them that the Spaniards were not invincible. Out of the sullen discontent of the Indian and a revival of their native religion led by the medicine man El Pope, came the Pueblo Revolt of 1680. Spanish officials probably hastened the revolt with their repressive measures of the 1670's, which attempted to destroy the native religion. Ceremonial dances were forbidden, ceremonial chambers (called kivas) were seized, and ritual articles confiscated. Suddenly in 1680 the Indians struck back in a general revolt, killing 21 of the 33 Franciscan friars and a large proportion of the white colonists, almost four hundred altogether. The remaining colonists retreated southward, finding refuge in El Paso, considerably to the south of the pueblo area. Magnificent mission churches were destroyed, like that at Pecos, as the remnants of Spanish rule were effaced, Christian faith itself being renounced by the Indians.

It was almost twelve years before Spanish rule was reinstated in New Mexico, but its return was inevitable. By 1697 the reconquest was complete, and the Franciscans were back, ministering once again to their Indian flocks, but "the missions were never again what they had been before 1680." [9] When the church at Pecos was rebuilt, it was on a much smaller scale. Some tribes, for example the Hopis, were not again brought under the control of the Spanish.

Other mission advances in the southwest occurred in what was eventually to be Arizona and Texas. A Franciscan friar had explored in Arizona as early as 1539, and Coronado's expedition entered it too, but the first permanent work was that of the Italian Jesuit Eusebio Francisco Kino who began missions in Northern Mexico in 1587. Eventually he founded mission churches farther north, at San Xavier del Bac (near modern Tucson), Tumacacori and Guevavi (both near present Nogales). He baptized thousands of Indians before his death in 1611, and commented that "I could have baptized ten or twelve thousand Indians more if the lack of father laboreres had not rendered it impossible for us to catechise them and instruct them in advance."[10]. Father Kino was succeeded in the area by several German Jesuits, but the missions declined.

Spanish missions in what is now Texas began as part of those of New Mexico, with Franciscans active in the region of El Paso and the lower Rio Grande. Some of these Franciscans penetrated farther eastward, but it was only after the threat of French expansion into the lower Mississippi valley that greater Spanish efforts were made to open and control the vast borderland of Texas. In the early 1690's a number of missions were founded in eastern Texas, but most were abandoned after a few years; it was not until more than twenty years later that a permanent settlement with both presidio and mission was made at San Antonio, and other missions followed. But little colonization took place in Texas and its missions remained weak. The story of Father Junipero Serra and the California missions is a later one.

When all of these Spanish efforts at colonization and church expansion are added together they constitute a movement of considerable cultural and religious impact, which gave much of its present character to what is now a large part of the United States. And though the typical image of religion in colonial America is shaped by the experience of the English colonies, these Spanish colonies with their Catholic faith constitute an important part of our national heritage.

French Catholicism in Areas That Became the United States

France, like England, was a latecomer in establishing colonies in the new world, but its expansion abroad, as was the case with that of Spain, coincided with a Catholic religious revival at home, giving great impetus to missionary labors among aboriginal peoples wherever Frenchmen adventured. The religious revival of seventeenth-century France was related to the defeat and suppression of Protestantism and found characteristic expressions in the creation of new religious orders and in the flowering of mystical piety. But religious revival in France was also intertwined with disruptive controversies. In the Gallican controversy there was division over the question of the extent to which the French church should be independent of the papacy, and in the Jansenist controversy the important Jesuit order found itself charged with minimizing divine grace and inculcating a worldly morality. Meanwhile French Catholic missionaries, like the Spanish before them, had scattered the seeds of their faith over vast areas of North America.

One of the first French attempts at colonization in what became the United States, however, was not carried out in order to extend the Catholic Church but was a Protestant venture. In the middle of the sixteenth century Admiral Coligny, political leader and staunch Protestant, saw possibilities for both his nation and his faith in colonization, and so promoted the settlement of Huguenots in the new world. Such an experiment brought French Protestants to Florida in 1564 but the Spanish quickly put an end to the colony, putting the colonists to the sword as both French interlopers and heretics. Coligny himself was murdered in the St. Bartholomew's Massacre of 1572 and thereafter Protestants were not prominent in French colonization, the later policy of

Cardinal Richlieu being to prohibit them altogether from residing in any French colony— a royal edict applying to one of the French trading companies engaged in colonization declared that they were "not to tolerate the exercise of any religion other than the Catholic, Apostolic and Roman, " and that the colonial governors were to "act firmly in this matter."11 In spite of this Protestants did occasionally turn up in the French colonies, especially since they were so prominent among French merchants and seamen who sailed out of important ports such as La Rochelle, where Protestantism flourished. In early Louisiana there were complaints from the Catholic clergy that Protestants were tolerated in the colony.

The religious history of New France however is mainly the story of French Roman Catholicism. It is also a story which began in the seventeenth-century and in those areas which became parts of the United States more a story of the daring enterprise of individual priests than of systematic attempts at colonization, though of course there were such attempts at the end of the century in the regions of the Great Lakes and Louisiana. Indeed the Church was one of the main reasons for the maintenance and permanence of the French colonies in the new world. Also responsible for the success of the French colonies in North America was the fur trade. Early in the seventeenth century small outposts for this trade with the Indians were established on the St. Lawrence River and at Port Royal (Nova Scotia); later the lure of profits in furs propelled the French much farther westward. From these beginnings the French presence in North America expanded until New France included the whole region of the St. Lawrence and the Great Lakes and also extended far southward through the Mississippi Valley to New Orleans.

Although several secular priests preceded them to New France, after the arrival of five of their members in 1625 the Jesuits were the Order most involved in missionary labors there. Only by the end of the century were they declining in influence, with the establishment of an episcopate at Quebec and the coming of members of other orders, including Récollets, a branch of the Franciscans, and the Sulpicians. These Jesuits set out to convert the Huron and later Iroquois Indians by living among them and gradually winning them to the faith. One of these Jesuits, Jean de Brebeuf, provided instructions: he advised prospective missionaries to be prepared to accept Indian customs and acquiesce in hardships without complaint, developing "sincere affection for the Savages," remembering that they cared little for your learning and that "All the fine qualities which might make you loved and respected in France" meant nothing to them. [12] The Jesuit story in New France is one of great heroism, nine of their number being martyred by the middle of the century, including Brebeuf.

The *Jesuit Relations*, consisting of the reports of the Jesuits in New France to their superiors, contain many dramatic stories of suffering and martyrdom. Isaac Jogues, canonized as a saint, was an example of Jesuit steadfastness, and also a missionary who labored in lands which came to be included in the United States. Captured and tortured by the Mohawks in New York, he escaped, only to be captured again by the Iroquois who killed him in 1646. The Iroquois destroyed most of the mission work which the Jesuits established among the Hurons.

Through much of the century Roman Catholic missionaries labored among the Abenaki Indians of Maine, and after the coming of the Jesuit Sebastian Rale in 1694 this mission succeeded in winning that tribe to the Catholic Church. Rale, however, was killed in skirmishing between the English and French and their Indian allies, and the English destroyed this mission in 1724.

French Exploration continued throughout the century to open up new areas in the Great Lakes region and the Mississippi Valley. Before the middle of the century Jesuits had accomplished some of these exploratory ventures into those regions but without permanent missionary effect. Rene Ménard travelled to the south shore of Lake Superior in 1660 in the company of some Chippewa Indians; the next year he left them and moved into Wisconsin in search of some Christian Hurons there of whom he had heard rumor. There Ménard disappeared, but soon thereafter Claude Allouez was sent into the same region where he founded a mission near what is now Ashland, Wisconsin. He established other missions nearby, including one at Green Bay. Appointed by the Bishop of Quebec as a vicar general with jurisdiction over all Catholics in the Western territories, he travelled widely, and later worked with Father Jacques Marquette among the Illinois tribes.

Marquette was remarkable as an explorer as well as a missionary. His journey down the Mississippi River with Louis Joliet is a familiar story, and before his death he was instrumental in founding the Kaskaskia mission on the Illinois River, opening up that area. Early in the next century forts and missions were flourishing in that region, in such places as Peoria (then Ft. Crèvecoeur), Detroit, and Vincennes. The Récollet father Louis Hennepin penetrated even farther west, reaching the present site of Minneapolis in 1680. In his account of this journey Hennepin was a good deal less sanguine about the possibilities of making any permanent Christian impact upon the Indians than many of his predecessors had been.

In 1731 the settlements in the Illinois region were incorporated into the jurisdiction of Louisiana, as French penetration of the Mississippi Valley from the south began to score some successes. The French had made their first settlement at the mouth of the Mississippi River in 1699, though for many years it was on the very edge of survival. Here Catholic activities were not primarily missions to the Indians but the provision of spiritual ministrations for the motley band of colonists who lived in these early settlements, the most important of which was soon to be New Orleans. From the beginning there were conflicts between the Jesuits and the government of the colony, the Jesuits withdrawing in 1704; until 1720 religious life was in the hands of priests of the Society of Foreign Missions. Later Capuchin priests were active in the colony. Gradually a regular parish life grew up.

Vast regions of the new United States came from lands first explored by the French and in which the first type of Christianity to penetrate was Roman Catholicism. Many traces of that French Catholic presence remained throughout the colonial period, eventually adding to the religious pluralism of the United States.

PART THREE

Dissenters, Latecomers and Outsiders

5
Puritan Separatism in the Colonies: Rhode Island,Baptists and Quakers

Puritan impulses were carried to a variety of extremes in the course of the seventeenth-century, and new ideas and movements flourishing on the edges of Puritanism luxuriated in England by the middle of that century. This Puritan radicalism also flowered in New England, but whereas the Separatists of Plymouth were gradually absorbed into the Massachusetts pattern the later radicalism of Baptists and Quakers was repelled. In Virginia too there was anxiety over the appearance of such Separatism. This chapter tells the story of these Puritan-inspired Separatist groups in their own right, beginning with Rhode Island where conditions allowed them to flourish, and then moving to their presence in other colonies and their leadership in Pennsylvania.

Radicals in Rhode Island

Rhode Island operated as a safety valve in New England, providing a haven for religious radicals unwelcome elsewhere. Among the banished Roger Williams and Anne Hutchinson and their followers were to be found many of the disturbing notions just beginning to appear in England and also the seeds of what would take shape as two major movements quite outside the Puritan mainstream, however indebted they were to essential and central Puritan impulses, the Baptists and Quakers.

Roger Williams, earlier a contender with the Massachusetts authorities over a number of theological ideas rooted in his Separatism, came to Rhode Island in 1636, founding a settlement on the Narragansett Bay called Providence, as he felt God's providence had guided him there. Receiving deed to the land from the Indians, he was soon joined by others and together they incorporated themselves as a town. In 1638 and 1639 Anne Hutchinson and a number of her associates and followers arrived, founding the town of Portsmouth; when differences arose among the colonists some moved on to establish Newport. These Rhode Island groups eventually formed themselves into one government, and later Williams went to England to assure the colony of a firm claim to their land, returning with a charter for "Providence Plantations" which granted them self-government. One of those who came with the Hutchinsonians, John Clarke, a Baptist dissident, spent a long time in England on behalf of the colony and received a renewed charter in 1663.

From the earliest arrival in the colony there was freedom of religion. In the agreement between Williams and his fellow townsmen, there was no mention of religion. But when the towns of Rhode Island came together on a common government, it was agreed that no one would be interfered with on account of religious belief. An elected assembly first met in 1647 and it ratified this liberty of religion.

To those outside, the colony seemed a fulfillment of their worst fears, and Rhode Island was dubbed "Rogues' Island." It had become to them what Nathaniel Ward feared people thought Massachusetts Bay was, "a colluvies of wild opinionists." One of the Dutch ministers in New York called it the "sewer" of New England. Radical religion flourished in Rhode Island according to John Winthrop:

> Mrs. Hutchinson and those of Aquiday Island broached new heresies every year. Divers of them turned professed anabaptists, and would not wear any arms, and denied all magistracy among Christians, and maintained

that there were no churches since those founded by the apostles and evangelists, nor could any be, nor any pastors ordained, nor seals administered but by such, and that the church was to want these all the time she continued in the wilderness, as yet she was.[1]

In Roger Williams, Edmund Morgan remarks, "we can watch Puritan thought exploding, hurling itself outward to its ultimate limits,"[2] and the religious positions adopted by him in Rhode Island bear this out. Puritanism had sought the pure church and now unhampered by interference Williams continued that search in Rhode Island. In 1639 he and some others in Providence, including a certain William Wickenden who had come there after being accused of Anabaptist views in Salem, formed a congregation by baptizing one another, with Williams and Ezekiel Holliman first baptizing each other and then ten others. Four months later Williams withdrew from this fellowship, along with several others, doubtful as to the validity of this baptism, and uncertain whether any existing church fellowship had a true authority from Christ to baptize; Richard Scott, who later turned Quaker, said of Williams:

> I walked with him in the Baptists' way about three or four months, in which time he brake from the society, and declared at large the ground and reasons of it; that their baptism could not be right because it was not administered by an apostle. After that he set upon a way of seeking (with two or three of them that had dissented with him) by way of preaching and praying; and there he continued a year or two, till two of the three left him.[3]

Leaving the Baptists, though he continued to speak favorably of them, Williams, as Richard Scott reported, adopted a position like that of the English Seekers, just then emerging. It was those beliefs which Winthrop described as the denial of the existence of any legitimate church or ministry. Unlike many Seekers, however, some of whom became Quakers,

Williams never abandoned Calvinist theology. Many of his later opinions had the flavor of both the Seeker denial of the existence of the true church and the Puritan thrust for withdrawal into the pure church: interested for a while in the conversion of the Indians, he finally concluded that preaching to convert others should only be done by apostles, and that none had been authorized since those sent by Christ himself. Earlier he had argued against sermons intended to convert others because the church fellowship where sermons were preached by definition included only those already converted. Indeed the other side of his contention that no one was to be forced to attend church was that church meetings in general and not just sacramental meetings were to be restricted to the regenerate and all others rigorously excluded. He objected to prayers said in common with unregenerate persons, even if of your own family—to such extent did his Separatism go!

The religious radicals who came to Newport evinced a similar variety in religious opinion. One group, in which John Clarke was prominent, developed a Baptist church; others followed the implications of the original Hutchinsonian doctrines of immediate sanctification and inner revelation to conclusions which adumbrated the theology of the later Quakers. Winthrop mentions Nicholas Easton in this group as teaching that the Christian is united to God's essence and that this divinity within a person becomes the spring of their actions. Easton was a prominent man in the colony who was several times governor, and his teachings were accepted by others who had come at the time of the Hutchinsonian expulsions. This group later joined the Society of Friends when Quaker missionaries appeared.

Another dissident who made his way to Rhode Island was Samuel Gorton. Charged in Massachusetts with claiming direct divine inspiration and with denying the validity of the sacraments, his Rhode Island settlement came to be known as Warwick. He had first stayed at Portsmouth, but there had quarreled with the town leaders and suffered a short imprisonment. Later at Warwick he was in continual dispute with neighbors over land boundaries and gained a reputation as a troublemaker. His religious opinions went even beyond his Quaker-like denial of ministry and sacrament to a denial of the Trinity and teaching of a conditional immortality dependent upon character.

Soon both Baptist and Quaker movements were growing in Rhode Island and started meetings. Both groups, in the roots of their ideas, go back to the first colonists of the place, to Roger Williams and the Hutchinsonians.

The Baptists

It has already appeared that Baptists emerged among the Separatist Puritans and that some members of the Massachusetts Bay community were won over to Baptist views. The logic of Puritanism and its search for the pure church led some in New England as in old to abandon the baptism of infants. The potential for Baptist growth was there, as is shown by both humble Baptist protesters and the Harvard president, Dunster. Evidence would suggest that many of the more pious persons of New England were attracted to the Baptists, and not just because of the logic of adult baptism; in explaining their reasons for dissent some Boston Baptists included such points as their rejection of the half-way covenant and the desire for greater liberty for laymen to "prophesy," thus protesting against the monopoly of a learned but not necessarily "spiritual" clergy, an issue to become very important a century later in the Great Awakening. The Baptist dissidents also declared that they felt that Quakers had been treated with unjust harshness.

Thus it is not surprising that individuals denying infant baptism and small Baptist house-fellowships began to appear in New England and that in Rhode Island, where the restraints against such groups were absent that they would develop into public meetings. Once churches in Rhode Island became firmly established, their influence and attraction in the rest of the region became strong. By 1700 there were six Baptist churches in Rhode Island, three within the area of the old Plymouth Colony, and one in Boston; in a few years there were to be several in Connecticut.

The Baptist church at Providence, Rhode Island, dates back to the mutual baptism of Williams and his associates in 1639. What was to be a more important Baptist congregation was soon founded nearby, at Newport, under the leadership of John Clarke, whom we have already met when he ventured into the Bay colony only to be stopped by persecution. This Newport meeting was formed at least by 1644 and Clarke was its pastor until his death in 1676. Another early Baptist church appeared at Rehobeth, in Plymouth Colony. There Clarke had gone in 1649 to baptize, and in 1663 an emigrant English Baptist, John Myles, formed a congregation. Arrested and fined for holding an illegal meeting, the leaders of this group moved to a place they called Swansea, on the Rhode Island border.

The Boston Baptists developed around the leadership of Thomas Goold. In trouble with the Boston church for his opinions, Goold was cited for not presenting his child for baptism: by his own account, "Then asking me why I did not bring my child to baptism, my answer was, I did not see any rule of Christ for it, for that ordinance belongs to such as can make profession of their faith, as the Scripture doth plainly hold forth...."4 Gradually a Baptist house fellowship grew up around Goold, in spite of harassment from the authorities, and although they met for a while on Noodle's Island, by 1674 they were meeting in Boston with some freedom. All civil punishments against Baptists in Massachusetts ended in 1682, and in 1686 the Boston Baptists had their own meetinghouse.

The dissidence so potent in the intensely felt personal religion of the Baptists was to lead to divisions within their own movement, as it had among the English Baptists, who were divided between the Calvinistic Particular Baptists and the Arminian General Baptists. The difference was greater than belief or not in predestination and related points, for the General Baptists were Puritan radicals who rejected many traditional doctrines and practices like the Quakers, whereas the Particular Baptists felt very close to the mainstream of Puritanism, always attempting to minimize their differences with Congregationalists and Presbyterians, and in England Particular Baptists often cooperated with the Puritan church establishment of the Cromwellian years. John Myles, already mentioned as the leader of the Rehobeth and Swansea Baptist fellowship, had held office, as a Baptist, in the Cromwellian church, serving as a "trier" on one of the commissions for the removal of unworthy clergy in Wales—he was one of the Puritan incumbents in the Church of England forced out in 1662. The first Particular Baptist church in England was perhaps that founded by John Spilsbury, a follower of the non-separatist principles of Ames and Jacob, which had had so much influence on New England congregationalism, and surprising as it seems, some of these Particular Baptists denied Separatism: Goold in Boston, for example, declared that he had not separated but only differed, along with his church, from the other Massachusetts churches on the one point of the baptism of infants; other individuals of Baptist opinion in Massachusetts attempted to retain their membership in Congregationalist churches, so long as their consciences were not forced in the matter of baptism. Nor did the Particular Baptists always insist on freedom of religion as completely as did the General Baptists: the Swansea congregation, which under Myles was Calvinistic, found acceptable a constitution for its settlement which would have excluded those who denied the fundamentals of Christian faith or morals. In England after 1662 Congregationalists and Particular Baptists sometimes practiced intercommunion with one another, and the English Congregationalists protested the mistreatment of Baptists by their brethren in Congregationalist Massachusetts.

This Baptist division first appeared in Rhode Island in

Providence, where, in 1652, the small congregation divided, the General or Arminian group being the majority while a Calvinistic minority withdrew under the leadership of Thomas Olney. The General Baptists were also called Six Principle Baptists because they added to the Baptist five principles a sixth, the practice of the laying on of hands for the reception of the Holy Spirit following baptism (the other five were repentance, faith, baptism, the resurrection of the dead, and eternal judgment, a list of fundamentals based on Hebrews 6:1-2). Roger Williams had apparently held this sixth principle, but had also been Calvinist, so his legacy can be seen on both sides. The Newport meeting divided over the same issue in 1656, with the General or Six Principle Baptists departing from Clarke's congregation.

Further schism occured with the appearance of the "Seventh-Day" principle among some Baptists. Strongly Sabbatarian in fulfilling the commandment to keep the Sabbath holy, as were most Baptists, these Baptists concluded that the true Sabbath day was Saturday, the last day of the week and the Jewish Sabbath. In 1671 some of the Newport Baptists formed themselves into a Seventh-Day Baptist church, and several other Baptist meetings trod the same path. An English Seventh-Day Baptist, Abel Nobel, came to the colonies and founded a church near Philadelphia in 1697.

The Rogerene sect represented another variation among the Baptists. Started by John and James Rogers of New London, Connecticut, who had imbibed Baptist and Seventh-Day principles through their contact with the Newport Baptists, they formed a fellowship at least by 1674 and gradually added ideas more distinctive of the Quakers than Baptists to their teachings (though the General Baptists had tended in the same direction). John Rogers adopted pacifism, the refusal of oaths, and the rejection of a paid clergy. Never growing large, the members of this sect were treated to whippings, fines and imprisonment by the Connecticut authorities, who prosecuted them under laws normally used against the Friends. It was not until 1705 when Valentine Wightman from Rhode Island founded a church at Groton, Connecticut that the colony had a Baptist meeting which was not Rogerene.

Most of the Rhode Island Baptists were General Baptists, but the future was to belong to the Particular Baptists, the main body of those we know in the United States as Baptists deriving from that side of the movement. One of the reasons for this was that as Baptists spread outside of Rhode Island the Particulars more and more predominated, abetted also by an influx of English Baptists of that outlook. Later the Great Awakening gave rise to an enormous expansion of Calvinistic Baptists whereas the General Baptists slowly withered away. And this meant that the influence of Baptists in American life was not to be of the same kind as that of the Quakers, but in time hardly distinguishable from that of other Calvinistic and Evangelical bodies such as Congregationalists and Presbyterians.

With the emigrating both of New England and English Baptists, churches of that faith began to appear outside of New England. A Baptist church was formed at Middletown, New Jersey, as early as 1665, made up mostly of emigrants from Rhode Island under the leadership of Obadiah Holmes, the Baptist who had been whipped in Massachusetts upon the occasion of his going there with John Clarke. The first pastor at Middletown was James Ashton, who had also come from the Newport church. Many New Englanders of radical religious views had gone to Long Island, and one of the Dutch ministers complained that many of the people there rejected infant baptism: William Wickenden of the Providence General Baptist fellowship went there in 1669; by the account of the Dutch minister, "Last year a troublesome fellow, a cobbler from Rhode Island in New England, came there saying, he had a commission from Christ. He began to preach at Vlissingen and then went with the people into the river and baptized them."[5] Wickenden was banished but the area continued a Baptist (and Quaker) stronghold. South Carolina received a group of Baptists from Maine in 1696, under the leadership of William Screven. Screven, an early resident of Kittery, Maine, having come to Baptist conclusions, went to Boston and received baptism from the Boston Baptists, returning to lead a Baptist church in Kittery in 1682. Unlike Wickenden and the Long Island Baptists he was a Calvinist, and with some of his congregation moved to near Charleston, South Carolina where by 1700 they had their own meeting-house.

These travelling New England Baptists however were not necessarily the first of their denomination to appear in the places to which they went. South Carolina had some Baptists since 1683 who had come there with an early governor of Puritan leanings, William Sayle. Elsewhere English Baptists had made a contribution: John Myles had come from England as a Baptist leader, the Boston church had grown partly through the accession of Baptists from England, and especially were the Baptists of New Jersey and Pennsylvania of recent English immigration. While many New England Baptists had moved into New Jersey, the organizing of churches there was greatly aided by the coming in 1687 of an English Baptist minister, Thomas Killingsworth, who helped in the founding of churches at Piscataway and Cohansey. About the same time churches were founded in Pennsylvania through the labors of such British Baptists as Thomas Dungan, earlier a preacher in Ireland, who formed a church in Bucks County and Thomas Griffiths, who emigrated with a group of Welsh Baptists and formed a church in what was known as the "Welsh Tract" of northern Delaware. Many Welsh Baptists settled in New Jersey and Pennsylvania. These British Baptists were mostly Calvinistic, though there were some Seventh-Day Baptists among them. These Baptists of New Jersey and Pennsylvania formed themselves into a Philadelphia Association in 1707 and in 1742 adopted the

London Confession of Faith which went back to 1688 and
was a Baptist version of the Calvinistic *Westminster Confession*, with the sections on church and sacraments altered
to teach Baptist tenets. Many individual churches had earlier
themselves adopted this confession.

In church life the Baptists reveal many similarities to the
New England Puritans, but with some significant differences,
the main difference being of course the separation of church
and state. Baptist churches were formed by "gathering" and
then "covenanting" with one another; for example, the original covenant of the Cape May, New Jersey fellowship (1712)
read:

> We whose names are hereunto subscribed who desire to
> walk together in the fear of the Lord being baptized on
> profession of faith, do in the sight and presence of God
> the Father and our Lord Jesus Christ by the assistance of
> his Holy Spirit profess our deep and serious humiliation
> for all our transgressions and we do...give up ourselves
> to the Lord in a church state...that he may be our God
> and we may be his people...6

In addition, they promised in this covenant to observe
Christ's laws and the ordinances of the church, and to watch
over one another and bear one another's burdens, obeying
their church officers. Baptist churches were not just places of
regular worship, but made a strenuous effort to create a real
spiritual fellowship—in this lay much of their appeal.

Baptist churches chose their own officers: deacons to dis-
pense the funds of the group and take care of the poor as well
as make provision for the elements used in the Lord's Supper
and their distribution to the congregation; ruling elders
whose task was discipline, presenting and trying offenders
who might be rebuked, suspended, or excommunicated
depending upon the gravity of their offenses; and a clerk who
kept records and led singing.

The pastor was also chosen by the congregation, and because of the Baptist emphasis upon lay prophesying, he was

often one of their own number chosen because of his "gifts." Such a person need not have any formal education, but he would be tried by the congregation as to the effectiveness of his "gifts" in preaching and instruction: when William Screven was chosen by the Maine Baptists to be their pastor they reported that they had found him "to be a man whom God hath qualified and furnished with the gifts of his Holy Spirit and grace, enabling him to open and apply the word of God...."7 When educated Baptist ministers from England came, however, they were often chosen as pastors, and in 1718 the Boston Baptists chose a pastor who was a Harvard graduate. Gradually higher educational standards for ministers became common among the Particular Baptists, but the General Baptists continued to call one of their number on the basis of gifts exercised in the fellowship.

Becoming more numerous the Baptists felt the need to join together in associations rather like those organized by Connecticut Congregationalists and the Presbyterians. The earliest such association was probably a "yearly meeting" (the term comes from the Quakers) of Six Principle Baptists in New England. But the main associational movement was that which created the Philadelphia Association in 1707, which was followed later by the Warren Association of the Particular Baptists in New England and several associations in the south. The Philadelphia Association eventually included the Calvinistic Baptist churches not only of New Jersey and Pennsylvania but also of Maryland, Delaware, parts of Virginia, and Connecticut. Having in theory only advisory powers, this association nonetheless exercised considerable authority, inquiring into internal problems in member churches and dealing with matters common to all the churches. Although its recommendations were not binding on member churches, it could withdraw fellowship from an offending congregation and in this way it built up considerable unanimity of belief and practice among the churches within its orbit.

The Quakers

The Quakers, or Society of Friends, emerged out of Puritanism in England, pushing to its limits the Puritan emphasis upon spiritual religion. In New England they disrupted the Puritan Zion. Their experience in colonial America was much wider than those New England incidents, however, as by the end of the seventeenth century they were to be found in all the colonies and in the leadership of some.

The expansion of the Society of Friends in the American colonies came first as a result of a conscious movement carried out by travelling missionaries and only later did colonial Quakerism grow through the emigration of Friends to the colonies and not through converts. In the period from 1655 to 1662 as many as eighty men and women announced the "truth" of the inner light of Christ in the colonies, travelling and founding meetings. It was a spontaneous effort in which individuals simply received a call from God to go to the colonies to publish the truth there; enthusiasm for this work was heightened by the recognition of the new world as an unparalleled opportunity to spread the truth. Filled with millenial expectations, the unfolding before them of a new land seemed providential: there people would respond to the truth, or so they hoped. They thought of themselves as taking up the long abandoned offices of apostles and prophets. These missionaries were voluntary and self-supporting, and sometimes spent years in this travelling ministry. Nor was it only to the colonies they came: their persistence and daring took them to the Sultan of Turkey, to Rome, where a Quaker denounced the papacy as an abomination and was hanged for his pains, and on an ill-fated expedition to the emperor of China, the outcome of which is unknown.

Quixotic as these itinerants sometimes were, their labors bore fruit in the English colonies and the continuation of the practice of the travelling missionary bound English and colonial American Friends closely together: by 1700 some one hundred and fifty English Quaker "ministers" had travelled in America and in the decade of the 1690's a number of colonial Friends were beginning to itinerate in the opposite direction. Frederick B. Tolles says "More than anything else it was the travelling ministry that welded Friends around the Atlantic rim into one people."8 Such travelling Friends were received "lovingly" by their fellows and listened to as having authority, with contributions often made by local groups to aid their ministry.

In 1656 Ann Austin and Mary Fisher appeared in Boston, and after imprisonment were banished. Both had first labored over a year in the island of Barbadoes in the West Indies, an important British colony at the time, where their publication of the "truth" had met with success; previously both had suffered for their witness in England, having been whipped at Cambridge. Josiah Cole and Thomas Thurston were also among the early Friends to arrive in Boston, and were sent back to England only to return immediately to the colonies; landing at Virginia, they walked all the way back to Boston, proclaiming their message to all along the way, including Indians. With no provisions for their maintenance, they relied on God: "we knew not how to supply ourselves, but without questioning or doubting, we gave up freely to the Lord, knowing assuredly that His presence was with us."9 They were probably the first Friends in Virginia, but in Maryland they had been preceded by Elizabeth Harris who had come out from London in 1656. In many cases such missionaries preceded any other kind of religious teaching: in what is now North Carolina the first religious groups of any kind were probably Quaker meetings formed there by these missionaries.

A little later some leaders among the Friends came to the colonies: after laboring in Barbadoes, John Burnyeat, an early pamphleteer among the Friends, came to Maryland in 1665 and eventually travelled southward in Virginia and the Carolinas. William Edmondson, an old Cromwellian soldier turned Quaker, travelled through the Carolinas, Virginia, Maryland, New Jersey, Long Island and Rhode Island, where he, with Burnyeat, represented the Friends in a debate with Roger Williams. Previously he too had been in the West Indies, active in Jamaica as well as Barbadoes. Edmondson kept a journal which gives insight into the Quaker experience. Asked in New England the difference between his teaching and that of the New England ministers, he replied "Your ministers are satisfied with talk about Christ and the Scriptures; we are not satisfied without the sure, inward experience of God and Christ."[10] In New York he reported that "We lodged at a Dutch woman's house who kept an inn. I was moved of the Lord to get a meeting in that town, for there had not been one there before. I spoke to the woman of the house to let us have a meeting. She let us have a large dining-room and furnished it with seats. We gave notice of it and had a brave, large meeting! Some of the chief officers, magistrates, and leading men of the town were at it; very attentive they were, the Lord's power being over them all."[11] Travelling in Virginia, he reported "I had eaten little or nothing that Day," but found a Quaker family living all by themselves who had not seen another Friend for seven years; there he held a meeting.

Most notable of the travellers in America, however, was George Fox himself, the founder of the movement, who from August 1671 to June 1673 moved throughout the colonies, including the West Indies. His Journal provides a first hand account. He says that "it was upon me from the Lord to go beyond sea, to visit the plantations in America," and so with twelve chosen associates he departed. On the voyage they were attended by various providences, including escape from pirates. Arriving first in Maryland he participated in a very large general meeting of Friends, and then crossed over to the eastern shore of that colony, travelling to New England through Delaware, and through "that wilderness country, since called West Jersey," finding some Friends even there however, and attending a large meeting on Long Island which lasted four days at which "The Lord's power broke forth gloriously." From thence he went to Rhode Island and took part in yet another general meeting, to which many people from Connecticut came who "had never heard Friends before." In his journeys, he met with both Burnyeat and Edmondson. Frequently in contact with Indians, "we declared the day of the Lord to them." Back in Maryland, he held meetings to which "some papists" came, one of whom offered to dispute with Fox but was instead converted. Then he and his associates went through much of Virginia and the Carolinas, proclaiming the truth in places where it had never been announced before. Finally, "having sounded the alarm to all people where we came, and proclaimed the day of God's salvation amongst them, we found our spirits began to be clear of these parts of the world, and draw towards Old England again."[12] The trip was less spontaneous than Fox's account suggests: he came purposely to further his plan to provide the Friends with a strong organization, and everywhere he went he attempted to create a system of general "monthly meetings" for dealing with matters of discipline and business which would be subordinate to the London Yearly Meeting. Such meetings would draw together Friends from many local meetings. Elders and Overseers were eventually appointed for the "monthly meetings" to look after spiritual and business matters respectively and to exercise greater discipline within the fellowship.

The accounts of the Quakers' travels betray their dependence upon God for succor and direction—their missionary efforts were a spontaneous response to the leading of the Spirit. When Margaret Brewster was tried in Boston for disrupting a meeting she told her judges that the Lord "laid this service upon me more than three years ago to visit this bloody town of Boston."[13] Perhaps the best example of such leading by the spirit is the story of Robert Fowler and his associates. A Yorkshire Quaker, the Lord 'laid it upon him' to build a ship and sail for America: he built a small craft, named the "Woodhouse," convinced that God would guide it, and gathered eleven Friends to go with him, six of them persons already expelled from Boston. Knowing little of navigation, they received "openings" from the "Lord" by which to steer the ship, God guiding them "as He did Noah's Ark to the hil Ararat." They ended up in New Netherland, and then proceeded to Newport, Rhode Island, where "The power of the Lord fell much upon us and an irresistible word came unto us, 'That the seed in America shall be as the sand of the sea!'"14 Claiming divine inspiration they scattered in all directions, and many of this twelve stayed in the colonies for years. Mary Clarke had a "special moving" to go to Boston, in spite of the inevitability of persecution. Two others went to Plymouth, where they were arrested "as extravagant persons and vagabonds" and banished. Humphrey Norton went to New Haven, Connecticut, where he underwent a whipping, and then to Boston where his companion, William Brend, received a whipping, one of the Congregationalist ministers justifying it by arguing that since the Quaker "endeavoured to beat the gospel ordinances black and blue" "it was but just to beat him black and blue."15 Five of the 'Woodhouse Twelve' remained on Long Island and two of the women, preaching in the streets of New Amsterdam, were promptly arrested and imprisoned. Three of the Woodhouse voyagers found their way to Virginia.

Everywhere the Friends met severe persecution, except for Rhode Island. To those in authority, whether Puritan, Dutch Reformed or Anglican, Quakerism represented the worst anarchism. In most colonies Quakers were first banished, but they soon came back, and upon their arrival would often pick some public spot to announce their return, forcing the authorities to take further steps. Four of them after repeated banishments were hanged in Boston, and one was almost beaten to death in New Netherland. Whippings and imprisonment were common elsewhere too. Executions came to an end because of the displeasure of King Charles II who brought pressure against Massachusetts, but he did little about the hundreds of Quakers who suffered whipping and imprisonment all over England. Having abandoned capital punishment for Quakers in May, 1661, the Bay colony passed the so-called "Cart and Whip" act which provided for the arrest of Quakers and their whipping at the tail of a cart through the streets; then they were to be transported to the next town, whipped in the same manner until they came to the border of the colony and were banished. Even this failed to keep them away; they seemed to thrive on punishment, and often gained the sympathy of the populace so that their suffering made new converts—the impression grows that the authorities were becoming desperate about the Quakers, whom no amount of cruelty seemed to discourage. When the authorities finally allowed them to remain within the colonies unmolested, Friends continued to trouble them by their refusal to pay taxes supporting the clergy or the militia. For such matters Quakers in New England were frequently in court up to the time of the American Revolution. Their insistence on certain "testimonies" characteristic of their special way of life also increased persecution. Refusing the use of all titles of human honor they would call magistrates simply "Friend" or refuse to address them with the polite form of address, using only the familiar second person singular, "thee" and "thou".

But if the Friends met persecution in the colonies, the ground had also been prepared for their coming. Just as with the Baptists, they grew up almost spontaneously out of the Puritan soil of New England, where many seemed to be immediately receptive to their message. Quakerism congealed into a system ideas long fermenting among New Englanders. Many Hutchinsonians in Rhode Island upon hearing the message of the Friends joined them, and the eccentric Samuel Gorton, having heard of their treatment in Boston, invited them to his settlement in Rhode Island, ad-

dressing his letter "To the Strangers and out-casts, with
respect to carnall Israel, now in prison at Boston." Mary
Dyer, who was hanged in Massachusetts, had been a close
friend of Anne Hutchinson, and Anne's sister Catherine Scott
was also a convert. At Plymouth Isaac Robinson, son of the
pilgrim pastor John Robinson, joined the Friends, and at
Salem, ever a place for dissidents, a number seem to have
been ready, considering themselves "Seekers" until the
Quaker message arrived. Long Island, to which like Rhode
Island many New England dissidents had removed, also
quickly adopted the Friends' teaching; many who did so had
apparently first been Baptists.

Penn and Pennsylvania

Another means by which the Society of Friends increased
in the colonies was by their emigration as a group. A small
group settled in South Carolina in 1675; in the same year
others founded the town of Salem in West Jersey, and in the
next few years more Quakers were settling in that area,
founding the town of Burlington. A group of Friends
including William Penn had taken control of West Jersey,
making such emigration possible.

Pennsylvania as a Quaker colony came a few years later.
William Penn arrived in his new colony in 1682, within a
year from the time he had received a charter to it from
Charles II as payment for a debt owed by the king to Penn's
father, who had been a successful admiral in the royal
service. The younger Penn has come gradually to his Quaker
convictions, earlier having consorted with Puritans while a
student at Oxford, where he came under the influence of the
Puritan theologian John Owen. His father was alarmed by
these religious tendencies and sent him to France to study and
perfect himself as a gentleman; later back in London, he
studied law. Having gone to Ireland in 1666 to stay at the
court of the Duke of Ormonde, he fell among "Friends." He
reached his "convincement" under the direction of Thomas

Loe, whom "Taking me by the hand," he says, "spake thus, 'Dear heart, bear thy cross: stand faithful for God and bear thy testimony in thy day and generation, and God will give thee an eternal crown of glory, that none shall ever take from thee. There is not another way."[16]

The young gentleman now adopted Quaker ways and was soon preaching in behalf of his new-found cause. Arrested and imprisoned for participation in an illegal meeting (the Friends in England suffered acutely under the provisions of the Clarendon Code), he wrote his devotional classic No Cross, No Crown while in prison, and was soon the author of other works of Quaker theology and of a history of the early movement. Many of these writings argued in behalf of religious freedom and much of his later activity, both in England and America, furthered that cause. Released from prison, Penn became involved in the relief of imprisoned and distressed Friends, and conceived the idea of founding a colony in the New World for their succor and for the relief of those persecuted for conscience' sake everywhere.

Having gained Pennsylvania as such a haven, Friends began to emigrate to it, not only from England but also from other English colonies like Jamaica and New England. Wesley Frank Craven says "Except for the great Puritan migration into Massachusetts after 1630, there is no parallel in the story of English colonization in North America for the immediate and phenomenal success attending the Pennsylvania venture."[17] The largest number of immigrants were suffering and impoverished Friends from England, where persecution had become more severe by 1680, often entailing burdensome fines which brought ruin to families. Friends also spoke of coming to Pennsylvania in order to flee the evils of the corrupt society of Restoration England, and like other colonists, to carry out missionary labors amongst the Indians. Some strict Friends warned against hasty removal: one should stay and bear "testimony" rather than seek material gain elsewhere!

In creating an ideal society, the Quakers had a great deal in common with the Puritans of New England. Sounding like them, Penn asserted that the purpose of his colonization was "that an example and standard may be set up to the nations."[18] The colony was to be an "holy experiment," an attempt to create the kingdom of God on earth; to Quakers, with their millenial enthusiasm, as Melvin B. Endy argues, "the kingdom of God was breaking into history" and "a truly Christian society of willing men in loving dependence on God and mutual service" was now to be realized.[19] Quakers had not been politically quietist in England: unable by law to participate in government they nonetheless continually criticized the state for various injustices and summoned men and society to repentance. In this respect they were unlike the spiritualist radicals of the continent who had tended towards political withdrawal—more millenarian than mystical in their early phase the Quakers were interested in the coming of God's kingdom.

But if in their thinking about society the Friends upheld the Puritan thrust towards the transformation of the social order, they also held to something of the perfectionism of radical spiritualism. Affirming that the light of Christ was in all men and rejecting the doctrine of predestination, they believed that all men could be saints and that a whole society could be built with a minimum of external restraints and could achieve a conformity to the teachings of the Sermon on the Mount: in the words of Frederick B. Tolles, "A land peopled largely by Friends, brought by the Spirit into a state of perfection like that of Adam before the fall, would become a second Eden. The coercive functions of the state could be expected to wither away from disuse, and a "holy community" of love and peace under the sway of God's Spirit would come into being on the banks of the Delaware."[20] It was at this point that they most differed from the Puritans of New England, who, however, much they dreamed of an ideal society, knew that restraint would always be needed since something of the sinful nature of man always remained—even the redeemed were, in Luther's phrase, 'at the same time righteous and sinners'.

As a "holy experiment" Pennsylvania had distinctly Quaker elements from the first. There was religious freedom, though office-holders were required to believe in Christ, there was no provision for any militia, affirmations were to be taken in court instead of oaths, and arbitrators or peace-makers were to be attached to the courts so that "brethren" might compose their differences without lawsuits. Penn wanted his colony to demonstrate to the world that the Quakers who had so frequently been charged with being fomenters of disorder could lead a peaceable and orderly society. In the event, however, the Friends with their individualism proved difficult to govern, the colonial government divided into factions and there were quarrels with the proprietor. As non-Quakers became more numerous, other issues arose, especially that of providing military protection against Indian raids on the expanding frontiers of the colony, peopled as they were by Germans and Scotch-Irish who did not share the pacifism of the Philadelphia government. Compromises had to be made, and under various evasions funds were voted for the support of the Empire's colonial wars; the tension remained, however, and in 1710 the Philadelphia Yearly Meetings warned Friends in public office against any deviations from principle.

With Penn's death, the colony devolved upon his three sons, none of whom was dedicated to Quakerism (two of them conformed to the Church of England) and gradually the colony slipped out of the control of the Friends, the issue which led to their political demise being that of defence: in 1756 a number of Friends resigned from the Assembly rather than support its military measures at the beginning of the French and Indian War. Thereafter the Friends retreated into a political quietism and emphasized the individual's own inner spirituality and the bearing of "testimony" against worldliness but avoided political responsibility. Quietism had already grown up among the English Quakers, and it now became characteristic of American Friends too.

In Quaker life and thought as a whole there was a similar turning inward. The millenarianism, ecstatic outbursts, and fiery enthusiasm of the first generations (people had "quaked" at those early meetings, and hence the name) gave way to a religious quietism paralleling the growing political one. The life of the Friends was now to be characterized by the orderliness of the silent meetings, the building up of a tightly-knit organization which exercised strict discipline over the membership, the importance of the "testimonies" of special modes of speech, dress and manners by which Friends were distinguished from the "world's people," and the mystical cultivation of the interior religious life. And emphasizing the virtues of industry and frugality, the Friends became a prosperous business-oriented community, their energies focused on commerce rather than statecraft.

The period of creative religious thought also came to a halt after the golden age of such writers as Fox, Penn, and Robert Barclay. Barclay, perhaps the greatest theologian the Friends produced, was appointed governor of the West Jersey province, and encouraged its settlement, though he never actually came over to take up his office. Penn, an able theological writer, was important in establishing the path later Quaker thought would take. Lacking, especially in his later years, the intense enthusiasm and millenialism of Fox, he and other Quaker thinkers opposed two opposite tendencies that soon appeared in the movement, that of John Perrot, who had travelled in Virginia as a missionary, and of George Keith, encountered earlier for his leadership in the history of colonial Anglicanism.

Perrot took to an extreme the Quaker protest against external forms, even denouncing the "form" of holding meetings and having worship at all—religion was the spirit of God within alone. Against Perrot the communal character of

Quaker life was stressed, an emphasis on the importance of the consensus of the religious fellowship as a whole.

George Keith caused trouble from the opposite direction, being concerned that in stressing the inner spiritual Christ Quakerism had lost hold upon the historical Jesus and his once-and-for-all redemptive work. It was over this issue that earlier in Rhode Island Roger Williams had debated the Quakers, his opponents including the close associate of Fox Edward Burrough, and written his 'punningly-titled' *George Fox Digged Out of His Borrowes*. Williams accused the Friends of rejecting the objective authority of scripture and claimed that they made Christ "a type and figure, a pattern and example how Christians ought to walk; not that the blood which he shed upon the cross at Jerusalem, was a sufficient price and satisfaction unto God for the sins of the whole world."[21] Fox and John Burnyeat, another one of the debaters, had responded in *A New-England Fire-Brand Quenched*, a long work of vituperation, where they asserted that "Roger hath discovered himself and his Blasphemy in Denying the Lord Jesus Christ and his Light."[22]

Williams' criticism was typical of the Puritans' reaction to Quakerism, and George Keith tried to respond to this criticism by stressing, as a Quaker, that objectivity of revelation in Christ and scripture which Williams found missing. An associate of Penn and other important Friends, Keith wished the Quakers to adopt a creed, but eventually found himself the leader of a schismatic party of "Christian Friends" in Pennsylvania and New Jersey, and later, going to England, left the movement altogether, denouncing his former associates for "deisme."[23] His conversion to the Church of England followed. Penn and other Quaker writers denied Keith's criticism of their beliefs, which was identical with Williams' criticism of them which Keith had first tried to answer, but it was difficult for the Quakers to show precisely why the historical Christ was necessary since what really mattered was the inner Christ in all men. In Penn's writings that inner Christ sometimes sounds like an inner reason, lending a sort of "rationalist" tinge to his thought which appeared often in later Quakerism.

6

Colonists from the European Continent

In addition to the colonists who have already appeared in these pages, many others came who were not of British background nor nurtured in the religious disputes of Great Britain. Their coming enriched the life of the colonies and increased their religious pluralism, but in the early years especially also increased the religious strife.

The Dutch in New Netherland

The Dutch colony in what is now New York was undertaken, as were several of the English colonies, as the venture of a trading company, the Dutch West India Company. Dutch exploration and fur trading in the area preceded colonization by more than a decade, the latter not being begun until 1624, when settlers located at New Amsterdam on Manhattan Island and at Fort Orange, up the Hudson at the present site of Albany. Very few colonists came at first, and in 1629 a system of "patroonships" by which large grants of land to patroons who would start plantations and bring out numbers of laborers was introduced. This failed to make the colony a success, and only in the last period of Dutch rule were efforts made to populate the colony with independent farmers.

The major motive for the colony from the beginning was profit. Building an outpost of Dutch empire or extending the frontiers of the Protestant faith were not foremost in the minds of the directors of the company. They increasingly represented a point of view developing throughout the century in the Netherlands, "one in which trade rather than religion would form the center of gravity and provide society's basic values."[1] This secular attitude came in conflict with the more traditional religious value of uniformity: those who represented secular commercial values were hardly scrupulous in inquiring into a prospective colonist's religious opinions. When the Dutch East India Company was chartered in 1602, no mention was made of religion, and that company, in its trade in Japan and other places in the orient instructed its agents to avoid such mention. Similarly, the charter for New Netherland, granted to the Dutch West India Company in 1621, omitted mention of religion. One of the leaders of that company, however, was Willem Usselinx, who had an interest in colonization as a means to create a Protestant empire in the New World and so thwart the expansion of Spain.

Nonetheless it was assumed from the beginning that the religion of the colony of New Netherland would be that of the Dutch Reformed Church, and in the course of the history of the colony efforts were made to suppress religious dissent. The loyalty of the Dutch to their Protestant religion was firm, the Reformation in that land having been achieved only through great struggle which brought about religious change along with the rejection of Spanish rule in a war for national independence. The Calvinists played a key role in that struggle, and with victory became the established church of Holland. A long controversy over predestination at the beginning of the seventeenth century hardened Dutch Reformed theology into a very scholastic and rigid version of Calvinism, climaxed in the decrees of the Synod of Dort, where the viewpoint of the more liberal type of Protestantism associated with the followers of Arminius was rejected. The Dutch Arminians, called Remonstrants, however, continued to go their own way as a separate Protestant sect. Dutch Calvinism also had a strong pietistic strain, an emphasis upon personal conversion and the individual's growth in the spiritual life which was partly the result of English Puritan influence in the Netherlands. In organization the Dutch Reformed Church was presbyterian.

The first stipulation concerning religion in New Netherland was a regulation drawn up by the company in 1624 which declared that no religion would be practiced within the colony except the Reformed as it existed in the mother-country, "without however persecuting any one on account of his faith, but leaving to every one the freedom of his conscience."[2] This allowed private or family worship of many kinds while permitting the public worship only of the Reformed Church, which was the pattern in Holland, where Protestantism having triumphed against the persecution of the Spaniard had less inclination than elsewhere to itself persecute others. This 1624 regulation also called for the punishment of anyone who committed blasphemy, and spoke piously of bringing the Indians "and other blind people" to the "knowledge of God and His Word." A directive of the following year requested the governor to provide for "divine service", protect the Sabbath from profanation, and prevent idolatry, the latter provision probably enjoining the suppression of any Roman Catholicism rather than the religion of the Indians! The Company was to provide ministers for the colony, but its actions in that respect were seldom generous. A 1638 regulation called for the support of a minister from the taxation of the colonists.

Among the colonists of the first few years there were no clergy, only two laymen who acted as "comforters of the sick." These comforters led services by reading prayers and sermons, and were authorized to baptize as well as to comfort the sick. The first minister of the colony, Jonas Michaelius, came in 1628 and remained only four years; he quarrelled with the governor and complained of his meagre maintenance from the company, which was in land rather than salary. A strict Calvinist educated at Leiden, Michaelius' ministry is known to us from two letters which he wrote and which were unknown until discovered in the last century. He described his formation of a church by selecting elders and his administration of the Lord's Supper to fifty communicants. Because many of the colonists were French-speaking Walloons (Protestants from the southernmost Netherlands, now Belgium, and exiles from Catholic persecution) he also conducted services in their language. The whole situation of New Netherland, however, he found discouraging: the Indians he thought wicked and devilish and the Europeans mostly "rough and unrestrained" though respectful of him.

Michaelius was succeeded in 1633 by Everardus Bogardus, also educated at Leiden, who also quarrelled with the government of the colony, and particularly with governors Wouter Van Twiller and Willem Kieft. Van Twiller proving unsatisfactory to the Company was soon recalled, but Bogardus' quarrel with Kieft dragged on for a long time. Bogardus denounced the governor from the pulpit as a "monster" and "villain". Kieft retaliated by boycotting services and later arranged for a drummer to play outside the service to disrupt it. Bogardus blamed Kieft for causing trouble with the Indians through an ill-conceived massacre the governor ordered which exposed the outlying colonists to Indian reprisals; Kieft charged the minister with stirring up rebellion in the colony and with appearing drunk in the pulpit. In 1647 both minister and governor left aboard the same ship and both were drowned when the ship sank.

Meanwhile a church building was erected, governor Kieft being told by one of the colonists that it was a great shame that the English settlers had everywhere built themselves fine churches whereas the Dutch were still worshipping in temporary quarters. A second minister also came to the colony, Johannes Megapolensis, and served the people at Fort

Orange up the Hudson river, where one of the more notable patroons, Kiliaen Van Rensselaer, had brought settlers. Megapolensis preached to a congregation in his home and also to the Mohawk Indians whose language he learned and about whose customs he wrote an account. But he too found the colonists a difficult lot, drunken and greedy, and prone to sleep through his sermons. After six years he was ready to leave the colony when he was invited to remain as pastor in the main settlement of New Amsterdam. There he was joined in 1652 by another minister, Samuel Drisius, sent to the colony by the Classis or Presbytery of Amsterdam, who was fluent in French as well as Dutch and could minister to the Walloons. According to a letter he wrote to the Classis he went every two months to Staten Island to conduct worship there for some French Protestants.

In 1647 New Netherland received an able if sometimes high-handed governor in Peter Stuyvesant, who was determined to reduce the colony to good order. He enforced strict observance of the sabbath, required church attendance, and restricted the sale of liquor. The colony by this time had considerable religious diversity: a Jesuit priest, captured by Indians and assisted by the Dutch in his escape, commented on religion in the colony that "No religion is publicly exercised but the Calvinist, and orders are to admit none but Calvinists, but this is not observed; for besides the Calvinists there are in the colony Catholics, English Puritans, Lutherans, Anabaptists...."[3] The Dutch ministers complained of this diversity, adding that within the colony were "many atheists and various servants of Baal among the English."[4] Stuyvesant saw religious uniformity as important for stability, and cooperated with the ministers in suppressing dissent. English Puritans, mostly on Long Island, were allowed to have their own meetings, since they were fellow Calvinists, and there were sometimes English ministers in these churches; but with others it was a different story. Stuyvesant forbade unauthorized religious meetings, prevented a group of Dutch Lutherans from having their own services, and was especially hostile to English sectarians like the Quakers. Stuyvesant had some Quakers severely beaten, enraged at their refusal to remove their hats or address him by his official titles of honor.

In 1654 the religious uniformity of the colony was also menaced (at least to Stuyvesant and the Dutch ministers) by the arrival of some Jews, exiles from the Dutch colony in Brazil which had recently been seized by the Portuguese. In these cases of persecution, however, the leadership of the Company recommended more tolerant courses than Stuyvesant favored, and even reprimanded him for his efforts to suppress dissent. In 1663 the Company directed him not to proceed so rigorously against dissenters, since this might stop immigration into the colony, but to 'shut his eyes', allowing people to follow their consciences if they did not disturb the peace.

In 1664 the colony was captured by the English and Dutch rule came to an end except for one short interlude ten years later. One of the articles of surrender provided that "the Dutch here shall enjoy the liberty of their consciences in Divine Worship and church discipline."5 Earlier the English efforts at Anglican establishment in what was renamed New York have appeared but the Dutch churches continued to flourish under English rule. Before the English conquest, Dutch Reformed churches had been founded on Long Island at Midwout and Breuckelen (Brooklyn) and farther north on Manhattan at Harlem, as well as at New Amsterdam and Fort Orange; across the Hudson in New Jersey a congregation had been formed at Bergen. At the time of the surrender the Dutch had six ministers in the colony, and their number continued to grow, as by the end of the century there were many new congregations, especially in New Jersey.

The whole Dutch experience in New Netherland reflects conditions and attitudes in the mother country: while a church establishment was maintained and the Reformed religion served by able ministers, considerable religious diversity was allowed as the needs of commerce and successful colonial development dictated religious tolerance, defeating efforts at uniformity.

New Sweden

A Dutch Lutheran pastor had come out to New Netherland, and in spite of harassment by Stuyvesant managed to minister to his little flock. But in 1655 when New Netherland added to its domains the territory to its south first settled by Swedes, it incorporated into itself many more Lutherans and allowed the continuation of Lutheran worship there.

The Swedish attempt at colonization in the New World had been carried out as a venture of a Swedish trading company and involved both Willem Usselinx, who left the Netherlands for the employment of the Swedish king and Protestant champion of the Thirty-Years War, Gustavus Adolphus, and Peter Minuit, one of the early governors of New Netherland, who came with the first Swedish colonists. Those first colonists, including many Finns along with the Swedes, established Fort Christina on the Delaware River near the present site of Wilmington, Delaware, an area claimed by the Dutch. More colonists arrived in succeeding years and other settlements were made, until in 1655 the Dutch seized the Swedish colony, only for it to fall to the English a few years later.

Having founded their colony, the Swedes made the same assumptions about its religion that we have seen others making: that the religion of the mother country would be established in the colony. One of the early governors was instructed to:

> Labor and watch that he render in all things to Almighty God the true worship which is his due,...and to take good measures that the divine service is performed according to the true confession of Augsburg, the Council of Upsala, and the ceremonies of the Swedish church,

having care that all men, and especially the youth, be well instructed in all parts of Christianity, and that a good ecclesiastical discipline be observed and maintained. [6] This of course meant the establishment of the Lutheran church, the Augsburg being the original confession of faith of the Lutheran movement. The ecclesiastical traditions and ceremonies of Sweden were a rather "high-church" version of the Lutheranism of Germany, in which much more of the liturgical and organizational usages of medieval times were retained than was the case with most Lutheran churches, putting the Church of Sweden in a relationship to the other Lutheran churches which was like that of the Church of England to the other Reformed churches.

Following these instructions, Reorus Torkillus came a year after the founding of the colony as its first minister, although he died in a few years; he was followed by others, one of whom translated Luther's Small Catechism into the language of the Delaware Indians. When the Dutch arrived, there were three Lutheran ministers in the colony, and one was allowed to remain. At the end of the century the Swedish king Charles XI became concerned about the spiritual needs of the Swedes in America and gave the responsibility for their care to the Archbishop of Upsala, who sent three ministers to America in 1697, one of whom became pastor at Wilmington and another at Philadelphia. Many more ministers came from Sweden in the next century, some preaching to the German Lutherans who began to arrive in substantial numbers. As time went on, the Swedish churches became English-speaking, and were absorbed into the Episcopal church rather than remaining Lutheran. Two of their early buildings, Holy Trinity Church in Wilmington, Delaware, and Gloria Dei Church in Philadelphia, built in 1699 and 1700 respectively, became Anglican and are still standing.

The French Huguenots
French Protestants, called Huguenots, settled all over the

north American colonies in the seventeenth century, although seldom in large groups; they first settled in the Dutch colony, which they considered to be governed by their co-religionists. French Protestantism went back to the earliest era of the Reformation, and counted among its founders some of the most important leaders and theologians of the whole Protestant movement, most notably of course John Calvin, who, although he spent his active years of leadership in Geneva, was from Picardy in France and filled Geneva with fellow French Protestant exiles. Geneva for Calvin was always a springboard for the larger and more important task of the conversion of France. French Protestantism had been tried in years of struggle and civil war against the Catholic monarchy, and had survived such disasters as the massacre of St. Bartholomew's Day, 1572, when several thousands of their number, including many of their ablest leaders, were murdered. With the accession to the throne of Henry IV in 1589 France had a Protestant king, but in order to retain that throne he found it expedient to change religions; but he did not forget his former fellows the Protestants, granting them toleration in the Edict of Nantes of 1598, which among other provisions, allowed the Protestants possession of certain fortified towns to insure their position; one of these, La Rochelle, gave its name to a Huguenot settlement in New York, New Rochelle.

But the toleration was far from complete, Protestant worship being forbidden in Paris, and later King Louis XIV set about systematically to crush French Protestantism which he feared not only as heresy but as a politically dangerous element within the state. His measures of suppression were climaxed with the revocation of the Edict of Nantes in 1685. In the long course of this persecution French Protestants in large numbers went into exile in Germany, the Netherlands, England, and other Protestant lands, and some chose to emigrate to the American colonies. In theological opinion the French Protestants were of course Calvinists and thus akin in faith not only to the Dutch but also to the Puritans; in organ-

ization they had developed a full presbyterian system with
elders in local congregations and provincial and national
synods. In fact this system was first developed and utilized
for a whole nation and not just a small city-state like Geneva
by the French.

A significant proportion of the early settlers of New
Netherland were French-speaking Walloons. To them were
added French exiles so that there were four French Protestant
churches in New York by the 1690's, with a number of ministers, including the prominent theologian Pierre Daillé who
had taught at the famous Protestant academy of Saumur
before its destruction by Louis XIV. In 1686 a French church
was established in Boston and called Daillé as its pastor; the
New Englanders welcomed the French as fellow-Calvinists,
as had the Dutch. In the south, many Huguenots went to
South Carolina and Virginia, and in the former founded
several congregations. These Huguenot churches usually
became Anglican in time, that being the established Protestantism of the colonies to which they went. They had no
objections, as did the Puritan Calvinists, to Anglican ritual
(the Church of England by its confession, the Thirty-Nine
Articles, they considered a Calvinist church). In other cases
these Huguenot churches became Presbyterian. One in
Charleston, South Carolina, simply remained independent,
keeping as its official name "The French Protestant Church in
the City of Charleston."

Because there were many ministers among these French
exiles they were frequently chosen to serve English-speaking
churches, especially Anglican, both in Virginia and South
Carolina, but also Presbyterian. Scattered among these
French Protestants were also a few Italian Protestant exiles,
or Waldensians, who were at the time subjected to increasing
persecution in their native Savoy.

German Protestants
More numerous in the colonial period than Dutch,
Swedes, or French, German Protestant immigrants swelled

the population of Pennsylvania and then poured down the southern inland valleys to fill up frontier areas. Most of this influx came in the eighteenth-century, but Germans were already arriving in the last years of the seventeenth and beginning to make their significant impact upon American culture, and not least upon religious life. They came from many regions of Germany, but especially from the Palatinate on the Rhine, which was a Protestant area greatly disturbed by the turmoil of the Thirty Years War and then by the invasion of a French Catholic king. Economic troubles also plagued the region, and thus there were many reasons for emigration when William Penn launched an advertising campaign urging Germans, especially those seeking a haven from religious persecution, to come to his "holy experiment" in Pennsylvania. Those who came represented the spectrum of German Protestantism (and included a few Roman Catholics too) from the established Lutheran and Reformed churches to the sectarian protest groups such as the Dunkers and Mennonites. It is usual to distinguish the former from the latter as the "Church-Germans" and the "Sect-Germans."

The "Sect-Germans" came first, attracted to Pennsylvania because of the persecution they suffered in the homeland and the similarity of many of their religious ideals to those of the inviting Quakers. Among these first German immigrants were Mennonites who traced their origins back to the Anabaptists, who arose almost simultaneously with Luther's revolt. These Anabaptists, appearing first in Switzerland and southern Germany, denounced the followers of Luther and Zwingli for not going far enough in their reformation of the church. They sought to reconstitute primitive Christianity in small fellowships of believers who practiced only adult baptism and emphasized the Christian life as a disciplined following of Christ. Persecuted by Catholic and Protestant alike, their lot was difficult, and much of this early Anabaptism was cruelly suppressed. Having survived persecution, some of them in the Netherlands and lower Rhine came under the steadying influence of Menno Simons, from whom they received their name. Under his leadership, more extreme ideas about the kingdom of God on earth were abandoned and the "Mennonites" settled down to a simple following of the New Testament which included pacifism and the rejection of oaths. They gradually drew into their orbit many of the remaining Swiss Anabaptists.

The first Mennonites to come to Pennsylvania settled at Germantown, north of Philadelphia, in 1683. They had emigrated from Crefeld, on the Rhine near the Dutch border, and were of mixed Dutch and German ancestry and as a result of contact with Quaker missionaries from England had modified some of their beliefs and practices. In Germantown they at first worshipped with Quakers, but in later years formed their own Mennonite meeting. In the next year, 1684, more Mennonites came from the Palatinate and from the canton of Berne in Switzerland. The Swiss Mennonites began settling the inland region of Lancaster County, which eventually became the heart of the Pennsylvania German area. By the middle of the eighteenth-century there were many modest Mennonite meeting-houses scattered about Pennsylvania, with several others located in towns of Western Virginia and Maryland.

Mennonite life and worship bore many resemblances to that of the Quakers, especially at first among Mennonites who had been stirred by Quaker witnessing. Their pacifism and rejection of oath-taking paralleled that of the Friends, and the Mennonites and other German sectarians lent support to the Quaker leadership in the government of the colony. However in other respects the Mennonites differed from the Quakers: there was no rejection of external rites since the Mennonites practiced baptism and the Lord's Supper as well as a rite of foot-washing, patterned after Jesus' washing of the feet of his disciples. Mennonite worship included hymn singing and a sermon, after which leaders in the congregation were encouraged to make edifying additions of their own. Discipline among the membership was strictly maintained, and those who violated the group's standards found themselves placed under the "ban," a kind of excommunication.

Another German sect were the "Dunkers," or as they usually preferred, "Brethren." The Brethren practiced adult baptism like the Mennonites but insisted that it be by a trine total immersion in the water. Though they shared many traits with the Anabaptists the Brethren had arisen later, under the influence of Pietism, a movement which spread through both the Lutheran and Reformed churches of Germany in the late seventeenth and early eighteenth centuries, and which sought to revivify the churches by an emphasis upon a warm, personal piety and the individual's own religious experience. The founder of the Brethren, Alexander Mack, raised in the Reformed Church, adopted Pietism and concluded that its ideals could only be realized outside of the state churches in small fellowships with ideals about Christian discipleship similar to those of the Anabaptists. The Brethren thus blended Anabaptist beliefs such as pacifism and the rejection of oaths and infant baptism with the evangelicalism of the pietists. Mack formed a congregation in Schwarzenau, Westphalia, in 1708 but the little groups of German Baptist Brethren were persecuted by the state churches so that in 1719 a group of Brethren led by Peter Becker came to Germantown, forming the first Dunker congregation in America. Later Alexander Mack too came with another band of Brethren, and the group ceased to exist in Germany. Small Dunker fellowships grew up in the same areas where Mennonites were to be found, with whom the Brethren had much in common. A colonial historian of the Baptists reported five congregations of them in Maryland prior to 1751; aggressively evangelistic, in the long run they grew more rapidly than the Mennonites.

A schism within the Brethren led by one of the early leaders from Germany, Conrad Beissel, occasioned the formation of the Ephrata Society in Lancaster County, Pennsylvania, in 1732. This group took the Bretheren emphasis on simplicity of life to the point of asceticism, organizing into a community which renounced both marriage and the ownership of property. An observer wrote a description of them for a friend in Germany:

> At Conestoga, some twenty miles from here, there has arisen a new awakening among some of the Brethren. Their leader is the well-known baker, Conrad Binsel [sic]. They find a great response among the people. They insist upon renunciation of the world and one's self. Their life, in clothing and nourishment, is limited to the bare necessities. They discard superfluous property and livestock. They greet no one whom they meet in the street, but walk straight ahead. To outward appearance they live in great harmony. Both sexes hold services and communion almost daily. They observe the seventh day and claim in general that it is their goal to achieve a perfect life and continual union with God, and this with great power and zeal.[7]

This schism attracted to itself many of the Brethren and was active in printing and disseminating the mystical writings of Beissel. With the leader's death it declined, though part of it continued on as the German Seventh-Day Baptists.

Also among the German sects were the Schwenckfelders, a small number of whom came to Pennsylvania in 1734. They were followers of Kaspar Schwenckfeld, a German religious radical who had at first been a follower of Luther but then took up spiritualist ideas of his own about the inner Christ as well as some of the ideas of the Anabaptists. Many of his views were similar to those of the later Quakers. Schwenckfelders in Pennsylvania held private meetings to cultivate their ideals of the inner life, and eventually organized a few congregations.

The German sectarians constituted a disproportionately large number of the German immigrants, attracted by the religious freedom of Pennsylvania. But other Germans came who had previously belonged to the established Lutheran and Reformed churches in the old land; they were somewhat later in arriving than the sectarians and also slower in forming churches. They did not so often emigrate as religious fellowships with their own leaders nor did they have the same kind of initiative and experience in forming congregations characteristic of the sect-people, but were accustomed to having religious matters ordered for them by the public authorities.

Among these German "Church People" perhaps as many as one-half were Reformed or Calvinist, even though Calvinists were far outnumbered by Lutherans in Germany. The reason for this was that so much of the emigration came from the Palatinate and surrounding regions, a part of Germany where the Calvinist church had been favored and in which the Reformed *Heidelberg Catechism* (also used by the Dutch) had been the prevailing confession. There were also German-speaking Swiss of Calvinist faith who came to Pennsylvania.

The first persons of German Reformed background in the colonies had settled in New York and New Jersey and been absorbed into the Dutch churches there, but that was of course not possible in Pennsylvania where no Dutch churches were to be found and to which most of the Germans were soon coming. There were several early German Reformed clergymen in the colonies too, one active along the Hudson river and another accompanying a group of German miners in Virginia, but the first important German Reformed leader was John Philip Boehm who came to Pennsylvania in 1720 as a farmer. Because of his piety and talent for leadership he was asked by his neighbors to preach to them and baptize their children, which he reluctantly agreed to do, although not ordained. He was soon preaching in private homes throughout Montgomery County, Pennsylvania. Two years later Michael Weiss, a Reformed minister, arrived among a group of Palatine immigrants and challenged Boehm's leadership since the latter was unordained. Boehm's people appealed to the Dutch ministers of New York who advised them to write to the "classis" of Amsterdam, the council of Dutch ministers in that city which had long been concerned with religious affairs in New Netherland and New York, and they did so in a long letter of 1728 which explained why they had requested Boehm's services, noting that he was a man of some learning and "as Reader, maintained the ministry of the Word, to the best of his ability and to the great satisfaction of the people," adding that they needed "pure religious worship" in a land, which while fertile and abundant, was also a "soul-destroying whirlpool of apostasy." To confirm this latter point they informed the classis "that we are living among all sorts of errorists, as Independents, Puritans, Anabaptists, Newborn, Saturday-folks, yea even the most horrible heretics, Socinians, Pietists, etc.."[8] The classis of Amsterdam was sympathetic to their appeal but concluded that Boehm must now receive regular ordination to continue his ministry; this he received from the Dutch ministers in New York, bringing to an end his dispute with Weiss. Thereafter the two of them served the growing number of scattered Reformed congregations in Pennsylvania. Soon other ministers were added, some coming from Germany and others from the Pennsylvania Germans, the latter receiving ordination from the nearby Presbyterians. Gradually Reformed congregations grew up beyond Pennsylvania, early ones appearing for example in Frederick and Monocacy, Maryland.

The most important of the German Reformed leaders was Michael Schlatter. Born in Switzerland and ordained in the Netherlands, he was sent to the colonies by the Dutch Church in 1746 with explicit instructions for the organization of the German Reformed congregations. In the next year, led by Schlatter, and with the cooperation of Boehm and Weiss, the clergy and lay elders of the German Reformed churches, having decided against union with the English-speaking Presbyterians in the area, organized a "coetus" or synod in Philadelphia. This coetus continued however to be under the authority of the classis of Amsterdam. The *Heidelberg Cate-chism* and *Canons of Dort* were adopted as the standards of belief.

In his later years, Schlatter founded many congregations and schools, and travelled in Europe to raise money for the nascent German Reformed Church in the American colonies. In 1751 he counted some fifty-three congregations of German Reformed.

Lutheran services were being held in Pennsylvania by the 1690's, and some assistance was given to German Lutheran immigrants by the Swedish ministers near Philadelphia, but German Lutheran congregations with their own pastors were not formed until early in the next century. One of the first was the church organized at New Hanover by Daniel Falckner in 1703; in 1709 a whole congregation of Lutherans, with their pastor Joshua Kochertal, came to New York from the Pala-tinate and located at Newburgh on the Hudson. Lutheran congregations were soon springing up in Germantown and Philadelphia, and beyond Pennsylvania in such places as Frederick and Hagerstown in Maryland and Winchester and Woodstock in Western Virginia. Active among these churches as ministers were the older and younger John Casper Stoever, father and son, who came to the colonies in 1718.

Much of this early colonial Lutheranism had connections with the movement in Germany known as Pietism. Such was the case with many of the earliest clergy and laity in Pennsyl-vania, amongst whom edifying services in private homes of the type encouraged by Pietism in Germany flourished. When colonial Lutherans sought aid from the mother country, they turned to the University of Halle, a Pietist center, partly because of its acknowledged interest in mis-sionary activities. This Lutheran Pietism was a movement within the German churches which sought to invigorate church life by a renewed interest in personal piety, devotion-al reading, and the demands of Christian discipleship. Often

Pietists protested what they considered the preoccupation of church people with formalities rather than the inner reality of religion.

Already inclined towards Pietism, the Lutheranism of Pennsylvania was further confirmed in this pattern by the arrival in 1742 of Henry Melchior Muhlenberg, the outstanding leader of colonial Lutheranism, who was responsible for the unification of the scattered congregations. Converted to a Pietist outlook in his youth, and closely associated with Halle, he responded to the standing invitation of the Pennsylvania Lutherans for Halle to send someone out to help them. Like Michael Schlatter among the Reformed he led in the formation of new congregations and of a larger organization: in 1748 he and other ministers and some laymen, meeting in Philadelphia to ordain a minister, proceeded to draw up a plan for a regularly meeting synod and a common liturgy. Later Muhlenberg held the office of "overseer" for the synod, travelling about and supervising its activities.

Lutheranism in colonial America thus achieved organization through the efforts of Muhlenberg, and because of his leadership and the influence of Halle, as well as its own earlier inclinations, gained a strongly pietist flavor, making it much more akin to the Puritan derived religiosity of so much of colonial America than a more traditionalist Lutheranism (like that of the Swedes, for example) would have been.

The last of the important German groups to come to the colonies were the Moravians, or Unitas Fratrum ("Unity of the Brethren"), who were not German in origin. They are difficult to categorize as either "church-people" or "sect-people", for they had characteristics of each, with a liturgical worship close to the Lutherans and a pacifism like the Mennonites. The Moravians go back to the Hussite religious protest of fifteenth-century Bohemia and Moravia (both regions of modern Czechoslovakia) part of which after the martyrdom of Hus in 1415 organized itself as the Unitas Fratrum and survived, in spite of persecution, until the time of the

Reformation, when it joined the Protestant cause. During the Thirty-Years War the Moravians were subjected to the full force of the counter-reformation and many went into exile. In 1722 a group of such exiles settled in Saxony on the estate of the Lutheran Count Nicholas von Zinzendorf, naming their center Herrnhut. There they met with German pietism as well as with the intense and very individual religious ideas of Zinzendorf, who had been educated at Halle and combined a very emotional love and adoration of Christ with visions of a united Christendom. Before long Zinzendorf was the leader of the "Herrnhuters", chosen as their "bishop", and the group itself was becoming a communal fellowship with a growing interest in world missions.

With missionary intent, small groups of Moravians began in 1735 to settle on land acquired by Zinzendorf in Georgia. This attempt at colonization proved a failure (although the young John Wesley was deeply impressed by the Georgia Moravians whom he met on shipboard) and most of them removed to Pennsylvania and founded the towns of Nazareth and Bethlehem on the Delaware River considerably to the north of Philadelphia. In 1736 Zinzendorf, banished from Saxony because of his unorthodox ideas, joined them there.

It was Zinzendorf's hope that he could unite all the German Protestants of Pennsylvania (and the Quakers and others) into a single "Church of God in the Spirit;" to that end he and the leaders of other groups met together on several occasions, and Zinzendorf served as pastor to some Lutherans in Philadelphia. But most of those whom he sought to unite became increasingly distrustful of Zinzendorf's motives, fearing that he wanted to unite everyone under his own authority, and soon he was being denounced by spokesmen for the other groups: John Philip Boehm of the Reformed accused Zinzendorf and his colleagues of being "false apostles" who had come "in sheep's clothing."[9] Eventually the Moravians formed their own congregations, and Zinzendorf returned to Europe, spending a considerable time thereafter in England. Leadership among the Moravians in America passed to Augustus Gottlieb Spangenberg, who had taught at Halle before joining the Herrnhuters, and who had originally come to Georgia with the Moravians who went there. He organized and led the group at Bethlehem. In 1753 the Moravians founded another community in North Carolina.

Jews in the American Colonies

At the time of the European colonization of America, Jews had no homeland of their own but were aliens resident in the societies of Muslims and Christians, subject both to harsh discriminatory laws and to the occasional rising of mobs inflamed by religious hatred. Indeed, in the very year of Columbus' great discovery the Jews of Spain were expelled; those of Portugal soon suffered the same fate, bringing to an end the impressive Jewish civilization of the Iberian peninsula.

Many of the exiled Spanish and Portuguese Jews (or Sephardim, as Jews of Iberian background were called) found their way to the Netherlands, which after its own independence from Spain was more tolerant than most of Europe. These Dutch Sephardim were active in the trading companies which carried out Dutch colonization, and some of them located in Brazil during the short period when part of that land was a Dutch colony. When this colony was retaken by Portugal in 1654 these Jews fled, some of them removing to the Dutch colony in North America, New Netherland. There were twenty-three persons in a group of Portuguese-speaking Jews which in that year arrived in New Amsterdam, and though some of them did not remain long, they were joined by other Jews from the Netherlands.

Much of the populace was hostile to the newcomers, and one of the Reformed ministers complained of their presence in the colony. Governor Stuyvesant wrote to the directors of the Dutch West India Company asking that these "hateful enemies and blasphemers of the name of Christ" be expelled that they might not "infect and trouble this new colony." 10 Prominent Jews in Amsterdam however interceded with the Company, pointing out that Jews had ventured much in its projects, and the directors responded to Stuyvesant that to expel the Jews would be unfair, noting that Jews had made considerable investment in the shares of the Company. Later Stuyvesant sought to prevent the Jews from enjoying certain privileges of citizenship and was reprimanded by the directors, who told him that the Jews "may quietly and peacefully carry on their business as heretofore and exercise in all quietness their religion within their houses."11

These Jews had private worship among themselves from the beginning, and this continued under English rule, although in 1685 a Jewish petition for public worship was rejected by the governor and council. They never had a rabbi (nor were there any rabbis anywhere in the North American colonies) but the service was led by voluntary "hazzanim", lay leaders of the community. Such a hazzan was Saul Brown, described by an observer as the "minister" of the Jews. One of his successors, Lopez de Fonseca, had come from a rabbinical family and had received a Hebrew education; he was given a salary for his services though he continued his activities as a merchant. In 1682 the Jews of New York purchased their own burial ground and in 1730 they completed a synagogue building, the first constructed on the mainland of North America. Other members of the community fulfilled the functions of circumciser of infant males and ritual slaughterer for kosher food.

Jews appeared elsewhere in the colonies besides New York. The British had encouraged the settlement of Jewish merchants in their West Indian colonies (there were early synagogues in Jamaica and Barbadoes) and a few of these established themselves in the mainland colonies. Individual Jews had come to Boston as early as 1649, and later one of them, Judah Monis, converted to Christianity and taught Hebrew

at Harvard, publishing both a Hebrew grammar and a treatise on the Trinity; he continued however to observe
Saturday as the Sabbath. There was a fairly substantial
Jewish community in Newport, Rhode Island, where eventually the second synagogue in the North American colonies
was built. Other groups of Jews sufficiently numerous to
hold services were to be found in Philadelphia, Savannah,
Georgia, and Charleston, South Carolina—by the time of the
American Revolution the Charleston group was probably the
largest in the thirteen colonies.

By any measure the Jewish community in colonial America
was tiny, but it represented a group of Jews who were free
from the restraints of European ghetto life and who were
rebuilding their way of life around the synagogue, which
served as a communal center.

7

Early Presbyterianism:
Puritans, Scots, and Irish

The Presbyterians were one of the largest religious groups in colonial America by the time of the Revolutionary War, and yet no colony had been settled as a "Presbyterian" one. The name itself, as seen in earlier chapters, had several different meanings. It referred most widely to the ecclesiastical polity of the Reformed churches of Switzerland, France, the Dutch Netherlands, Scotland and parts of Germany in which all clergy were on a parity, and assisted by lay elders, governed the church through an ascending series of church courts or assemblies. Presbyterianism in England meant also the Puritan attempt to force such a polity upon the Church of England, but by the later seventeenth century it had also come to refer to a conservative party amongst the English Puritans which held to wider and more "churchly" patterns of sacramental administration, a meaning which it had in New England. Even after the ejections of 1662, these Presbyterian Puritans did not abandon hope for "comprehension" within the Church of England. Never establishing a complete Presbyterian system of government for themselves as a separate denomination, these English Presbyterians represented that end of the Puritan spectrum which, unlike the Congregationalists and Baptists, did not restrict the ministry to local congregations but thought of ministry as related to the church as a whole and thus continued to seek inclusion in a national church. Presbyterianism in the American colonies contained elements of all these strands and others as well, and may be considered as a bringing together in the colonies of at least six different groups and experiences.

The first experience going into the make-up of colonial Presbyterianism was that of New England Puritanism, in which there were "presbyterian" elements and tendencies, and from which migrants to other colonies came, forming churches most of which eventually became Presbyterian. One "presbyterian" tendency had to do with broader sacramental practice, and both the half-way covenant and the broadening of admission to the Lord's Supper represented such a tendency. Another "presbyterian" element in New England Puritanism came to the fore later in the century, and predominantly in Connecticut, the adoption of a system giving a greater role to associations. With the Saybrook Platform of 1708 the Connecticut churches had become "half-presbyterian" and this influence extended to many of those moving beyond the confines of New England.

From quite early in the seventeenth century New Englanders moved into Long Island and northern New Jersey, and formed churches. Where these churches practiced a less inclusive admission and administration of the sacraments they often became Baptist, and where their practices were more inclusive, Presbyterian. In the seventeenth century, churches were founded by New Englanders at such places on Long Island as Southampton, Southold, East Hampton, and Setauket; the first two formed in 1640, out of migrants from Lynn, Massachusetts and New Haven, Connecticut, respectively. The Lynn group, Winthrop tells us, emigrated in search of more land. In these churches, especially as they were strengthened by new immigrants from Connecticut and under the influence of Connecticut's modified congregationalism, Presbyterian tendencies were present. Even the name was sometimes used: in a deed of 1707 land was granted to "the church or congregation of Presbyterians at Southampton."1 A stipulation contained in a grant of land made by the town of Setauket provided that it was for a "presbyterian" ministry. Churches founded at Newark and Woodbridge in New Jersey, the former as early as 1667, also became Presbyterian. Groups of New Englanders also moved farther south and formed churches which were frequently considered Presbyterian. Individuals and small groups had settled in Virginia, Maryland and the Carolinas and such persons naturally gravitated towards churches some of which were or became Presbyterian (Baptists and Quakers also recruited such people). Francis Doughty would be a good ministerial example of this. Having settled in Taunton, Massachusetts, he left there, probably in 1642, because of his belief that all children of persons themselves baptized should be baptized. For a while he served a congregation of New Englanders on Long Island, but later itinerated in both Virginia and Maryland preaching to scattered "Presbyterian" fellowships meeting in private homes. A Puritan church was established in Charleston, South Carolina in 1690 with a New England minister; it was called both "the New England Meeting" and the "Presbyterian Church." Another such church was founded about the same time at Dorchester, South Carolina.

Close ties were maintained between these churches and New England, even when the churches included many not of New England background. In 1698 the ministers of Boston sent two of their number to serve congregations in Philadelphia and New Castle, Delaware; the early Presbyterians of Philadelphia corresponded frequently with New England ministers and associations, seeking advice. Thomas Barrett was sent by New England ministers to North Carolina, where he was preaching in the Ashley River area by 1684. In the eighteenth century the Presbyterian churches of New York and New Jersey were usually served by ministers educated in the New England colleges. This "Presbyterianism" which was something of a New England "spill-over" remained close to Congregationalism.

The second experience which went into colonial Presbyterianism was that of the English Puritan Presbyterianism of the late seventeenth and early eighteenth centuries. This English Presbyterianism not only favored a wider sacramental usage but included some who had moved away from strict Calvinism towards a more liberal theology. Following Richard Baxter and the French Reformed theologian Moise Amyraut they minimized the doctrine of predestination without moving all the way to the free will theology of Arminianism. Such Presbyterians were nonetheless taxed by the more strictly Calvinist Congregationalists and Particular Baptists as nearing Arminianism, and some of them later in the eighteenth-century abandoned the orthodox doctrine of the Trinity, giving rise to English Unitarianism. Benjamin Colman, whom we have earlier seen participating in the liberalization of New England religion, had consorted with such English Presbyterians during his years in England.

English Puritans of Presbyterian views came in small numbers to the colonies, and one whole group settled at Hempstead, Long Island. Some ministers who came were important in the development of colonial Presbyterianism: one such was Richard Denton, who began a long ministry at Hempstead in 1644—one of the Dutch ministers wrote of him that he was "a pious, godly and learned man, who is in agreement with our church in everything."[2] It was from members moving away from the Hempstead church that the church at Jamaica, Long Island was founded, the oldest Presbyterian congregation in the New World with a continuous history. Later came Matthew Hill, who had been ejected from his parish in the Church of England in 1662, and who settled in Maryland, preaching in the area of Port Tobacco. In 1669 he wrote Richard Baxter in England that in Maryland "We have many also of the reformed religion who have a long while lived as sheep without a shepherd." Apparently strong Puritan opinions still flourished among them, for he commented that they "are not at all fond of the liturgy or ceremonies." Hill also deplored the fact that the "Quakers have gained a great many proselytes in this place," and hoped that Baxter could send him some books "necessary for my work."[3]

In 1690 a General Fund was established by the English Presbyterians and Congregationalists at London which was to be used to aid struggling churches, including those in the colonies. After theological differences, the two denominations divided in their administration of the fund and after 1696 there were two funds; frequent appeals to the London Presbyterians for financial help came from the colonies. They provided funds to support two ministers for the colonies in 1704, and John Hampton, who was Irish, and George McNish, who was Scottish, were sent out.

To English and New English Puritans were added Scottish immigrants in the building up of colonial Presbyterianism. They came directly from experience in the Church of Scotland which was the favored and established religion, and tended to be more strictly "presbyterian" than the English Presbyterians in their understanding of the government of the church, believing in a strong presbytery. The Scots also were usually more strict in their Calvinism. Scattered groups of Scots settled in the colonies after the middle of the seventeenth century, and sometimes became an element in already existing Presbyterian congregations: such occurred when some who settled along the Patuxent river in Maryland in the 1650's joined the Puritans there in their churches. The same thing happened at Woodbridge, New Jersey, where Puritans had already settled—there one of the Scots became the pastor. At Freehold, New Jersey, a group of Scots settled and formed a church, though having no pastor they had to be satisfied with a lay leader. Several small groups of Scots came to South Carolina, with some attempting a Scottish colony on the Isthmus of Darien; a failure, one of those who came to provide religious leadership, Archibald Stobo, remained and later organized several Presbyterian congregations in the area and helped secure the coming of several more Scottish ministers. Somewhat later in the eighteenth century Scottish Highlanders involved in one of the rebellions over a pretender to the throne emigrated to North Carolina, but they had no minister until 1757. Within a decade of the founding of the Philadelphia presbytery in 1706 it numbered among its ministers eight from Scotland.

Also among the Scottish immigrants, though coming later, were members of the smaller groups which had broken away from the Church of Scotland. Some of these were called "Covenanters" and had refused to accept King Charles II as their ruler because of loyalty to the Solemn League and Covenant of 1643; some settled in Pennsylvania, and in 1753, with drawn swords, a group of them "renewed the Covenants", remembering what they had suffered earlier under the English monarchy. The "Seceders" had a later origin, deriving from a protest over lay patronage in the church of Scotland. Settling in Pennsylvania and the Carolinas, these groups formed into several small sects and kept alive their ancient grievances.

Most important of all, at least numerically for the future of American Presbyterians, were the Irish, or more properly, Scotch-Irish, who came to the colonies in small numbers in the late seventeenth-century but who constituted a veritable wave of immigrants by the middle of the next century, so that James Logan of Pennsylvania noted in 1729 that "It looks as if Ireland is to send all its inhabitants hither for the last week not less than six ships arrived."[4] It has been estimated that by the time of the American Revolution one-third of the Protestant population of Ireland had come to the colonies. These Irish Protestants are termed Scotch-Irish because most of them were descended from Scots who had been transplanted to Ireland in the seventeenth century as a matter of English policy, in an attempt to reduce Ireland to Protestantism by encouraging large numbers of Protestants to settle there. Most of the settlers were drawn from the poorer classes of lowland Scotland and settled on the large estates of English Protestant landlords. But in their adopted Irish home they were confronted with several conditions which led to their further emigration after a generation or two: one of these conditions was economic depression and famine and another was the religious disabilities they suffered as dissenters from the established Anglican Church of Ireland. They also met with the hostility of the yet poorer native Irish Roman Catholic peasantry. In religion these Scotch-Irish were of course Presbyterian, and formed their own churches and presbyteries throughout Ireland; they developed a very militant and strict Presbyterianism, rigidly orthodox yet with a strong component of emotional piety.

Coming to the colonies, the Irish Presbyterians settled in the largest numbers in the middle colonies of New Jersey and Pennsylvania, especially pushing out to the frontier of Pennsylvania where they came into contact with the Indians and caused the colony considerable trouble by their seizure of Indian lands. A rough lot, they tended to simply "squat" on land and so claim it. Filling up the Pennsylvania frontier, they spilled over into the back country of the south, pouring down the inland valleys into Western Maryland, Western Virginia and the Carolinas. By the 1720's such Scotch-Irish settlers had formed Presbyterian churches at Londonderry, New Hampshire, Goshen, New York, and a number of places in Pennsylvania. Writing from Pennsylvania, a minister informed his Scottish correspondent that "There are a great many congregations erected, and now errecting; for wthin the space of five years by gone, near to two hundred Families have come into our parts from Ireland, and more are following...."[5]

Ministers from Ireland also constituted a substantial proportion of the whole number of early Presbyterian ministers in the colonies: Samuel Davis was preaching at Snow Hill, Maryland and Lewes, Delaware in the last two decades of the seventeenth century; Josias Mackie was preaching in Virginia at about the same time; and Francis Makemie was beginning his travels on behalf of Presbyterianism. The next generation saw many more come from Ireland, including William Tennent, who was pastor at Neshaminy, Pennsylvania, and founded there an academy for the training of ministers, derisively dubbed the "log college", which represents the remote beginnings of the College of New Jersey, or Princeton, later to be the major institution in the training of Presbyterian clergy.

The sixth and last group which went into the making of colonial Presbyterianism consisted of persons and groups of continental Reformed background who found their way into Presbyterian churches. The Dutch Reformed and later the German Reformed had their own congregations, where their native languages were used; but many scattered individuals of these backgrounds and also from the French Calvinists joined congregations which were or became Presbyterian. In New Rochelle, New York, a whole French congregation affiliated with the Presbyterians. The church at New Castle, Delaware, originally founded by the Dutch, gradually added members of British extraction and in 1698 called as its minister John Wilson of Boston, probably the grandson of the first Boston pastor of that name; it was one of the original member churches of the 1706 presbytery. The New Jersey congregations, mostly founded by New Englanders, soon had numbers of French and Dutch members. And the first Presbyterian congregation in Savannah, Georgia, included numbers of French and Swiss Calvinists along with Scots and Irish, and had for its first pastor the Swiss John Zubly. Several Frenchmen served Presbyterian churches as pastors, especially in the south.

The vicissitudes of early Presbyterianism in the colonies are best typified in the experiences of Francis Makemie. To his biographer, "In his twenty-five years in the New World Francis Makemie had become colonial Presbyterianism's chief exponent, its leading literary apologist, main defender of its liberties, foremost overseer of its congregations, and the moving force in the formation of its first presbytery."[6] Makemie was born in northern Ireland in 1658, of Scottish parentage. Educated at the University of Glasgow, in 1681 he was ordained by a Presbytery in Ireland for work in the colonies. Arriving in Maryland in 1683, he began a series of travels which took him through many colonies, preaching to small groups of Presbyterians and striving to organize them. In 1684 he was in North Carolina; the next year in Virginia; later he settled in Accomack County, Virginia, on the eastern shore, and preached to small congregations there and across the border in Maryland at Snow Hill and Rehobeth. He went to England, probably in 1689, spent some time later in Philadelphia, and was in Barbadoes in the West Indies for several years, where he was successfully engaged in commerce. During these travels he took time for a theological debate with George Keith, then still a Quaker, publishing an attack on Keith who had first criticized a catechism Makemie had earlier written. This writing shows him a learned defender of Calvinist orthodoxy who saw in Quakerism the denial of many Christian fundamentals. In 1704-1705 he was back in England, persuading the London ministers to support missionaries for America out of their General Fund.

Under the conditions of the English Toleration Act of 1689 Makemie had secured a license to preach as a dissenting minister, but in spite of this met with difficulties in 1706. Travelling to Boston in that year in the company of another minister, he stopped in New York and there preached to a small assembly in a private home, as a result of which he was arrested by the royal governor, Lord Cornbury, for preaching without the governor's license. In the ensuing trial (after Makemie had suffered a month's imprisonment) Lord Cornbury charged him with being a disorderly "strowling" preacher, and denied that Makemie's license had any force in New York. Makemie's defense was that the license was good anywhere in the British dominions, and that it was outrageous that a Presbyterian, with a license, "and likest the Church of England of any Dissenters," should be so hindered when many other dissenters met freely. Makemie was acquitted but assessed the entire costs of his trial.

Lord Cornbury had earlier, under the pretext of the law establishing the Church of England in New York, obtruded Anglican ministers, often missionaries of the Society for the Propagation of the Gospel, into parishes which had long been Puritan churches. In 1705, the Hempstead, Long Island, church, being vacant, and in spite of being a town church on the model of New England, had an Anglican minister forced upon it, to whom was given possession of the parsonage and church building. Unable to get their church back, most of the members withdrew and built another meeting-house. This also happened with the church at Jamaica, Long Island. Shortly after Makemie's trial Lord Cornbury was recalled, blamed for a number of high-handed actions.

Back in Virginia, Makemie died in 1708. His greatest achievement was the leadership he had provided in the formation of an organization to bring together the various struggling Presbyterian congregations. The Philadelphia Presbytery was founded in 1706 and included seven ministers at first, three New Englanders, two Irishmen and two Scotsmen; besides the area of Philadelphia most of its churches were in Delaware and Maryland. During the next decade churches of Puritan origin in New Jersey (including the congregations at Newark and Elizabeth) and New York affiliated with the presbytery. In 1716 it formed itself into the synod of Philadelphia and subdivided into three presbyteries, Philadelphia, New Castle, and Snow Hill, the last of which never organized; in 1717 the presbytery of Long Island formed and joined the synod. In 1738 the New Brunswick Presbytery in New Jersey was organized, and before long several others grew up in western Pennsylvania and the backcountry south.

These early presbyteries and the synod fulfilled many purposes for the congregations which made them up, as their early minutes show. The Philadelphia presbytery in its first years was concerned with the credentials of ministers coming to them, inquiring into their education and piety before ordaining them or approving them for pastorates. They commissioned their members to do missionary work, resolving "That every minister of the Presbytery supply neighbouring desolate places where a minister is wanting, and opportunity of doing good offers."[7] Cases requiring discipline came before them: one member was admonished for washing on the sabbath, another suspended from the ministry for bigamy. They also settled quarrels between pastors and their churches (usually over unpaid salaries) and between warring factions within congregations. An extensive correspondence was carried on by the presbytery, keeping the London ministers, presbyteries in Scotland and Ireland, and the churches of New England informed of their activities. They had a strong sense of being closely united with both Presbyterians abroad and the Congregationalists of New England.

The most important issue to come before this early organized Presbyterianism was that of creedal subscription, which was settled by a compromise in 1729. Subscription to a creed (usually the *Westminster Confession* and its Congregationalist recension, the *Savoy Confession*) had become a controversial matter in England and Scotland at the beginning of the eighteenth century, as conservatives began to fear a decline of Calvinist orthodoxy. Subscription was required for Scottish ministers by law although there had been some resistance to this, but in England the Presbyterians and Congregationalists had divided over the issue, the more strictly Calvinistic Congregationalists favoring subscription while most Presbyterians resisted it. In the Philadelphia synod, the tendency was for those of Irish and Scottish background to favor strict creedal subscription (and give greater authority to synods and presbyteries in enforcing orthodoxy) whereas those of English Puritan and New England background tended to either resist subscription or leave it to individual congregations. Thus the synod included the quite different viewpoints of men like John Thomson, educated at Glasgow and pastor at Lewes, Delaware, who argued that the acceptance of the Westminster Standards was essential "for preventing the ingress and spreading of dangerous errors" and of Jonathan Dickinson, pastor at Elizabeth, New Jersey, and educated at Yale College, who argued that it would be enough to acknowledge "our Lord Jesus Christ for our common head," "the sacred Scriptures for our common standard both in faith and practice," and "the same essential and necessary articles of Christianity" without the subscription of a detailed creed.[8] The resulting compromise prevented a split in the synod and provided that the ministers must declare agreement with and approval of the *Westminster Confession* and catechisms "as being in all the essential and necessary articles, good forms of sound words and systems of Christian doctrine" but each individual was to be allowed to state his "scruples" or take exception to those things in the Confession with which he disagreed, it being left up to the presbytery to then decide whether or not these scruples constituted essential disagreement or merely minor differences which could be overlooked. At the same time the Synod adopted the "Directory for Worship" and "Form of Government" "commonly annexed to the Westminster Confession" which provided the new denomination with standards for liturgy and polity.

One motive behind the formation of the synod and presbyteries was to enable Presbyterians to unite against Anglican encroachments which were feared more and more in the course of the eighteenth century with the coming of the aggressive missioners of the S.P.G. and their agitation for the bringing of a bishop to America. In fact, many of the Presbyterians came from a background where they were either the established church or wanted to be included within it (as the English Presbyterians did) but found themselves instead dissenters from the established religion. Unable to form themselves as the established church in the middle colonies and the south, they sought an organization whereby they could unify their efforts, maintain their liberties, and conduct their own affairs. As a result they created in their joint synod a voluntary religious organization which drew together a membership scattered through many colonies, and which, as such, was a "national" organization, transcending the limits of colonial governments and churches. The Friends, with their various monthly meetings, provide the closest parallel, along with the Baptists of the Philadelphia Association, but the Baptist body was merely advisory and the Friends' meetings subordinate to the London Friends, whereas the Presbyterians created a fully independent but tightly disciplined body throughout the colonies. In this they prefigured what was later to develop in American denominationalism, nation-wide church institutions which were independent of secular government and which in turn depended upon religious voluntarism for their support and membership.

8

Religion, Indians and African Slaves

Both the American Indians and Black slaves have appeared in this story in relation to other matters; it is appropriate now to consider their religious history. They constituted important groups: the American Indians had threatened to destroy the first intrusions of Europeans into their domain but had also contributed much to the agriculture of the colonists; the African slaves became an integral part of the economy of several colonies and numbered at least one-sixth of the population by the end of the Revolutionary War. There were similarities in the relation of both slaves and Indians to the European colonists: both had their long-standing patterns of life and religion disrupted by contact with Europeans and attempts were made to incorporate both into the religion of the colonists.

Religion and the American Indian

The native inhabitants of North America had been there for thousands of years by the colonists' arrival. In that time, there had been many shifting patterns of social and cultural development, producing such varied results as the cliff-dwelling and pueblo cultures of the Southwest, the mound-builders of the Ohio and Mississippi valleys and the nomads of the plains. They had domesticated the dog, established agriculture, learned to make pottery and use such metals as copper, and engaged in trade, sending commodities great distances across America.

Most of the Indians on the coasts of eastern North America with which the colonists came in contact were of the Algonquian group, which designates a number of tribes of a common language-family. Farther inland there were other Indians whom the colonists eventually met, including in the north such Iroquoian tribes as the Mohawk and the Seneca. The Algonquians engaged in mixed farming and hunting and lived in agricultural villages consisting of houses built of bark—one early colonist in Maryland commented that "They live for the most part in Townes, like Countrey villages in England."[1] These tribes frequently engaged in war with one another, but casualties were few. Politically they formed powerful confederations, some almost becoming "empires", such as the Powhatan confederation which was being built up in Virginia and adjacent regions at the time of European settlement.

The attitudes of the Indians towards the Europeans who were encroaching upon them is difficult to determine. Well before the settlements of Jamestown and Plymouth they had had experience with white men. Spaniards had raided and plundered well up the North American coast, seeking slaves; explorers and fishermen farther north had occasionally seized Indians. In all this there was little to predispose the Indians to friendliness, but in fact many reports told of the friendly approach of Indians. Indians befriended the early Plymouth settlers, the Dutch in New Netherland, and the early inhabitants at Jamestown, John Smith reporting that "It pleased God (in our extremity) to move the Indians to bring us Corne, ere it was half ripe, to refresh us, when we rather expected...they would destroy us."[2] No doubt the Indians were curious and eager for bartering and also had their own traditions of hospitality, but Roger Williams commented on the general "cheerfulness" of the Indians, and thought that they were less given to crime and gross vices than Englishmen, adding "I have heard of many English lost, and have oft been lost my selfe, and my selfe and others have been found, and succoured by the Indians."[3] Certain Indian chiefs, like Powhatan in Virginia and Massasoit in Massachusetts be-friended the colonists hoping to gain powerful allies who might help them in their own intertribal empire-building.

Nor was there as much reason for fear of the newcomers as is sometimes thought, when imagining the pitting of a highly developed society with its technology against a far more prim-itive people: "From the viewpoint of the twentieth century," a modern historian comments, "it is difficult to realize that the material differences between the Indians and the European colonists, who lived before the full development of the in-dustrial revolution, were equalled if not outweighed by the similarities of culture."[4] When the colonists spoke of repre-senting powerful but far-off kings this was no doubt often received as boastful exaggeration. Even the advantage of fire-arms was quickly overcome when the Indians learned their use.

It is not easy to reconstruct the details of the religious life of the Algonquians because the colonists had scant interest in it for its own sake and when later ethnographers tried to reconstruct their beliefs it was after a long period of contact with Christianity and based upon the memories of a few indi-viduals long out of touch with anything like original tribal life. What we do know of their religion indicates similarity with North American Indian religion elsewhere: a nature religion with the personification of animals and the employ-ment of shamans and priests to cure disease and ward off evil spirits. They acknowledged the existence of a supreme spirit but more often propitiated the more accessible spirits believed to inhabit and empower the various forces of nature: accord-ing to the first Jesuits in Maryland, they knew "one God of Heaven," but did not worship him; instead, the Jesuits noted, they tried to appease certain harmful spirits. The Jesuits also asserted that they had knowledge of Noah's flood. The early Virginia minister Alexander Whitaker also claimed that they acknowledged a great God but did not worship him.

Roger Williams, who spent much time among the Indians, learning their language and holding theological conversations with them, related many interesting things about their religion. He too found that they believed in a great God who was the creator and also that the soul lived on after the death of the body. He approved these beliefs, and also found acknowledgement of God's omnipresence in their willingness to deify anything desirable or powerful, although he disputed with them as to whether fire was a God. Williams was also puzzled because "They have many strange relations of one Wetucks, a man that wrought great miracles amongst them, and walking upon the waters, etc., with some kind of broken resemblance to the Son of God."[5]

All of the colonies were launched with high expectations concerning the conversion of the Indians, and although much of this was perhaps merely rhetorical, nonetheless such expectations both reflected and shaped the attitudes of the Europeans. Richard Hakluyt, who told the story of the English explorations, wrote enthusiastically of missions to the Indians and saw such efforts as a means of thwarting Catholic Spain. Sir Walter Raleigh agreed that conversion of Indians would stop the boasting of the Spaniards. The promoters of Virginia asserted in a tract of 1609 that their first aim was the conversion of the natives; a year later the Virginia Council claimed that "the eyes of all Europe are looking upon our endevors [sic] to spread the Gospell among the heathen people of Virginia."[6] In New England similar claims were made. William Penn included conversion of the Indians among his reasons for requesting a charter; as late as the founding of Georgia in 1734 it was claimed that conversion of the Indians was a major purpose, and General Oglethorpe had an English bishop draw up a manual for the settlers to further this purpose. Missionary rhetoric was not always pure in its motives: Lord Cornbury in 1703 as governor of New York sought missionaries to win the Indians on the frontier to the Church of England, thus keeping them out of the clutches of the French.

Hopes of their conversion notwithstanding, the colonists feared the Indians. Early writers had stressed their savagery, William Bradford commenting that the Plymouth colonists had heard harrowing tales of their cruelty. A Dutch minister declared them to be utterly savage, ungodly, and devilish. Frequent are the references to the barbarism and treachery of the Indians.

But a more positive view of the Indian was often implied by the religious ideology of mission and conversion. Those who sought their conversion usually insisted that they were full human beings, capable of learning and understanding all that a European could. Alexander Whitaker in Virginia reminded his readers that the Indians "have reasonable soules and intellectuall faculties as well as wee," and that while they were children of the devil, so are all men as sons of Adam. He found good qualities in them:

> ...let us not thinke that these men are so simple as some have supposed them: for they are of bodie lustie, strong, and very nimble: they are a very understanding generation, quicke of apprehension, suddaine in their dispatches, subtile in their dealings, exquisite in their inventions, and industrious in their labour."7

Whitaker added that the law of nature dwelt in them, as could be seen by their ability to frame a civil government and obey just laws. The Jesuits in Maryland felt the Indians, "once imbued with Christian precepts," would become virtuous and humane. As already noted, Roger Williams found much about them praiseworthy, and enjoyed discussing theology with them, finding that they were prepared for Christian truth. He was however distressed that they spent so much time in idle pastimes when they could be laboring productively. Early Quaker preachers frequently commented on the responsiveness of the Indians to their message, attributing this to the light of Christ which illuminated all mankind. Colonial spokesmen usually seemed to have no idea of racial inferiority in speaking of Indians, many regarding them as descendents of the lost ten tribes of Israel who had somehow found their way to America. Another view did come however from the Dutch minister Michaelius who thought that people in Holland had been misled about the teachableness of the Indians and the presence within them of a natural law, declaring that he was unable to find a single good point about them!

In contrast with the stated intentions the actual accomplishments appear small, but when considering the problems involved, were fairly significant, especially in New England. Comparison is often made to the more successful missions of Spain and France, but not only were the Catholic religious orders better organized for mission work but they also received more support from the mother country. For the most part the English Protestant colonists had to maintain their own missions, and when as in New England they received significant help from individuals in the mother country, the results were substantial. Moreover, the approach was quite different: Catholic missions tended to baptize numbers of converts and gradually accustom them to a Christian pattern of life and worship; Protestant missions concentrated more on individual converts from whom they expected fairly high standards of theological comprehension involving the ability to read the Bible. The Puritans especially were hindered by their exalted expectations of what true conversion and church membership meant—most white settlers found it impossible to fulfill the requirements!

In Virginia very little was done for the conversion of the Indians in spite of the initial high hopes. To be sure, John Rolfe thought that marrying Pocahantas would open the door to the conversion of the natives and there were plans for an institution at Henrico to educate and convert Indians, but these were abandoned when George Thorpe, who was in charge of that effort, was killed by Indians in 1622. A Virginia statute had anticipated that each town would educate a few Indian children whom they would adopt in the ways of Christianity, but after the Indian uprising of 1622 little was done until the coming of S.P. G. missionaries in the next century.

Some missionary effort was made in New Netherland and New York. The Dutch pastor Michaelius, in spite of his low opinion of the Indians, tried to learn their language, as did pastor Megapolensis later. The latter in fact preached to the Indians, but complained that they laughed at his sermons and asked him why the Christians did all the things he preached against. In 1669 the minister Johannes Fabricius reported to Amsterdam that he was instructing some Indians. Thoroughgood Moore, missionary of the Anglican Society for the Propagation of the Gospel, settled at Albany in 1704 to labor among the Mohawks; discouraged, he soon left and was drowned at sea. But this mission was later reestablished and by the middle of the century the Mohawks were Church of England, remaining loyal to the British in the coming French and Indian Wars.

Among the German settlers, the Moravians carried on extensive and successful Indian missions, with almost fifty persons engaged in this work by the middle of the eighteenth century.

There were of course also Roman Catholic missions. The story of French and Spanish missions, integral to the activities of those nations in North America, has been told elsewhere, but the Jesuits in Maryland also had some missionary success. Although they complained at first of the hostility of the colonial authorities and other colonists to their efforts, these Jesuits eventually baptized many of the Indians dwelling along the Potomac and Patuxent rivers.

Only in New England were missionaries to the Indians drawn out of the colonial population itself and anything resembling the missionary hopes of the early rhetoric realized. In that region the work was carried on by individuals who took it upon themselves to exercise leadership in this matter.

One of the first of these was Roger Williams. He had

learned an Algonquian dialect while at Plymouth and wrote to Governor Winthrop in 1632 that he intended to preach to the Indians. After leaving Massachusetts Bay he lived with the Indians and they considered him their friend. In 1643 he published in London *A Key into the Language of America* which was a combination Indian dictionary and description of their customs. His interest however did not produce converts.

Thomas Shepard was another Puritan leader who took an early interest in the Indian. In 1648 he published in London *The Clear Sunshine of the Gospel Breaking Forth Upon the Indians in New England* which described "Indian lectures" to which the natives came and asked questions. Commented Shepard: "I have heard few Christians when they begin to looke toward God, make more searching questions that they might see things really...."[8]

One of the most successful missions in New England was that carried out by the Mayhew family on Nantucket and Martha's Vineyard. The elder Thomas Mayhew established himself on Martha's Vineyard and developed good relations with his Indian neighbors. His son Thomas Jr. was a minister, and knowing the language of the Indians preached to them, forming them into a church of which he was eventually pastor. Among his converts was one named Hiacoomes who was soon himself preaching to his fellow Indians. In 1657 when the younger Mayhew was killed at sea, his father took over the mission and before long most of the Indians of Nantucket were converts too, with several Indian congregations springing up.

The most notable of the missionaries in New England was John Eliot. He came to Boston in 1631, having been educated at Cambridge, and became pastor of the church at Roxbury. A well-loved figure of saintly character, he began to take time from his regular duties to work among the nearby Indians, an activity which his congregation found acceptable, granting him an associate for the work of the church. His converts were numerous, and in 1651 at Natick he founded the first of his special villages for "praying Indians," hoping to insulate them from their unconverted fellows as well as from the bad example of many colonists; the town was to have its own church with its own native leadership. This established the pattern for New England missions before King Philip's War, and by 1674 there were fourteen of these towns with thirty-seven Indian ministers by the end of the century.

For their training an Indian college was founded at Harvard—its 1650 charter had declared its purpose to be the education of both English and Indian youth. A building was constructed to house "hopefull Indian youthes" and before long a few Indians were attending and studying Latin and Greek. Unfortunately almost all who attended died early of disease, including Caleb Cheeshateamuck who was the only Indian to graduate in the early period. In many lower schools of New England Indians were taught to read and write.

Support for all this came from the government of Massachusetts Bay and also from interested Englishmen through the Society for the Propagation of the Gospel in New England, founded in 1649 by Puritan merchants in London. This society survived the Restoration in England and received money from many philanthropists, being later befriended by Sir Robert Boyle. It provided money for the Indian college at Harvard and for the projects of John Eliot. For a few years after 1651 the society paid a salary to Abraham Pierson to enable him to preach to the Indians.

Testifying to the indefatigible labors of Eliot was his translation of the whole Bible into Algonquian which was printed in Cambridge, Massachusetts. The tasks of typesetting and proofreading were so complicated that they required the assistance of trained Indian helpers. Prior to this Eliot's own catechism for Indians in their native tongue had been printed, and the Bible translation was followed by other translations, including one of the devotional works of Richard Baxter. Eliot and his helpers also produced a grammar of the Algonquian language. To publicize their work letters of Eliot were published in England accompanied by sermons preached by Indian converts.

These missionary efforts received a serious setback with the advent of King Philip's War when the villages of Christian Indians met with the distrust of their English neighbors in spite of the fact that they remained loyal to the government of the Bay colony. But the missions continued, and in the next century Cotton Mather was to show great interest in them, laboring himself to educate Indian youths. Mather described the Puritan mission to the Indians as "one of New England's peculiar glories," and in an *Address to the Christianized Indians* he told them in his inimitable style to

> Behold, ye Indians, what care, what cost, has been used by the English here for the salvation of your precious and immortal souls. It is not because we have expected any temporal advantage, that we have been thus concerned for your good; no, it is God that has caused us to desire his Glory in your salvation; and our hearts have bled with pity over you, when we have seen how horribly the Devil oppressed you in this, and destroyed you in another world. It is much that has been done for you; we have put you into a way to be happy both on earth while you live, and in Heaven when you die.[9]

Colonial rhetoric and missionary work dealing with the Indians were not just window-dressing to camouflage less sanctified behavior. At least in early New England, as a recent book by Alden Vaughan argues, "...the New England Puritans followed a remarkably humane, considerate, and just policy in their dealings with the Indians. In matters of commerce, religious conversion, and judicial procedure, the Puritans had surprisingly high regard for the interests of a people who were less powerful, less civilized, less sophisticated, and—in the eyes of the New England colonists—less godly."[10] The Puritans were usually scrupulous in purchasing Indian lands; they offered them medical care; they allowed Indians to sit on juries and intermarriage with

Europeans was legal; in a number of cases colonists suffered capital punishment for crimes against Indians. Indians were educated at Harvard and considered capable of mastering the classical curriculum and were admitted to full membership in congregational churches. In the Quaker colony of Pennsylvania there was an even better record of good relations between Indians and colonists, although this deteriorated when Quakers lost control of the colony.

Yet there were fearful clashes between Indian and colonist and relations worsened as the colonial period elapsed. It was after all into a country in which the Indians had long had sole possession that the Europeans came. And Europeans in that age seemed to feel that whenever a Christian people came upon a land hitherto unknown to them they had the right to claim it and possess it if they could in the name of their sovereign. Thomas More argued in *Utopia* for example that it was perfectly creditable for the Utopians when too crowded in their own country to colonize other lands, settling alongside the natives if possible, but driving them out if they resisted. The Pope, in an effort to silence the rival claims of Spanish and Portuguese adventurers had in 1493 decreed the non-Christian world to be divided between them.

At first Indians acceded to the coming of scattered colonists and were happy to sell them land. They were not necessarily pushed to the frontiers of settlement for in both Virginia and New England Indians owned land throughout the areas of white settlement. Nor is it certain, as so often has been asserted, that the Indians had no idea of private property so that they did not know what they were doing when selling land. But when the number of colonists swelled and their encroachment upon Indian society began to severely dislocate it, causing them economic disaster, it is no wonder that they struck back at the newcomers. The major Indian wars, the attacks of 1622 and 1644 in Virginia and King Philip's War in 1675 in New England were desperate attempts to rid the land altogether of the interlopers.

The colonists were insensitive to the disruption of Indian

life they were causing and seldom concerned about their encroachment upon the land—Roger Williams was an exception when he argued that the King's charter for Massachusetts was worthless since the Indians, not he, had sovereignty in the area, as was the Reforming Synod of 1679 which declared deceitful and oppressive dealings with the Indians to be one of the sins of the colonists for which God was angry. In the first years of settlement the Puritans often noted that God had prepared for their coming by destroying many of the Indians in a plague and was still striking them down to make room for the English (the Indians had a high mortality rate because of their susceptibility to new diseases brought by the colonists such as smallpox). To John Winthrop, God must have been pleased with the colonists' coming since he made room for them by diminishing the number of natives. More than once New Englanders justified their coming into the land and driving out those who would not live peaceably with them on the grounds that they were God's people come into a promised land—similarly an early Virginia tract asserted the right to cast out the "Canaanites," as conquering Israel had done of old.

Ultimately it was the wars and massacres which embittered relations between colonists and Indians. Nor did these always begin with Indian attacks, as in Virginia: in 1643 the Dutch governor ordered a massacre of Indians near New Netherland, including women and children, which begot a long period of strife there. Even when the Indians struck first, the reprisals of the colonists were likely to be out of all proportion to the provocation. But even in the midst of strife and cruelty there were those who spoke in behalf of milder courses: John Eliot protested the treatment meted out to Indians in the wake of King Philip's War, declaring that "The design of Christ in these last days is not to extirpate nations, but to gospelize them;" men rightly, he added, "condemn the Spaniard for cruelty upon this point in destroying men and depopulating the land. The country is large enough. Here is land enough for them and us too." [11]

Slavery and Religion in the Colonies

If the Indian was dispossessed of his land and his culture disrupted, the Black slaves experienced an equal if not worse disruption, spirited away from their native lands as captives, subjected to a horrifying experience of transportation across an ocean under unbelievably crowded and diseased conditions, and then compelled to work for strange masters in an alien land, treated as mere property.

Slavery had long existed in Western society as it had in many societies of the world, and had anciently received the sanction of philosophers and theologians, neither of whom found anything inherently wrong with the principle that some men, because of captivity in war or other causes, were to be held in bondage by others. But the medieval West, while it had a system of serfdom with those of inferior status bound to the land, had much less of chattel slavery than the ancient world. The older kind of slavery however was kept alive in the Middle Ages in Mediterranean lands, where slaves, usually household servants, were supplied by captives taken in wars such as those of the Spaniards against the Moors. In the age of discovery Spain and Portugal pioneered the transition to a new phase in the long history of slavery by enslaving Africans and sending them to their new world colonies to provide a much needed labor force, especially after the enslavement of the native Indian population proved unsuccessful. In 1488 King Ferdinand sent one hundred African slaves to the Pope, who divided them among his cardinals as household servants. Such enslavement of non-Christian peoples was sometimes justified on the ground that their captivity gave them the opportunity of conversion to the true religion and was therefore a favor done them.

Several characteristics of New World slavery made it peculiarly virulent: it came to be more and more racial in character, making the slave class more distinct and manumission less likely, and thus drawing to itself justification by way of the assertion of the inferiority and naturally "slavish" character of the enslaved group; and it ceased to be primarily a way to provide servants, becoming instead an economic system for the working of vast plantation lands by labor-gangs bossed by adventurers in new lands among whom those traits which might have ameliorated the inhumanities of the system were at a minimum. Also, this type of slavery coincided with the rise of a very exploitative kind of capitalism and commerce in which many of the traditional paternalistic bonds between master and inferior were being replaced by a cash-nexus—the slave trade itself became a very callous kind of capitalist exploitation in which owners could figure how to write off as a probable loss the lives of that percentage of captives likely to die on a voyage and still make a profit.

England had little precedent in law or practice for slavery. Sir John Hawkins in 1562-1563 was the first Englishman to engage in the trade, and eventually slavery became an important part of English commercial life. By 1650 there were many slaves in the English colony of Barbadoes as there were soon to be also in Jamaica—slavery became an integral part of the sugar plantations of the West Indies. In 1619 the first slaves arrived in Virginia; within a decade of the founding of Maryland they were there too, and they were eventually to be found in all the colonies. Even the Quaker colony of Pennsylvania recognized slavery, and William Penn himself owned slaves. New England ports became important in the slave trade.

It was only gradually that English law in the colonies recognized perpetual bondage and the buying and selling of persons. At first the status of the Blacks was not so clearly distinguished from that of white indentured servants and in the early years in Barbadoes and Virginia Africans and white indentured servants worked side by side on the plantations. In fact, many Blacks worked under contracts of indenture, and in the early transitional period Africans were sometimes given their freedom after periods of bondage. There were thus free Blacks in the colonies from the earliest times. The law in Virginia did not fully recognize slavery until 1661; two years later Maryland law acknowledged the system. Black Codes containing special provisions relevant to Black slaves grew up, especially in the southern colonies. Under these conditions slaves often ran away, fleeing to the Indians on the frontier and in Florida, where they found refuge.

Slavery grew to be an important economic institution in the southern colonies, with their large plantations for raising sugar, rice and tobacco. In the north slaves were usually servants, working in the household or on small farms alongside of their masters. As a result, the life of the Blacks in such places as New England was very different from that of slaves on southern plantations, and their condition continued to be similar to that of indentured white servants. In New England Blacks had closer social and working relations with whites, were allowed their own social gatherings, and held certain legal rights, such as trial by jury, the right to sue in court and to testify in court against whites. As John Hope Franklin comments, "The Negro in New England was unique in colonial America. He was not subjected to the harsh codes or the severe treatment which his fellows received in the colonies south of the region."12 Some New England Blacks even amassed a certain amount of wealth.

Much of this better treatment in New England resulted from the Puritan religious interest in the African. John Eliot took time from converting Indians to instruct slaves in the faith. Such efforts at conversion also meant teaching Africans to read and write, and later, in the eighteenth century, schools for Blacks were opened. New England also insisted upon legal marriages for slaves, allowing them thereby to build up stable family life.

Eventually slaves and freed Blacks became members of Congregational churches. Probably the first example of this was reported in 1643 in *New Englands First Fruits*, concerning an African servant-girl:

There is also a Blackmore maid, that hath long lived at

Dorchester in New-England, unto whom God hath so blessed the publique and private means of Grace, that she is not only indued with a competent measure of knowledge in the mysteries of God, and conviction of her miserable estate by sinne; but hath also experienced the saving work of grace in her heart, and a sweet savour of Christ breathing in her; insomuch that her soul hath longed to enjoy church fellowship with the Saints there, and having propounded her desire to the Elders of the Church after some triall of her taken in private, she was called before the whole Church, and there did make confession of her knowledge in the Mysteries of Christ and of the work of Conversion upon her Soule: And after that there was such a testimony given of her blamelesse and godly Conversation, that she was admitted a member by the joynt consent of the church, with great joy to all their hearts."[13]

Interesting for its revelation of Puritan attitudes is Cotton Mather's treatise *The Negro Christianized*, published in 1706. In this work Mather insisted upon the need to bring the slaves to Christianity, assuring his readers however that this would improve their usefulness—they would be better servants as Christian servants. Mather was convinced that some of the Blacks were among God's elect and that all of them were fellow-men, neighbors and brothers. He protested against any attempt to deny them souls and argued that their educability showed them to possess reason. Nor should their color be made to count against them: not only is the major part of mankind not white—most, he claimed, were 'tawny' or "Copper-Coloured"—but God looks only upon the heart and not the color of the skin. He recommended special catechisms for their instruction, and also that they be given the Sabbath day to receive such instruction.

Cotton Mather also touched upon a delicate point when he assured his readers that the reception of baptism did not necessitate the freeing of a slave but that it was lawful to hold

a fellow Christian in bondage. This had been an issue elsewhere in the colonies, where masters had feared the effects of
baptism upon the legal status of their slaves and had accordingly resisted efforts at Christianization. Apparently in New
York some of the Dutch ministers had assumed that baptism
would lead to manumission and so found their labors to
convert slaves hindered by slave-owners. In Virginia in 1667
a statute explicitly declared that "the conferring of baptisme
doth not alter the condition of the person as to his bondage
or freedome; that diverse masters, ffreed from this doubt,
may more carefully endeavour the propagation of christianity by permitting children, though slaves, or those of greater
growth if capable to be admitted to that sacrament."14
Maryland adopted a similar law in 1671, and the other colonies followed—a New York law of 1706 asserted that "The
Baptizing of any...Slave shall not be any Cause or reason
for the setting them or any of them at Liberty."15

In spite of the convenience of these laws, missionary work
directed towards the slaves outside of New England was
slight. Later in Virginia Commissary Bray organized a group
for the purpose of missionary work among slaves, and the
Society for the Propagation of the Gospel showed some
concern in the matter. Quakers preached to slaves and made
occasional converts too, and the Jesuits in Maryland had
some success, but probably before the Great Awakening in
the middle of the next century and the evangelical enthusiasm
which it engendered most of the slaves had received no instruction at all in Christianity.

Attempts to instruct Blacks in Christianity, however, did
not necessarily imply any criticism of the slave system, as
Cotton Mather made clear. Such criticism came only at the
very end of the seventeenth-century. The first real protests
seem to have come from the German sectarians, the Mennonites and Brethren in Pennsylvania having no sympathy for
slavery. In 1688 the Germantown Quakers, a group made up
almost entirely of Germans and Dutch, drew up a protest

against slavery and sent it to the monthly, quarterly and yearly meetings of the Friends, none of which approved it. In their remonstrance they said:

> Now, though they are black, we cannot conceive there is more liberty to have them slaves, as it is to have other white ones.
>
> In Europe, there are many oppressed for conscience-sake; and here are those oppressed which are of a black colour.
>
> Pray, what thing in the world can be done worse towards us, than if men should rob or steal us away, and sell us for slaves to strange countries; separating husbands from their wives and children.
>
> ... have these poor negers [sic] not as much right to fight for their freedom, as you have to keep them slaves? [16]

A few years later the Keithan Quakers protested in a memorial against the practice and cruelties of slavery. But it was only much later, through the witness of John Woolman and others, that the Friends as a whole came to disapprove of human bondage.

At about the same time as these early memorials the New England judge Samuel Sewell published in Boston his tract *The Selling of Joseph* which was the first significant Puritan objection to the system of slavery. Sewell argued that all men, as sons of Adam, have equal rights to liberty and that the slave trade was the greatest cruelty. As for the argument that bringing them from Africa exposed them to Christianity, he responded that one must not do evil to bring about good.

Epilogue

The first theme of this story of the religious side of the settlement of the American colonies has been that settlement was carried out primarily by those interested in transplanting to the new world religious patterns developed in the old. The colonial period saw traditional state churches formed in most of the colonies which operated on the assumption that religious opinion was a legitimate concern of public life. Certainly in New England the ties between religion and the social order were close and the necessity of religious uniformity assumed. But south of New England in the predominantly Anglican colonies there were also close ties between church and state and a belief in the importance of religious uniformity: Virginia, Maryland and parts of New York had Anglican establishments and Anglicanism had favored status in the other southern colonies too. And in the short periods of Dutch and Swedish rule on the Hudson and the Delaware the same assumptions about the closeness of religion and the state prevailed. Only in Maryland in its early years (and there because a Roman Catholic proprietor who had received a colony as a gift from a Protestant king could scarcely do otherwise) and in the Quaker-dominated colonies of Rhode Island, West Jersey and Pennsylvania did religious freedom exist—often to the scandal of neighboring colonies. The Quakers, and a little later the Baptists and German sectarians, were the only groups who in principle accepted the notion of private choice in matters of religion.

And if there was such consensus in most of the colonies about the matter of religious uniformity, there was an equally widespread theological consensus of Calvinist opinion. The Puritans, the early (and some later) Anglicans, the Dutch, the French Protestant exiles, the majority of the Baptists, Scottish and Scotch-Irish Presbyterians, and those German immigrants who were Reformed all shared Calvinist theology. The Quakers certainly rejected that theology, but like the General Baptists and other British sectarians, had been thrown off, like sparks from a grindstone, by the vigorous Puritan Calvinism of the British Reformation. Only clearly unrelated to Calvinism were the Roman Catholics, Lutherans, Jews, and German sectarians, who altogether would have numbered a very small percentage of colonial American religionists.

And yet by the end of the period of the religious settlement of the American colonies what would have been most striking was not religious uniformity but variety, pluralism, and dissent. Thus we come to the major conclusions growing out of a second theme, that factors of inner tension and outer environment in the new world defeated the religious uniformity which was so commonly the original ideal. The best example of defeat by inner tension is the story of religion in New England, as we have seen. There the powerful conflict between religious uniformity and establishment on the one hand and the demands of intense and inner piety striving towards perfection on the other continually disrupted the church establishment, rendering it less and less effective, and throwing off combustible material for the newer religious sparks of Antinomian, Baptist, Seeker and Quaker which burst the limitations of that church establishment. In the Anglican colonies it was not so much inner tension but outer environment which hindered the success of the old pattern. In Virginia and elsewhere in the South the scattered nature of the population and the scarcity of able clergy in a new and remote land meant an ineffective church establishment.

This problem of space, so important in Virginia, combined with the inner tensions of religion, most acutely felt in New England, to help create that other factor of the new world so inimical to the old pattern, religious pluralism. Dissenters thrown off from New England could simply remove themselves from its authority, going to Rhode Island or the western frontiers. Available space seemed to encourage dissent.

Dissent and pluralism were further encouraged simply by the coming of new emigrants, who, even if they came from traditions which might have preferred an established church, like the Lutherans, Presbyterians, or Roman Catholics, found themselves a religious minority and potential dissenters. Other new immigrants, like the Quakers, English Baptists, and German sectarians, rejected in principle a state church and where they came not only added to pluralism but created a population resistant to any efforts to maintain religious uniformity. Furthermore, Indians and slaves constituted a not very malleable element in the population, scarcely making uniformity easier to achieve. And as the United States expanded westward its pluralism increased by the incorporation of areas first touched by French and Spanish Catholic missions.

The old ways of religious and theological uniformity were passing away. Already there were signs of that with which they would be replaced, as the inhabitants of the American colonies, thrown back on their own resources economically and also spiritually, began to create religious patterns and institutions independent of the public order by their own efforts, such as the creation of organized but voluntary denominations by Presbyterians and Quakers or the creation of associations and societies for mission and church purposes, like the Anglican Society for Propagation of the Gospel. This religious voluntarism was to be vastly abetted by that religious conflagration known as the Great Awakening which swept through the colonies at about the time when the original religious settlement of the colonies had reached its conclusion.

References

Chapter One

1. A.G. Dickens, *The English Reformation* (New York: Schocken Books, 1964), p. 107.

2. Ibid., p. 271.

3. Patrick Collinson, *The Elizabethan Puritan Movement* (Berkely: Univ. of Calif. Press, 1967), p. 34.

4. John S. Coolidge, *The Pauline Renaissance in England, Puritanism, and the Bible* (Oxford: Clarendon Press, 1970), p. vii.

5. Leonard J. Trinterud, ed., *Elizabethan Puritanism* (New York: Oxford University Press, 1971), pp. 146, 159.

6. Paul Elmer More and Frank Leslie Cross, eds., *Anglicanism* (London: S.P.C.K., 1957), pp. 551-552.

7. A.B. Grosart, ed., *The Complete Works of Richard Sibbes* (Edinburgh: James Nichol, 1852), vol. I, pp. 45, 47.

8. Alan Simpson, *Puritanism in Old and New England* (Chicago: University of Chicago Press, 1955), p. 26.

9. Stephen Foster, *Their Solitary Way, the Puritan Social Ethic in the First Century of Settlement in New England* (New Haven: Yale Univ. Press, 1971), p. 127. Used by permission.

10. Christopher Hill, *The World Turned Upside Down, Radical Ideas During the English Revolution* (New York: Viking Press, 1972), p. 151.

11. Thomas Edwards, *The First and Second Part of Gangraena...* (London, 1646), pp. 57-58, second series of pagination.

12. Ibid., pp. 24-30.

13. Ephraim Pagitt, *Heresiography* (London, 1662), p. 167.

14. Hugh Barbour, *The Quakers in Puritan England* (New Haven: Yale Univ. Press, 1964), p. 2. Used by permission.

15. George Gifford, *A Dialogue betweene a Papist and Protestant...* (London, 1599), p. 2.

16. quoted in H.R. Trevor-Roper, *Men and Events* (New York: Harper and Bros, 1957), p. 93.

17. Dickens, p. 311.

Chapter Two

1. H. Shelton Smith, Robert T. Handy, and Lefferts A. Loetscher, *American Christianity, An Historical Interpretation with Representative Documents*, vol. I, *1607-1820* (New York: Charles Scribner's Sons, 1960), pp. 86-87.

2. William Bradford, *Of Plymouth Plantation*, ed. Harvey Wish (New York, Capricorn Books, 1962), p. 38.

3. Michael McGiffert, ed., *God's Plot, the Paradoxes of Puritan Piety, Being the Autobiography and Journal of Thomas Shepard* (Univ. of Mass. Press, 1972), pp. 49, 55.

4. Alden T. Vaughan, ed., *The Puritan Tradition in America* (New York: Harper and Row, 1972), p. 64.

5. J. Franklin Jameson, ed., *Johnson's Wonder-Working Providence* (New York: Charles Scribner's Sons), pp. 52, 54, 49.

6. Quoted in Clifton E. Olmstead, *History of Religion in the United States* (Englewood Cliffs, N.J.: Prentice-Hall, Inc., Reprinted by permission. 1960), p. 71.

7. John Norton, *Abel being Dead yet speaketh; or, the Life and Death of that deservedly Famous Man of God, Mr. John Cotton* (London, 1658), p. 9.

8. Kenneth A. Lockridge, "The History of a Puritan Church, 1637-1736," *The New England Quarterly* XL (March-Dec., 1967), pp. 399-424.

9. Williston Walker, ed., *The Creeds and Platforms of Congregationalism* (1893; rpt. Boston: Pilgrim Press, 1960), p. 116.

10. Smith, Handy and Loetscher, pp. 127-128.

11. Perry Miller and Thomas H. Johnson, eds., *The Puritans, A Sourcebook of Their Writings* (1938; rpt. New York: Harper and Row, 1963), p. 185.

12. Smith, Handy and Loetscher, pp. 124-126.

13. Bradford, pp. 166-167.

14. James K. Hosmer, ed., *Winthrop's Journal*, 2 vols., (New York: Charles Scribner's Sons 1908), I, 209.

15. Ibid., p. 206.

16. John Cotton, *The Keyes to the Kingdom of Heaven, and Power Thereof, according to the Word of God* (London, 1644), p. 44.

17. *Winthrop's Journal*, II, 177.

18. Smith, Handy, and Loetscher, p. 167.

19. Quoted in Olmstead, p. 87. (Reprinted by permission of Prentice-Hall, Inc.)

20. Quoted in Edmund Morgan, *Visible Saints, The History of a Puritan Idea* (1963; rpt. Ithaca, N.Y.: Cornell Univ. Press, 1965), p. 138.

21. Robert G. Pope, *The Half-Way Covenant, Church Membership in Puritan New England* (Princeton: Princeton Univ. Press, 1969), pp. 261-262. Reprinted by permission.

22. Miller and Johnson, p. 244.

23. Walker, pp. 423-437.

24. Quoted in Chadwick Hansen, *Witchcraft at Salem* (New York: George Braziller, 1969), p. 21.

25. David D. Hall, *The Faithful Shepherd, A History of the New England Ministry in the Seventeenth Century* (Chapel Hill: Univ. of N.C. Press, Institute of Early American History and Culture, 1972), p. 10.

26. Isaac Backus, *A History of New England. With Particular Reference to the Denomination of Christians Called Baptists*, ed., David Weston 2 vols, (Newton, Mass.: Backus Historical Society, 1871), I, 308.

27. Norton, p. 27.

28. Bradford, p. 83.

29. Vaughan, ed., p. 79.

30. Miller and Johnson, p. 348.

31. *The Diary of Michael Wigglesworth 1653-1657*, ed. Edmund S. Morgan (1946; rpt. New York: Harper and Row, 1965), p. 18.

32. Quoted in Ola E. Winslow, *Meetinghouse Hill 1630-1783* (1952; rpt. New York: W.W. Norton & Co., 1972) pp. 183-184.

33. Christopher Hill, *Society and Puritanism in Pre-Revolutionary England* (second ed., New York: Schocken Books, 1967), p. 446.

34. Norton, p. 18.

35. Quoted in Edmund S. Morgan, *The Puritan Family, Religion and Domestic Relations in Seventeenth-Century New England* (1944; rpt. New York: Harper and Row, 1966), pp. 103, 105.

36. Miller and Johnson, pp. 563, 564, 570, 579.

37. Donald E. Stanford, ed., *The Poems of Edward Taylor* (New Haven: Yale Univ. Press, 1960), pp. 11, 54, 18. Used by permission.

Chapter Three

1. Quoted in Clifton E. Olmstead, *History of Religion in the United States* (Englewood Cliffs, N.J.: Prentice-Hall, Inc., Reprinted by permission. 1960), pp. 41-42.

2. H. Shelton Smith, Robert T. Handy and Lefferts A. Loetscher, *American Christianity, An Historical Interpretation with Representative Documents*, vol. I, *1607-1820* (New York: Charles Scribner's Sons, 1960), p. 43.

3. George Maclaren Brydon, *Virginia's Mother Church and the Political Conditions Under Which it Grew*, 2 vols. (Richmond: Virginia Historical Society, 1947), I, 426, 429. Includes the text of many documents and statutes relating to religion in Colonial Virginia.

4. Ibid., p. 444.

5. Quoted in Perry Miller, "Religion and Society in the

Early Literature of Virginia," in Perry Miller, *Errand Into the Wilderness* (Cambridge: Belknap Press of Harvard Univ. Press, 1956), pp. 104, 102.

6. Quoted in Sydney Ahlstrom, *A Religious History of the American People* (New Haven: Yale Univ. Press, 1972), p. 187. Used by permission.

7. Alexander Whitaker, *Good Newes from Virginia...* (London, 1613; rpt. New York: Scholars' Facsimiles & Reprints, n.d.), pp. 23-24.

8. Quoted in Brydon, p. 24.

9. Quoted in Babette M. Levy, *Early Puritanism in the Southern and Island Colonies* (Worcester, Mass.: American Antiquarian Society, 1960), p. 114. Used by permission.

10 Quoted in Ernest Trice Thompson, *Presbyterians in the South*, vol. I *1607-1861* (Richmond: John Knox Press, 1963), p. 12.

11. Brydon, p. 493.

12. Ibid., p. 512.

13. Ibid.

14. William H. Seiler, "The Anglican Parish in Virginia," in James Morton Smith, ed., *Seventeenth-Century America, Essays in Colonial History*, pp. 119-142 (Chapel Hill: Univ. or North Carolina Press, Institute of Early American History and Culture, 1971), p. 38.

15. Quoted in Olmstead, p. 46.

16. Brydon, p. 404.

17. Parke Rouse, Jr., *James Blair of Virginia* (Chapel Hill: Univ. of North Carolina Press, Institute of Early American History and Culture, 1971), p. 38.

18. Seiler, p. 134.

19. Smith, Handy, and Loetscher, pp. 54-55.

20. Alexander S. Salley, Jr., ed., *Narratives of Early Carolina 1650-1708* (New York: Charles Scribner's Sons, 1911), p. 71.

21. Ibid., p. 124.

22. Quoted in Raymond W. Albright, *History of the Protestant Episcopal Church* (New York: Macmillan Co., 1964), p. 81.

23. "The Journal of the Reverend George Keith 1702-1704," *Historical Magazine of the Protestant Episcopal Church*, XX (no. 4, December, 1951), p. 388.

Chapter Four

1. Quoted in John Tracy Ellis, *Catholics in Colonial America* (Baltimore: Helicon, 1965), p. 379.

2. John Tracy Ellis, ed., *Documents of American Catholic History*, rev. ed, 2 vols. (Chicago: Henry Regnery Co., 1967), I, 109.

3. Ibid., p. 104.

4. Ibid., p. 98.

5. Ibid., pp. 113-114.

6. John E. Pomfret, *Founding the American Colonies 1583-1660* (New York: Harper and Row, 1970), p. 93.

7. C.C. Hall, ed., *Narratives of Early Maryland 1633-1684* (New York: Charles Scribner's Sons, 1910), p.

8. Quoted in Ellis, *Catholics in Colonial America*, p. 369.

9. Ibid., p. 59.

10. Ellis, *Documents*, p. 26.

11. Charles Edward O'Neill, *Church and State in French Colonial Louisiana* (New Haven: Yale Univ. Press, 1966), pp. 5-6. Used by permission.

12. Ellis, *Documents*, pp. 49-51.

Chapter Five

1. James K. Hosmer, ed., *Winthrop's Journal*, 2 vols. (New York: Charles Scribner's Sons, 1908), II, 39.

2. Edmund S. Morgan, *Roger Williams: the Church and the State* (New York: Harcourt, Brace, Jovanovich Inc., 1967), p. 4. Used by permission.

3. Quoted in Isaac Backus, *A History of New England. With Particular Reference to the Denomination of Christians Called Baptists*, ed. David Weston, 2 vols (Newton, Mass.: Backus Historical Society, 1871), I, 89.

4. Quoted in Backus, I, 291-292.

5. J. Franklin Jameson, ed., *Narratives of New Netherland 1609-1664* (New York: Charles Scribner's Sons, 1909), p. 397.

6. Quoted in Norman H. Maring, *Baptists in New Jersey, A Study in Transition* (Valley Forge, Pa.: the Judson Press, 1964), p. 19. (Used by permission)

7. Quoted in Backus, I, 401.

8. Frederick B. Tolles, *Quakers and the Atlantic Culture* (New York: Macmillan Co., 1960), p. 14.

9. Quoted in Rufus Jones, *The Quakers in the American Colonies* (1911; rpt. New York: W.W. Norton Co., 1966), p. 73.

10. Quoted in Ibid., p. 122-123.

11. Quoted in Ibid., p. 231.

12. *The Journal of George Fox*, ed. Rufus Jones: New York: Capricorn Books, 1963), p. 533.

13. H. Shelton Smith, Robert T. Handy, and Lefferts A. Loetscher, *American Christianity, An Historical Interpretation with Representative Documents*, 2 vols, (New York: Charles Scribner's Sons, 1960), I, 176.

14. Quoted in Jones, p. 51.

15. Quoted in Ibid., p. 71.

16. Quoted in W.C. Braithwaite, *The Second Period of Quakerism*, 2nd edition prepared by H.C. Cadbury (Cambridge: Cambridge Univ. Press, 1961), pp. 60-61.

17. Wesley Frank Craven, *The Colonies in Transition, 1660-1713* (New York: Harper and Row, 1968), p. 192.

18. Quoted in Melvin B. Endy, Jr., *William Penn and Early Quakerism* (Princeton: Princeton University Press, 1973), p. 349.

19. Ibid., p. 314.

20. Frederick B. Tolles, *Meeting House and Counting House, the Quaker Merchants of Colonial Philadelphia* (Chapel Hill: Univ. of North Carolina Press, Institute of Early American History and Culture, 1948), pp. 10-11.

21. Quoted in Backus, I, p. 368.

22. George Fox and John Burnyeat, *A New-England Fire-Brand Quenched...*, (no. pl., 1679), p. 69.

23. George Keith, *The Quakers Proved Apostates and Heathens and a Specimen of the Quakers Great Malice and Ignorance* (no pl., 1700), p. 6.

Chapter Six

1. George L. Smith, *Religion and Trade in New Netherland* (Ithaca: Cornell Univ. Press, Copyright© 1973 by Cornell Univ.), p. 93.

2. H. Shelton Smith, Robert T. Handy, and Lefferts A. Loetscher, *American Christianity, An Historical Interpretation with Representative Documents*, 2 vols. (New York: Charles Scribner's Sons, 1960), I, 60-61.

3. J. Franklin Jameson, ed., *Narratives of New Netherland 1609-1664* (New York: Charles Scribner's Sons, 1909), p. 260.

4. Quoted in G.L. Smith, p. 13.

5. Quoted in Ibid., p. 236.

6. Quoted in William Warren Sweet, *Religion in Colonial America* (New York: Charles Scribner's Sons, 1951), pp. 203-204.

7. Quoted in Donald F. Durnbaugh, ed., *The Brethren in Colonial America* (Elgin, Ill.: Brethren Press, 1967), p. 117.

8. Smith, Handy, and Loetscher, I, 278.

9. Quoted in Durnbaugh, p. 134.

10. Morris U. Schappes, ed., *A Documentary History of the Jews in the United States 1554-1875* (New York: Citadel Press, 1950), p. 2.

11. Ibid., p. 12.

Chapter Seven

1. Robert Hastings Nichols, *Presbyterianism in New York State*, ed. and completed by Robert Hastings Nichols (Philadelphia: Westminster Press, 1963), p. 12.

2. J. Franklin Jameson, ed., *Narratives of New Netherland 1609-1664* (New York: Charles Scribner's Sons, 1909), p. 397.

3. Charles Augustus Briggs, *American Presbyterianism, Its Origin and Early History* (New York: Charles Scribner's Sons, 1885), pp. xlii-xliii.

4. Quoted in William Warren Sweet, *Religion in Colonial America* (New York: Charles Scribner's Sons, 1951), p. 252.

5. Maurice W. Armstrong, Lefferts A. Loetscher, and Charles A. Anderson, eds., *The Presbyterian Enterprise, Sources of American Presbyterian History* (Philadelphia: the Westminster Press, 1956), p. 21.

6. Boyd S. Schlenther, ed., *The Life and Writings of Francis Makemie* (Philadelphia: Presbyterial Historical Society, 1971), p. 28. Used by permission.

7. *Records of the Presbyterian Church in the United States of America....1706-1788* (Philadelphia: Presbyterian Board of Publications, 1904) p. 10.

8. Quoted in Leonard J. Trinterud, *The Forming of an American Tradition, A Re-examination of Colonial Presbyterianism* (Philadelphia: Westminster Press, 1959), pp. 45-46.

Chapter Eight

1. Clayton C. Hall, editor, *Narratives of Early Maryland 1633-1684* (New York: Charles Scribner's, 1910), p. 86.

2. Quoted in William Brandon, *The Last Americans* (New York: McGraw Hill, 1974), p. 9.

3. Roger Williams, *A Key Into the Language of America* (London, 1643), p. 70.

4. Nancy O. Lurie, "Indian Cultural Development to European Civilization," in James Morton Smith, ed., *Seventeenth-Century America, Essays in Colonial History* (Chapel Hill: University of North Carolina Press, Institute of Early American History and Culture 1959), p. 38.

5. Williams, *A Key Into the Language of America*, sig. A5r.

6. Quoted in Robert Pierce Beaver, *Church, State, and the American Indians* (St. Louis: Concordia Publishing House, 1966), p. 12.

7. Alexander Whitaker, *Good Newes from Virginia* (London, 1613; rpt. New York: Scholars' Facsimiles and Reprints, n.d.), p. 25.

8. Thomas Shepard, *The Clear Sunshine of the Gospel Breaking Forth Upon the Indians in New England* (London, 1648; rpt. New York: Joseph Sabin, 1865) p. 10.

9. Quoted in R. Pierce Beaver, "American Missionary Motivation Before the Revolution," *Church History*, XXXI (June, 1962), p. 217.

10. Alden T. Vaughan, *New England Frontier, Puritans and Indians 1620-1675* (Boston: Little, Brown and Co., 1965), p. vii.

11. Louise Ruchames, ed., *Racial Thought in America*, vol. I, *From the Puritans to Abraham Lincoln* (New York: Grosset and Dunlap, 1970), pp. 34-35.

12. John Hope Franklin, *From Slavery to Freedom* (New York: Alfred A. Knopf, 1961), p. 111. Used by permission.

13. *New England's First Fruits*... (London, 1643; rpt. New York: Joseph Sabin, 1865), p. 10.

14. George Maclaren Brydon, *Virginia's Mother Church*, vol. I (Richmond: Virginia Historical Society, 1947), p. 186.

15. Gerald F. DeJong, "The Dutch Reformed Church and Negro Slavery in Colonial America," *Church History*, XL (December, 1971), p. 431.

16. Ruchames, pp. 38-40.

Suggested Readings

Chapter One

Clebsch, William A. *England's Earliest Protestants 1520-1535.* New Haven: Yale Univ. Press, 1964.

Collinson, Patrick. *The Elizabethan Puritan Movement.* Berkeley: Univ. of Calif. Press, 1967.

Davies, Horton. *Worship and Theology in England, From Cranmer to Hooker, 1534-1603.* Princeton: Princeton Univ. Press, 1970.

Dickens, A. G. *The English Reformation.* New York: Schocken Books, 1964.

Eusden, John Dykstra. *Puritans, Lawyers and Politics in Early Seventeenth-Century England.* New Haven: Yale Univ. Press, 1958.

Haller, William. *The Rise of Puritanism.* 1938; rpt. New York: Harper and Bros., 1957.

Little, David. *Religion, Order, and Law, A Study in Pre-Revolutionary England.* New York: Harper and Row, 1969.

Nuttall, Geoffrey. *Visible Saints.* Oxford: Basil Blackwell, 1957.

Porter, H. C. *Reformation and Reaction in Tudor Cambridge.* Cambridge: Univ. Press, 1958.

Rose, Elliot. *Cases of Conscience, Alternatives Open to Recusants and Puritans....* Cambridge: Cambridge Univ. Press, 1975.

Simpson, Alan. *Puritanism in Old and New England*. Chicago: Univ. of Chicago Press, 1955.

Trimble, W. R. *The Catholic Laity in Elizabethan England*. Cambridge: Harvard Univ. Press, 1964.

Walzer, Michael. *The Revolution of the Saints*. Cambridge: Harvard Univ. Press, 1965.

White, B. R. *The English Separatist Tradition*. London: Oxford Univ. Press, 1971.

Chapter Two

Demos, John. *A Little Commonwealth, Family Life in Plymouth Colony*. London: Oxford Univ. Press, 1970.

Hansen, Chadwick. *Witchcraft at Salem*. New York: George Braziller, 1969.

Jones, Mary Jeanne Anderson. *Congregational Commonwealth, Connecticut 1636-1662*. Middletown, Conn.: Wesleyan Univ. Press, 1968.

Langdon, George D. Jr. *Pilgrim Colony, A History of New Plymouth, 1620-1691*. New Haven: Yale Univ. Press, 1966.

Middlekauf, Robert. *The Mathers, Three Generations of Puritan Intellectuals*. New York: Oxford Univ. Press, 1971.

Miller, Perry. *Errand Into the Wilderness*. Cambridge: Belknap Press, 1956.

_____. *Orthodoxy in Massachusetts 1630-1650*. Cambridge: Harvard Univ. Press, 1933.

Morgan, Edmund S. *The Puritan Dilemma, The Story of John Winthrop*. Boston: Little, Brown and Co., 1958.

Morison, Samuel Eliot. *Builders of the Bay Colony*. Boston: Houghton Mifflin, 1930.

Petit, Norman. *The Heart Prepared: Grace and Conversion in Puritan Spiritual Life*. New Haven: Yale Univ. Press, 1966.

Powell, Sumner Chilton. *Puritan Village*. Middletown, Conn.: Wesleyan Univ. Press, 1963.

Rutman, Darrett B. *Winthrop's Boston*. Chapel Hill: Univ. of North Carolina, 1965.

Chapter Three

Brydon, George Maclaren. *Virginia's Mother Church and Political Conditions Under Which it Grew.* 2 vols. Richmond: Virginia Historical Society, 1947.

Levy, Babette May. *Early Puritanism in the Southern and Island Colonies.* Worcester, Mass.: American Antiquarian Society, 1960.

Chapter Four

Bolton, Herbert E. *The Mission as a Frontier Institution in the Spanish-American Colonies.* El Paso: Texas Western College Press, 1960.

Ellis, John Tracy. *Catholics in Colonial America.* Baltimore: Helicon Press, 1965.

Shea, John Gilmary. *Catholic Missions Among the Indian Tribes of the United States.* 1855; rpt. New York: Arno Press, 1969.

Chapter Five

Bronner, Edwin, B. *William Penn's "Holy Experiment," The Founding of Pennsylvania 1681-1701.* New York: Temple Univ. Publications, 1962.

Endy, Melvin B. Jr. *William Penn and Early Quakerism.* Princeton: Princeton Univ. Press, 1973.

Jones, Rufus. *The Quakers in the American Colonies.* 1911; rpt., New York: W. W. Norton Co., 1966.

McLoughlin, William G. *New England Dissent, 1630-1833: The Baptists and the Separation of Church and State.* 2 vols. Cambridge: Harvard Univ. Press, 1971.

Chapter Six

Marcus, Jacob R. *The Colonial American Jew 1492-1776.* 3 vols. Detroit: Wayne State Univ. Press, 1970.

Smith, George L. *Religion and Trade in New Netherland.* Ithaca: Cornell Univ. Press, 1973.

Chapter Seven

Trinterud, Leonard J. *The Forming of an American Tradition, A Re-examination of Colonial Presbyterianism.* Philadelphia: Westminister Press, 1959.

Chapter Eight

Beaver, Robert Pierce. *Church, State, and the American Indians.* St. Louis: Concordia Publishing House, 1966.

Davis, David Brion. *The Problem of Slavery in Western Culture.* Ithaca: Cornell Univ. Press, 1966.

Jordan, Winthrop D. *White Over Black, American Attitudes Toward the Negro, 1558-1812.* Chapel Hill: Univ. of North Carolina Press, 1968.

Scherer, Lester B. *Slavery and the Churches in Early America.* Grand Rapids: Wm. B. Eerdmans, 1975.

Vaughan, Alden T. *New England Frontier, Puritans and Indians 1620-1675.* Boston: Little, Brown and Co., 1965.